POLISH CINEMA NOW!
FOCUS ON CONTEMPORARY POLISH CINEMA

**EDITED BY
MATEUSZ WERNER**

LONDON – WARSAW 2010

Polish Cinema Now!
Focus on Contemporary Polish Cinema
Edited by Mateusz Werner

Published by:
Adam Mickiewicz Institute
Mokotowska 25
00-560 Warsaw
Poland
www.culture.pl

John Libbey Publishing Ltd.
3 Leicester Road
New Barnet, Herts
EN5 5EW
United Kingdom
www.johnlibbey.com

Copyright © 2010 Adam Mickiewicz Institute
ISBN 978-83-60263-22-1
Copyright © 2010 John Libbey Publishing Ltd.
ISBN 9780-86196- 691-2

Editor: Mateusz Werner
Produced by: Monika Derenda
Translation (from Polish): Mark Bence, Paul Coates, Wojciech Góralczyk, Bartłomiej Reszuta, Ewa Kanigowska-Gedroyć
Proofreading: John Libbey, Simon Włoch
Technical editor: Bożena Kowalkowska
Designed by: Edgar Bąk
Dtp: Magdalena Heliasz
Printed by: Druk Intro

The publisher would like to thank Grzegorz Boguta for his help with the publishing of this book.

DVD "Polish Short Films Since 1989" made with the support of Filmoteka Narodowa.
www.fn.org.pl

6 From the publishers

MATEUSZ WERNER
8 Whatever happened to Polish cinema after 1989?

MICHAEL BROOKE
22 Resolving a crisis of identity: how central-eastern European cinema adjusted to the changes of 1989

ANDRZEJ KOŁODYŃSKI
40 The arrival of the new documentary. Two decades 1989–2009

ANDRZEJ WERNER
58 Cinema and history

MARIUSZ FRUKACZ
80 The second youth of a sixty year old. Polish animation after 1989

ANITA PIOTROWSKA
104 Is Poland a woman? Feminist and homosexual themes in Polish film from 1989–2009

JOANNA ROŻEN-WOJCIECHOWSKA
130 The phenomenon of Polish independent cinema in 1989–2009

JERZY PŁAŻEWSKI
150 Polish cinema – a return to market economy

JANUSZ WRÓBLEWSKI
170 Polish cinema success stories

MAŁGORZATA SADOWSKA
194 Strategies of Polish commercial cinema after 1989

KRZYSZTOF ŚWIREK
220 Tradition and diversity: an outline of Polish film education

242 Contributors

246 DVD

256 Index of names

262 Index of films

FROM THE PUBLISHERS

Twenty years have passed since Polish cinema was once again able to speak with its own voice, without having to worry about political censorship, and having broken the production monopoly of the communist state. For twenty years now, Polish film artists have been able to enjoy the same freedoms and possibilities as their colleagues from France or Germany. Over five hundred feature films and a few thousand documentaries have been produced over this time – some representing the highest artistic quality. Paradoxically, however, it is this cinema which is much less known to the international audience than the Polish films which had been made behind the "Iron Curtain", when the cultural exchange with the western world was limited to a small trickle, entirely controlled by the communist regime. Now the communication barriers are no longer there, and Poland is in the international circuit of film production and distribution, the most recent Polish cinema remains an unknown land awaiting to be discovered, and awaiting viewers from the entire world. We believe this publication will be helpful in this discovery.

WHATEVER HAPPENED TO POLISH CINEMA AFTER 1989?

MATEUSZ WERNER

The revolution of 1989

This was a strange revolution indeed. Firstly, because it was anti-communist; and in the eyes of the then Polish rulers, it must have looked like a counter-revolution. Happily, we are no longer obliged to follow this view. Secondly, the revolution was strange because this time, contrary to Polish Romantic tradition, it lacked all its typical external symptoms: tanks on streets, bloody demonstrations, setting fire to police stations. Still, the results of the first semi-democratic elections of 4 June 1989, which were shattering to the Polish communist authorities, was what Timothy Garton Ash termed "revolution of Solidarity". And so, a few months later began the "Autumn of Nations" with the grand finale in the form of the fall of the Berlin wall. At that time, in mid 1989, pretty much the entire country was back on its feet, after having wobbled on its head for over forty years. For Polish cinema, which had always been very linked to the current political situation, and which had been socially involved and attentively listening to the goings on in the lives of its viewers, the events of that period were of the magnitude of a "Copernican Revolution". Today, from the perspective of twenty years, we see that once the dust settled after this bloodless breakthrough, a new chapter was opened in the history of Polish cinema. The revolutionary changes have taken place in three dimensions: political censorship vanished, the market began to be ruled by the logic of supply and demand, and entirely new technologies appeared on the horizon, offering opportunities for film creation beyond the official system of production.

Freedom of expression

One of the properties of Polish cinema at the time of the communist state was its political nature, which was definitely in surplus even if we take into consideration the specificity of the very means of expression. As we know, film as such is a means of artistic expression which is predestined to play a political role. This is due to the persuasive properties of the language of the genre, whose possibilities of pictorial metaphorical quality equips it with the ability to impact the collective sub-consciousness, allowing for the creation of symbolic icons, and, in particular, the characters. Another reason is the nature of film's public perception: its mass reach, inclination to draw public attention by means of raucous promotion mechanisms, international festivals, tabloids and glossy press. Obviously, authoritarian politicians were well aware of how exceptionally convenient the cinema was in shaping public opinion. No wonder Lenin believed cinema to be one of the "most important of arts", and provided extra care to creators who were useful in propaganda terms, such as Dovzhenko, Pudovkin or Eisenstein. Before the appearance of television, cinema had been treated on equal footing to press and radio as a tool of ideological indoctrination and a tube for propaganda broadcasting, which is the reason why it was so scrupulously supervised in the countries of the Soviet block. Nevertheless, film artists who had to work in conditions of limited freedom of expression and under ideological and economic pressure, were more than often able to play an important role in broadening the field of freedom, criticising the authoritarian regimes, and undermining the intellectual bases of political systems in which they had to function. This is proved by the importance a number of phenomena had in the forming of democratic opposition movements, such as the "Polish Film School",[1] which was the flagship of the Polish "thaw" of "October 1956", the Czech "New Wave", which had played the same role during the "Prague Spring" of 1968, Polish cinema of "moral anxiety" in 1970s, accompanying the activities of the underground press publishing circles and the Workers' Defence Committee, or – to give an example from a different political reality – "Nueva Cine Español", which had contributed to the crumbling of Franco's propaganda system in the mid-1960s. The Palme d'Or in Cannes in 1981 for Andrzej Wajda for his *Man of Iron* (*Człowiek z żelaza*, 1981) was one in a series of political events in support of anti-communist opposition, weakening the authoritarian regime – similar to Czesław Miłosz's winning the Nobel Prize for literature, or Karol Wojtyła becoming Pope John Paul II. It was most probably this very aspect of the cinema's influence on reality that Robert Rehme, President of the Academy of Motion Picture Arts and Sciences had in mind when presenting the justification for awarding Andrzej Wajda with an Oscar – Lifetime Achievement Award. He said that the author of *Danton* offered his audience an "artistic take on history, democracy, and freedom". It is the same order that should be applied when assessing the international successes of Miloš Forman, Jiži Menzel, Luis Buñuel, Juan Antonio Bardem, Andrey Tarkovsky, Miklós Jancsó, Vasili Shukshin and Kira Muratova.

The political nature of Polish cinema is particularly apparent in the convergence of the rhythm of historical turning points with the generational gaps among artists – instead of the definition "Polish Film School" we could say "cinema of Polish October" and everybody would know what it applies to. The next phase was "cinema of the small stability period" of the 1960s, which after the events of March 1968 turned into "cinema of moral anxiety", and which was to later transform into the "cinema of Solidarity" and "cinema of martial

---

[1] "Polish Film School" is a current in Polish cinema which originated in the times of the political "thaw" in the latter half of the 1950s. The common denominators linking the artists were their war experiences and the political breakthrough in post-war Poland. The artistic formation began to take shape with the success of Andrzej Wajda's *Canal* (*Kanał*, 1956) in Cannes in 1957. Among the canonical films of the current, there are: *Canal*, *Ashes and Diamonds* (*Popiół i diament*, 1958), *Speed* (*Lotna*, 1959) by Andrzej Wajda; as well as *Eroica* (1957) and *Bad Luck* (*Zezowate szczęście*, 1959) by Andrzej Munk, *Birth Certificate* (*Świadectwo urodzenia*, 1961) by Stanisław Różewicz, *Cross of Valor* (*Krzyż Walecznych*, 1958) by Kazimierz Kutz, or *Farewells* (*Pożegnania*, 1958) by Jerzy Wojciech Has. Many of the later films from the 1960s – 1990s referred to the *oeuvre* from that time, e.g. *Man of Marble* (*Człowiek z marmuru*, 1976) by Wajda; *Salto* (1965) by Tadeusz Konwicki or *Death as a Slice of Bread* (*Śmierć jak kromka chleba*, 1994) by Kazimierz Kutz. See: *The Polish School – Returns* („*Szkoła Polska" – powroty*, ed. E. Nurczyńska-Fidelska and B. Stolarska, Łódź 1998.

law". All these terms assign a certain poetics of communicating with the viewer in a given fragment of political history of communist Poland, an artistic reaction to that fragment of this history. There is no coincidence in the fact that this political language of description is still used by historians, as it really does correspond to the logic of the development of Polish cinema. Giving it up, therefore, would be an artificial gesture, a fictitious attempt which would falsify the picture of events. Polish filmmakers touched on political themes, undermining the official version of reality – not only because they were so outrageously brave or so ideologically passionate. This stance was, to an extent, the result of marketing calculations. Wherever there is political censorship, taboo subjects are much more effective in luring audiences than sex, fights or car chases. Andrzej Wajda was perfectly aware of that, hence it was no wonder that his films always showed something for the first time. Warsaw Uprising in *Canal* (*Kanał*, 1956), or the post-war fight of the communists for power in *Ashes and Diamonds* (*Popiół i diament*, 1958) are immediate examples. Crowds would go to see the films not only because it was Wajda who had directed them. After ten years of Stalinist propaganda, people simply wanted to see a film about the soldiers of the Home Army [Armia Krajowa], played by nice and good looking actors. The strategy had many followers. It required the authors to create their own "Aesopian language", which would convey forbidden messages, eagerly picked up by the audience. These codes ensuring an alibi for the creators against possible repercussions from the authorities and, at the same time, perfectly deciphered by the public, were also a part of the historical moment. The allusions after the "thaw" of 1956 were formulated differently from the times of the triumphant Solidarity. The gradation of the disloyal messages could even be presented in a graph form: from the still socialist realist films by Andrzej Munk and Wajda (*Man on the Track* [*Człowiek na torze*, 1956]; *Generation* [*Pokolenie*, 1954]), which, however, had already carried a breeze of the new air, to the works from the early 1980s, which were directly negating the political foundations of the communist country, such as *Man of Iron* (1981) by Wajda, or *Interrogation* (*Przesłuchanie*, 1982) by Ryszard Bugajski.

The "ciphered political code", which had been applied to smuggle messages integrating the public who came to the cinema to taste the forbidden fruit, was no longer needed after the transformation of the political system into a democracy. The phenomenon of the "Aesopian language" vanished from Polish cinema. The language, once constantly developed in confrontation with censorship, was no longer needed. As from 1989 anything could be talked about "directly" in films, without the need to resort to allusions. One even no longer had to go to the cinema – it was enough to switch on the TV for live broadcasts of sessions of the Parliament. For that reason, the cinema lost its status of a public forum, of an unofficial surrogate for the exchange of ideas. Politics abandoned film clubs and alternative movie theatres and moved in to the Parliament. Artists, like priests, ceased to be the "speakers of the nation", and could no longer enjoy the feeling of one with a public

*Death as
a Slice of Bread*,
dir. Kazimierz Kutz

mission and an extraordinary position in society. Many literally moved to politics, such as Andrzej Wajda, who was elected to the Sejm (lower chamber of Polish Parliament), or Kazimierz Kutz, who became a Senator.

The most visible consequence of the transformation – apart from the personal aspects in the lives of the artists – was the disappearance of political cinema. It is difficult to grasp now why the tumultuous end of communism never became a source of inspiration for cinema artists. True, there were a few films which were more journalistic in nature, such as *Players* (*Gracze*, 1995) by Ryszard Bugajski, or *Hijacking of Agata* (*Uprowadzenie Agaty*,1993) by Marek Piwowski, which had applied a language of simplified, cartoon-like sociology in describing the so-called "period of transformation", and in doing so, taking full advantage of the most recent political events, or economic changes (such as *Capital, or How to Make Money in Poland* [*Kapitał, czyli jak zrobić pieniądze w Polsce*, 1989] by Feliks Falk). But no films have been made which would really use the opportunity presented by the newly regained freedom, and which would use a loud voice to speak about the political past of this country – about the Soviet attack on Poland in 1939, the Stalinist crimes after the war, or the brutal repressions against the Church and democratic opposition. The failure of Andrzej Wajda's *Ring with a Crowned Eagle* (*Pierścionek z orłem w koronie*, 1992), in which the filmmaker wanted to pay tribute to the heroes of the Warsaw Uprising, was more off-putting and, with few exceptions, such as *Poznan '56* (1996) by Filip Bajon or *Death as a Slice of Bread* (*Śmierć jak kromka chleba*, 1994) by Kazimierz Kutz – there were virtually no films in the 1990s that would "settle accounts" with the painful past.[2] It was taken for granted that this is a topic which would be entirely uninteresting to the young public, which statistically comprised the majority group of movie goers. Actually, if it were'nt for documentaries, it could be said that history was eradicated from the cinema of the 1990s. Luckily, there was a number of gems among documentary cinema, such as *Katyn Forest* (*Las katyński*, 1990) by Marcel Łoziński or *Hear My Cry* (*Usłyszcie mój krzyk*, 1991) by Maciej Drygas, which did not only present anew the facts which had been falsified earlier, but also which would introduce the viewer to facts thus far unknown. In a few cases the documentary was not only a carrier of certain interpretations of history but also a tool of learning about it and, at the same time, a testimony as important as historical sources. The

---

2
The film by Bajon is a story of the massacre which ended the workers' protests in June 1956 in Poznań, seen through the eyes of a child, while Kutz' film is a faithful presentation of the tragic pacification of the miners' strike in the "Wujek" coalmine at the beginning of martial law in 1981.

situation of feature films was very different. Suffice to say that the first film about Solidarity did not appear until 2006, and was made by a German artist, Völker Schlöndorff *Strike* (*Strajk – Die Heldin von Danzig*, 2006). At the same time, Andrzej Wajda had to wait over ten years to finally decide on making a film about the Katyn crime, in 2007. It was not until the great success of the The Warsaw Rising Museum[3] that it became apparent that interest in the tragic Polish history was not limited to a handful of sentimental old-timers and a marginal group of politicians fossilised in their outdated pretensions, but that it is something important, vivid, alive, and evoking much emotion among the youth and the so called "regular folk". This success caused a sensation and once more set alight the discussion about the purposefulness of making "historical politics" in Poland, the sense of which had been most often questioned or even mocked.

The only one part of the most recent history which caused no doubts among the intellectual *élite*, and which was well worked through by Polish cinema, touched on Polish-Jewish relations, which in the times of communist Poland had been a topic subjected to extreme political censorship, in particular after 1967, when Polish communist authorities and the regimes of other countries of the Soviet Block broke their diplomatic relations with the state of Israel. The abundance of topics, genres, the multifaceted perspectives, and courage in dealing with the most sensitive and inconvenient motifs – all these properties show what a fantastic tool cinema can be in understanding and taming the past, as long as there is a

---

[3] The Warsaw Rising Museum was opened on 1 August 2004, on the 60th anniversary of this tragic revolt against the German occupation. This is the first museum in Poland which is a of a narrative type, similarly to the Holocaust Museum in Washington D.C. The popularity of the exposition, particularly among young viewers, was a great surprise, as it had been commonly thought that "history and martyrdom are no longer "in". The success of the Museum encouraged many filmmakers to consider dealing with historical subjects in their work.

common agreement in the most important triangle of viewers, producers, and the media, that such cinema is really worth making. Furthermore, it turns out that historical politics in Polish cinema is possible, even when there is no "centre of power". It is enough to have the mentioned commonly shared feeling of sensitivity. For this to happen, however, the public opinion has to be worked on, so as to create a standard acceptable by the majority.

Free market

Another element specific to Polish cinema in the times of communism was the extraordinarily strong position of ambitious, artistic films which would seek new forms of expression, and which would make it possible to touch on the most important existential and philosophical issues, just as literature would. Such was the attitude presented not only by filmmakers like Jerzy Wojciech Has, or Grzegorz Królikiewicz, who would follow the best "artistic" patterns and reveal their *désintéressement* with the broad audience by playing with the art of film for its own sake. This was also a stance shared by filmmakers who cared for communication with a wider public, and who included Andrzej Wajda, Roman Polański, Jerzy Skolimowski and Andrzej Munk, Kazimierz Kutz and Tadeusz Konwicki. For them the point of reference was European artistic cinema – Italian neorealism, French "New Wave", or the English "Angry Young Men" – and not popular Hollywood movies. It is noteworthy that even the lighter films, such as comedies of manners, crime dramas etc. were judged according to the criteria adopted from artistic cinema. This is what hap-

pened to the interesting output of Stanisław Bareja, author of a series of comedies from the 1970s which now enjoy cult status and popularity. At the time they were created, they were attacked and mocked, accused of representing the conventional tastes of the *petit-bourgeois*, despite the fact that they represented an entirely different category, namely entertainment, hence being intentionally in a different style than films by such directors as, say, Krzysztof Kieślowski or Krzysztof Zanussi.

Of course, there were also films made which were intentionally non-political entertainment, and there were also politically correct films ... But they passed, and having evoked no emotions, they simply fell into oblivion. The relatively large number of authors who followed the political guidelines belonged, however, to the margins of the filmmaking community, and represented no strong personalities or outstanding talent. An exception to the rule was perhaps Sylwester Chęciński, author of extremely popular but politically safe comedies, as well as television series directors – Jan Łomnicki and Jerzy Gruza. The first filmmaker who wanted to create good quality "pure" entertainment in the western style, and who had the divine spark for it, was Juliusz Machulski (made his first film in the early 1980s). But even in his light comedies, there were still nuances discovered, such as the subtle stylistic dialogue with the conventions of gangster films *Hit the Bank* (*Vabank*, 1981), or political allusions (*Sexmission*, [*Seksmisja*, 1983]). The tone of Polish cinema was set by artists – artists who were politically engaged.

The transformation of the economic system into capitalism revealed the existence of a new dictator: the mass consumer. For fear that the audience would turn their back on them, and feeling the breath of strong Hollywood competitors flooding Polish movie theatres on their necks, Polish filmmakers fell into a frenzy of seeking a formula which could substitute the old political ties with the viewers. Moreover, the more sublime artists felt that capitalism would mean problems with finding the finances for their ambitious experiments. The atmosphere, in which the "mass audience is always right", offered no consensus to the sophisticated stance of artistic extravagance, particularly cinema that was still predominantly sponsored by the state, and not by eccentric sponsors who could afford to finance their caprices. Very few directors, such as Jan Jakub Kolski, were able to stand guard of their creative individuality, and create a work, written out into a series of separate films, which would be devoted to the same subject matter, contribute to the development of the film language, and share the same type of imagination (*The Burial of the Potato* [*Pogrzeb kartofla*, 1990]; *Pograbek*, 1992; *Johnnie Aquarius* [*Jańcio Wodnik*, 1993]; *History of Cinema in Popielawy* [*Historia kina*

Johnnie Aquarius,
dir. Jan Jakub Kolski
←

w Popielawach, 1998]). Among the artists who made their first films after 1989, it was pretty much only Kolski and Dorota Kędzierzawska (*The Devils, The Devils* [*Diably, diably*, 1991]; *The Crows* [*Wrony*, 1994]; *Nothing* [*Nic*, 1998]) who were able to hold ground. The new situation caused a serious feeling of being lost both among the authors who had thus far been focusing on the political ties with the viewers, as well as filmmakers who were more inclined to experiment formally. This was a period of many works which were mixtures of artistic and commercial ambitions, a compromise between the expectations of the public and the artists' own creative explorations. Such "artistic popular cinema" held an internal contradiction, thus was insincere, full of forced and fake ideas, but at the same time, a reflection of the organisational and financial situation of the Polish film industry – the whole production and financing system had been adapted to art creation, while the projected expectations of the viewers were "populist" and "mass". The schizophrenia of the situation was further magnified by the feeling of temporariness and awareness that some kind of a major change would have to take place soon so as to reestablish the model for the entire industry. Discussions about the future of Polish cinema kept constantly returning to the subject of a few possible scenarios: advocates of cultural Darwinism kept referring to the American model of production, where there are no state donations, or even a ministry of culture, but which was able to create the most productive and expansive, and at the same time, most commercially competitive machine of the Hollywood "Dream Factory". An extreme option of this "neoliberal" discourse went as far as accepting the disappearance of Polish cinema as such – should it not survive the severe competition of the free market ruled by supply and demand. On the other hand, however, there were voices praising the old system of state tutelage over cinema, demanding that a policy of cultural protectionism be continued. Both extremes were devoid of rational bases; however they set the direction for the public discussion, dominating its tone and blocking, by means of their raucous presence, any possibility to work out more moderate solutions, which could combine elements of market mechanisms with the European model of protecting national culture. It wasn't until the late 1990s that the French model of supporting the domestic film industry was offered as a possibility. The concept finally won but it wasn't until 2005, pursuant to a new Cinematography Act, that the Polish Film Institute was established.

New technology

Approximately at the time when censorship in Poland disappeared, a technological revolution began. Already in the early 1990s it brought with it a new format of film image: *high definition*, and cheap digital cameras, which enabled professional film production in "no budget" conditions. Another equally important circumstance was the declaration of the "Dogma" manifesto, which gave artistic prestige to such types of artistic creation, and which opened up unprecedented and quite overwhelming possibilities for young creators.

"Dogma" made a huge psychological impact in Poland, as it helped weakness be forged into strength. The young filmmakers who previously had had to wait for an eternity to make their first full length feature film, grabbed HD cameras, talked actors and crew into working for free (for the uncertain potential future profits in case somebody turned out to want to buy the production one day), and take on a risk of a "home" production. Of course, they would spice up their endeavours by adding a legend of anti-systemic independence. It was a situation shared by both the young artists, fresh graduates of film schools, such as Dariusz Gajewski, Anna Jadowska and Ewa Stankiewicz, as well as amateurs – Jacek Borcuch, Przemysław Wojcieszek, Piotr Matwiejczyk or Bodo Kox. Gajewski's modest but visually interesting *AlaRm* won the 2002 edition of the youth film festival in Koszalin, as a result of which the film was later purchased by Polish public television, which created an opportunity for the author to begin work on his full length feature *début*. This is how the film *Warsaw* (*Warszawa*) was made – the great winner of Polish Film Festival in Gdynia in 2003. Similar was the story with the independent first film by Jadowska and Stankiewicz, *Touch Me* (*Dotknij mnie*, 2003) – a sensation, as it later appeared, at the independent films competition in Gdynia 2003, giving both the artists a spectacular career boost. The eruption of independence in the film industry, which exploded in the late 1990s, was a reaction of young artists to having no chance in the mainstream. But this eruption would not have been possible without the availability of digital technology, drastically cutting the costs of professional film production. Neither would it have been possible without the aesthetic ideology of "Dogma", which introduced this type of artistic expression to film salons. This is the true story of Polish "independent cinema": it came out of necessity and was turned into a virtue. Amateur filmmakers also benefited from this wave of "garage" production. Without these circumstances, they would have probably remained stuck in the ghetto of hobbyists with a passion. The new situation also helped create a new mechanism of professional co-optation. Today, nobody would ask Jacek Borcuch, who began with an entirely amateur production of *Cauliflower* (*Kalafiorr*, 1999), or Przemysław Wojcieszek with his *Kill Them All* (*Zabij ich wszystkich*, 1999) to show their art school graduation diplomas. It is their films, the wonderful *Louder Than Bombs* (*Głośniej od bomb*, 2001) by Wojcieszek, or *All That I Love* (*Wszystko co kocham*, 2009) by Borcuch which are their best certificate in the arts. This is how the breakthrough in the hermetic film production circuit happened – now this world was also open to artists who had no state diplomas of their professional skills, but who were willing and able to fight for what's theirs, who had talent and … something to say.

BEGINNING OF THE NEW SYSTEM

A few events took place in the late 1990s which started a period of transformation and maturation of Polish cinema. Entertainment cinema, which tried to lure the mass

audience in the country was predominantly drawing on the more or less successful attempts of copying Władysław Pasikowski's mechanism applied in his two films *Kroll* (1991) and *Pigs* (*Psy*, 1992). It was based on the idea that the familiar Polish car thieves and drug dealers were presented like the bosses of dangerous mafias, while the former officers of security police and militia adopted the rough charm of "Dirty Harry". The current of "bandit cinema", represented by such directors as Jacek Skalski *Private Town* (*Miasto prywatne*, 1995), Jarosław Żamojda *Fast Lane*, (*Młode wilki*, 1995), Marcin Ziębiński *Anger* (*Gniew*, 1997), Maciej Ślesicki *Sara* (1997), Łukasz Zadrzyński (*Billboard*, 1998) substantially changed its orientation following the unprecedented success of Juliusz Machulski, who shifted the course of "bandit cinema" steering it on a path of comedy with his *Killer* (*Kiler* (1997). The mysterious "godfathers" of the gloomy world of crime and played with all due seriousness, were here replaced by thick rednecks fed on steroids, who happen to encounter different comic mishaps and adventures. Soon other directors followed in the footsteps of Machulski: Jacek Bromski (*It's Me, the Thief* [*To ja złodziej*, 2000]; *The Career of Nikos Dyzma*, [*Kariera Nikosia Dyzmy*, 2002]), and Olaf Lubaszenko (*Boys Don't Cry*, [*Chłopaki nie płaczą*, 2000]; *Coyote's Morning* [*Poranek kojota*, 2001]; *E=mc2*, 2002) to name a few. What is more important is that the great success of *Killer*, which was a modest low budget production that managed to attract an audience of over a million, and whose rights for a remake were bought by the The Walt Disney Company for

← *All That I Love,* dir. Jacek Borcuch

↓ *With Fire and Sword,* dir. Jerzy Hoffman

US$ 600,000, finally convinced producers that domestic cinema did have commercial potential. The success also drew the attention of private investors, which made it possible to produce films with budgets unheard of before in Polish cinema, such as *With Fire and Sword* (*Ogniem i mieczem*, 1998) by Jerzy Hoffman and *Pan Tadeusz: The Last Foray in Lithuania* (hereafter: *Pan Tadeusz*, 1999) by Andrzej Wajda – both blockbusters to the extent that in 1999 these two titles attracted over half of the annual number of cinema goers. The example of both these productions, which were film adaptations of Polish classical literature, was so infectious that it led to the creation of what was somewhat ironically termed "school reading-list cinema". Though usually neglected by critics, they were met with a great interest by the public and revived the public's trust in Polish films. The current would eventually give rise to a more professional field of entertainment cinema, producing not only in response to the ever better recognised market needs, but also being more effective in reaching the audience. In effect, we have the present situation, in which an audience of a million viewers coming to see a Polish comedy is no longer something surprising. This is seen as normal, and expected by producers.

On the other hand, the late 1990s were marked with the appearance of a new tone in art cinema, as ambitious filmmaking was beginning to regain its vigour and self-confidence.

The Dark House, dir. Wojciech Smarzowski

Debt, dir. Krzysztof Krauze

Krzysztof Krauze's *The Debt* (*Dług*, 1999) about a group of young friends, ordinary and decent people who, as a result of intimidating threats by gangsters start behaving like the gangsters themselves, as well as *Hi, Tereska* (*Cześć Tereska*, 2001) by Robert Gliński, a film about the difficult life of a girl from a poor housing project, with nobody to care for her, and with no prospects for a better life, are both pieces in which their makers have explicitly revealed their effort to strike an authentic communication with the viewer, who is no longer treated as a silly consumer or a "target" of marketing tricks, but who is a partner of the director, and a trustee of his/her thoughts and fears. These are films for a mature audience, the type of cinema that the 1990s lacked. This is also the direction that the young generation of film artists is following. Let us mention a few examples: *Louder Than Bombs* (2001) by Przemysław Wojcieszek – a film about rebellious teenagers in love, who come from a small sleepy town, and who, as much as it is possible, refuse to participate in the provincial version of a rat race; *Edi* (2002) by Piotr Trzaskalski about an anti-hero in the times of rapacious capitalism – a homeless collector of recyclable metal scrap who has more dignity and life wisdom than all those "respected citizens"; *Squint Your Eyes* (*Zmruż oczy*, 2003) by Andrzej Jakimowski about a self-taught philosopher, who decided of his own free will to move to the outskirts of the world so as

to be able to contemplate better its ups and downs; finally *The Wedding* (*Wesele*, 2004) and *The Dark House* (*Dom zły*, 2009) by Wojciech Smarzowski – cruel and merciless depictions of the Polish provinces, where – by means of the metaphysical fatalism of the author – human passions will always reveal their destructive, vicious force. There is also *33 Scenes From Life* (*33 sceny z życia*, 2008) by Małgorzata Szumowska, in which the director decides on a surprising and subversive way to grapple with her own youthful experience of having lost both parents. All these films of artists debuting in recent years, though very stylistically and thematically different, have a common denominator in that they all need to define the autonomy of the individual, have a gesture of freedom against the economic, social and cultural systems. A fact that serves as a sign of maturity is that these artists create their world without giving a second look to fads, trends and commercial ratings. At the same time, their cinema is not arrogant; it has nothing to do with artsy ventriloquism. These films search for their audience in want of conveying an intimate, personal experience. Interestingly, they lack any sort of an ideological framework – they do not fit in any of the ready and convenient political discourses. They are a private voice telling stories which have happened here, in Poland, but which can be understood anywhere.

Translated by Ewa Kanigowska-Gedroyć

RESOLVING A CRISIS OF IDENTITY: HOW CENTRAL-EASTERN EUROPEAN CINEMA ADJUSTED TO THE CHANGES OF 1989

MICHAEL BROOKE

East European cinema in the West

Contrary to expectations engendered by the near-universal euphoria that greeted the end of Communism in central and eastern Europe in 1989, its impact on the relevant countries' national cinemas has turned out to be largely malign. The long-desired abolition of bureaucratic censorship on ideological grounds was accompanied by the economic near-collapse of previously state-subsidised film industries and a sudden flood of previously unavailable western (mostly Hollywood) titles invading local cinemas, leading to unprecedented competition. Perhaps the most sobering statistic from this period is that the most successful film at the Czech box office in 1990 was *Emmanuelle* – not a remake, but Just Jaeckin's 1973 French original, given a legitimate release for the first time.

More damagingly, following an initial flurry of interest in central and eastern European cinema at major film festivals (including Berlin and Edinburgh) in 1990, the region's cinema largely vanished from commercial distribution outside their native countries. While they never matched the appeal of French or Italian films, at least twenty Polish films[1] (all with clear linguistic and cultural roots in the country) were given a British cinema release during the fifteen years prior to 1989. However, during the equivalent period between 1990 and 2004 (the year Poland joined the European Union), the total fell to just nine[2] – including co-productions primarily or entirely in languages other than Polish. Worse, between 1994 and 2007, British distributors seemingly showed no

---

[1]
The *Monthly Film Bulletin*, the British Film Institute's official journal of record, cites the following films as having been screened commercially in Britain between 1974 and 1989 - dates refer to the Polish premiere followed by the British release: *The Third Part of the Night* (*Trzecia część nocy*, Andrzej Żuławski, 1972/74), *Illumination* (*Iluminacja*, Krzysztof Zanussi, 1973/75), *The Deluge* (*Potop*, Jerzy Hoffman, 1974/76), *The Story of Sin* (*Dzieje grzechu*, Walerian Borowczyk, 1975/76), *Family Life* (*Życie rodzinne*, Zanussi, 1971/76), *Landscape After Battle* (*Krajobraz po bitwie*, Andrzej Wajda, 1970/77), *Camouflage* (*Barwy ochronne*, Zanussi, 1977/79), *Man of Marble* (*Człowiek z marmuru*, Wajda, 1977/79), *Rough Treatment* (*Bez znieczulenia*, Wajda, 1978/81), *The Conductor* (*Dyrygent*, Wajda, 1980/81), *The Constant Factor* (*Constans*, Zanussi, 1980/81), *Man of Iron* (*Człowiek z żelaza*, Wajda, 1981/81), *The Contract* (*Kontrakt*, Zanussi, 1980/82), *The Beads of One Rosary* (*Paciorki jednego różańca*, Kazimierz Kutz, 1980/82), *Camera Buff* (*Amator*, Krzysztof Kieślowski, 1979/82), *Maids of Wilko* (*Panny z Wilka*, Wajda, 1979/83), *Sexmission* (*Seksmisja*, Juliusz Machulski, 1984/85), *Year of the Quiet Sun* (*Rok spokojnego słońca*, Zanussi, 1985/86), *No End* (*Bez końca*, Kieślowski, 1985/88), *A Short Film About Killing* (*Krótki film o zabijaniu*, Kieślowski, 1988/89).

---

[2]
The *Monthly Film Bulletin* and *Sight & Sound* (which merged with the *MFB* in April 1991) cite the following films as having been screened commercially in Britain between 1990 and 2004: *A Short Film About Love* (*Krótki film o miłości*, Krzysztof Kieślowski, 1988/90), *Interrogation* (*Przesłuchanie*, Ryszard Bugajski, 1989/90 – originally completed 1982), *Korczak* (Andrzej Wajda, 1990), *The Double Life of Véronique* (*La double vie de Véronique/Podwójne życie Weroniki*, Kieślowski, 1991/92), *The Silent Touch* (*Dotknięcie ręki*, Zanussi, 1992/93), *The Decalogue* (*Dekalog*, Kieślowski, 1989/93 – British television premiere 1990), *Three Colours: Blue* (*Trois couleurs: Bleu/Trzy kolory: Niebieski*, Kieślowski, 1993), *Three Colours: White* (*Trois couleurs: blanc/Trzy kolory: Biały*, Kieślowski, 1994), *Three Colours: Red* (*Trois couleurs: rouge/Trzy kolory: Czerwony*, Kieślowski, 1994).

interest in Polish cinema whatsoever. It took the Poles themselves to start making serious efforts to get Polish films back on British cinema screens via the annual Kinoteka film festival (launched in 2003 by the Polish Cultural Institute) and a distribution initiative called The Polish Connection.[3]

Very similar patterns could be observed by comparing any central-eastern European film culture with any foreign marketplace. While 1989 remained a totemic year for western media, they subsequently showed little interest in anything but the most obviously seismic events, such as the reunification of Germany and the collapse of the Soviet Union in 1991, Czechoslovakia's split into the Czech Republic and Slovakia at the beginning of 1993 or the conflict in the former Yugoslavia throughout the 1990s. At a time of significant change in western Europe (symbolised by the renaming of the European Community as the European Union, the introduction of the single European market and, eventually, the Euro), it is perhaps not surprising that the often traumatic economic and social upheavals occurring eastwards received minimal coverage. It didn't help that the facts on the ground usually contradicted the widespread myth that a switch was flicked in 1989 that turned the eastern bloc from centrally-planned communist to free-market capitalist overnight, with no complications along the way.

Accordingly, with little interest being expressed in national cinemas outside festivals and short seasons at specialist cinémathèques, films had to stand or fall on individual merit. Independent arthouse distributors and exhibitors, a conservative group even at the best of times (and the early 1990s was far from the best of times), understandably tended to favour work by long-established auteurs such as Krzysztof Kieślowski, István Szabó and Nikita Mikhalkov, with only occasional forays elsewhere. A major award, ideally a top prize from the "big three" (Cannes, Berlin, Venice) or an Oscar for Best Foreign Film would also guarantee distribution, but it was comparatively rare for such honours to go to central-eastern European films.[4]

3
Films given British theatrical distribution by The Polish Connection, an offshoot of independent distributor Dogwoof Pictures, included Krzysztof Krauze's *My Nikifor* (*Mój Nikifor*, 2004), Wojciech Smarzowski's *The Wedding* (*Wesele*, 2004), Michał Kwieciński's *The Extras* (*Statyści*, 2006), Marek Koterski's *We're All Christs* (*Wszyscy jesteśmy Chrystusami*, 2006), Tomasz Konecki and Andrzej Saramonowicz' *Testosterone* (*Testosteron*, 2007), Stanisław Mucha's *Hope* (*Nadzieja*, 2007) and Maciej Żak's *Midnight Talks* (*Rozmowy nocq*, 2008) – in other words, a far more varied blend of arthouse and commercial titles than had been the case in the more auteur-focused 1970s and 1980s.

4
This is a complete list of Berlin Golden Bear, Cannes Palme d'Or, Venice Golden Lion and Best Foreign Film Oscar winners falling within the scope of this essay – 1990: Golden Bear – *Larks on a String* (*Skřivanci na niti*, d. Jiří Menzel, Czechoslovakia); 1991: Golden Lion – *Urga* (d. Nikita Mikhalkov, Russia); 1993: Golden Lion – *Three Colours: Blue* (*Trzy kolory: Niebieski*, d. Krzysztof Kieślowski, France/Poland/Switzerland); 1994: Golden Lion – *Before the Rain* (*Pred dozhdot*, d. Milcho Manchevski, Macedonia); Oscar – *Burnt by the Sun* (*Utomlyonnye solntsem*, d. Nikita Mikhalkov,

Times of Transition

It is likely that the region's cinema would have encountered these difficulties even without massive internal upheavals, but they certainly didn't help. As Dina Iordanova acknowledged in her overview of the period:

> The abolition of the centralised management of culture divorced film production from exhibition and distribution, and earlier distribution networks were ruined before new ones had come into being. Most of the new private distributors who emerged subsequently chose to abide by market rules and rather than play the losing card of domestic productions opted for Hollywood box office winners. Although well-received at festivals, productions carrying an east European label continued to be considered hard sells at film markets.[5]

They were equally hard to make in the first place. Without a reasonable prospect of international sales, most domestic markets were simply too small to sustain much production activity, and in the 1990s the number of films being made declined sharply. While Poland, with a population approaching 40 million, could occasionally sustain large-scale blockbusters like Andrzej Wajda's *Pan Tadeusz* (1999) and Jerzy Hoffman's *With Fire and Sword* (*Ogniem i mieczem*, 1999) despite negligible international income, the Czech Republic and Hungary had populations of just 10 million apiece, Slovakia 5 million, and Slovenia just 2 million.

This left central-eastern European filmmakers with several challenges. They needed to maintain what in many cases (certainly in Poland, Czechoslovakia, Hungary and Russia) was a very strong film tradition. Their veterans must continue to find work (not least because their work would usually have greater international appeal), but not at the expense of nurturing new talent that would ultimately supplant them. Given the total transformation of the structure of the various film industries, this would require imaginative new fundraising strategies and a willingness to consider alternative distribu-

---

Russia); 1995: Palme d'Or – *Underground* (*Podzemlje*, d. Emir Kusturica, Yugoslavia); Oscar – *Kolya* (*Kolja*, d. Jan Svěrák, Czechoslovakia); 2001: Oscar – *No Man's Land* (*Ničija zemlja*, d. Danis Tanović, Bosnia-Herzegovina); 2003: Golden Lion – *The Return* (*Vozvrashcheniye*, d. Andrei Zvyagintsev, Russia); 2004: Palme d'Or – *The Pianist* (d. Roman Polański, France/Poland/Germany/UK); 2006: Golden Bear – *Esma's Secret* (*Grbavica*, d. Jasmila Žbanič, Bosnia-Herzegovina); 2007: Palme d'Or – *4 Months, 3 Weeks and 2 Days* (*4 luni, 3 săptămâni și 2 zile*, d. Cristian Mungiu, Romania).

5
Iordanova, D. (2003) *Cinema of the Other Europe: The Industry and Artistry of East Central European Film*, London, Wallflower Press, pp. 144–145.

Pan Tadeusz,
dir. Andrzej Wajda

tion models. Governments needed persuading that national film industries were worth supporting, even at a time of deep financial crisis, while critics and audiences at home and abroad needed convincing that the films had sufficient artistic and/or commercial appeal to justify their existence. Above all, how were notions of national identity to be maintained at a time when international co-production would become more the rule than the exception?

Although these core problems were common to all the region's film industries, in practice they were often addressed in strikingly different ways, relating to various economic, social, cultural and historical factors peculiar to individual countries. The nature of the transition from communism to capitalism itself was a factor. The totalitarian regimes of East Germany, Czechoslovakia and Romania fell very rapidly in the space of a few weeks towards the end of 1989, amidst much breathless coverage by the world's media. By contrast, the political transitions in Poland and Hungary occurred earlier and more gradually,[6] with more attention being paid to conventional democratic process. After the fall of the Berlin Wall, East Germany underwent a total purge of communist officials and those associated with the Stasi, or secret police, followed in 1991 by a "reunification" that in practice was more of a corporate takeover by the country's richer western counterparts. That same year, the sudden, wholly unexpected collapse of the USSR created a similarly abrupt break between Russia, its former Soviet satellites and their still very recent history.[7] Other European regions that experienced decisive or symbolic breaks with their past in the 1990s included Northern Ireland and the former Yugoslavia (especially Bosnia-Herzegovina), both of which underwent processes similar to those conducted by the South African Truth and Reconciliation Committees. The past was discussed and analysed at exhaustive length, with the primary aim of bringing cathartic closure at a national level.

---

[6] There was, of course, a pivotal election in June 1989 in which Solidarity decisively demonstrated its popular mandate, but this had the misfortune to take place at exactly the same time as the Tiananmen Square massacre and the death of Iran's Ayatollah Khomeini. Consequently, the election result and its ramifications received much less international attention at the time than would normally have been its due.

---

[7] Or at least up to the election of Vladimir Putin, former KGB agent and protegé of former Soviet leader Yuri Andropov, as Russian President in 2000, after which various elements of the Soviet Union gradually inveigled themselves back into the national narrative.

However, Poland did not experience anything similar, partly because the country's true anticommunist revolution had taken place a decade earlier, between the election of the Archbishop of Kraków, Karol Wojtyła, as Pope John Paul II in September 1978 (an event of far greater political significance for Poland than was often recognised by the west) and General Jaruzelski's declaration of martial law in December 1981. In terms of illuminating how communism worked (or didn't work) in Poland, the events of 1981 are as important as those of 1956 in Hungary and 1968 in Czechoslovakia. However, while there are numerous Hungarian and Czech films dealing with those eras, the martial law period has been comparatively absent from Polish cinema screens. The first film to tackle the subject was premiered as early as May 1982: Jerzy Skolimowski's *Moonlighting* is not technically a Polish film, though it certainly qualifies for honorary status, and obviously couldn't have been made in Poland itself at the time. Specifically Polish "1981" films include Maciej Dejczer's *300 Miles to Heaven* (*300 mil do nieba*, 1989), Sylwester Chęciński's satirical comedy *Controlled Conversations* (*Rozmowy kontrolowane*, 1992), Kazimierz Kutz' 1994 diptych *Death as a Slice of Bread* (*Śmierć jak kromka chleba*) and *The Convert* (*Zawrócony*) and, most recently, Wojciech Smarzowski's *The Dark House* (*Dom zły*, 2009), but they remain in the minority. One explanation for this apparent reluctance to probe too deeply into this period is that while the Hungarian "1956" and Czech "1968" films could take the easy option of characterising the events as foreign invasions, the events of 1981 were entirely internal affairs, and therefore difficult to explore in any depth without shedding unwelcome light on aspects of specifically Polish history and behaviour.

A rare example of a recent Polish film that directly confronts emotive issues arising from the Communist past is Michał Rosa's *The Scratch* (*Rysa*, 2008), in which a woman suffers intolerable cognitive dissonance after hearing a rumour that her warm and loving husband of several decades was a secret police agent who only married her for espionage purposes. In its exploration of all-consuming paranoia, it tackles similar themes to Florian Henckel von Donnersmarck's enormously successful *The Lives of Others* (*Das Leben der Anderen*, 2006) about an East German Stasi surveillance agent who develops a conscience – with the difference that von Donnersmarck's film views its events from a reassuring historical distance, is set in a state that no longer exists, and even contrives a plausibly upbeat ending without undermining the force of its central situation.

The other immensely popular "East German" film of recent years was Wolfgang Becker's *Good Bye Lenin!* (2003), whose preposterous but winningly-performed central conceit concerned an ardent Communist waking from a long-term coma to find herself in a post-1989 world – though her family goes to increasingly farcical lengths to prevent her from finding this out, lest the shock ends up killing her. This situation neatly allowed Becker to criticise the DDR period while simultaneously indulging in barely – concealed nostalgia for many of its trappings (an emotion that even has its own specific term: "Ostalgie", or "nostalgia for the east"). Similarly rose-tinted views of the past underpinned the Hungarian musical comedies *Dollybirds* (*Csinibaba*, 1997) and *Made in Hungária* (2008), both set in the early 1960s at a time when János Kádár's more relaxed form of "goulash Communism" was giving Hungarians a higher standard of living than elsewhere in the eastern bloc – something vociferously recalled by many Hungarians as the economic reforms of the 1990s began to bite. These splashily artificial quasi-Technicolor musicals are clearly not intended to be anything other than idealised caricatures of the past (western cinema has frequently fallen prey to similarly rose-tinted historical indulgences throughout its entire lifespan), but their popularity is revealing enough in itself – as is the fact that Poland, lacking an equivalent of the Kádár era, has produced nothing similar.

Although in the 1970s and 1980s, Polish filmmakers were amongst the most outspokenly critical of all their central and eastern European peers, they were emboldened by a situation that Marek Haltof characterised as: a polarised world, in which the only meaningful distinction was between the pro-communist side ("them") and the "right side" ("us"). The artistic criteria in Poland were repeatedly subordinated to political criteria. To be a dissident meant to be a true artist.

But what did "being a dissident" mean in a post-communist world, when former dissidents were now in government and, in the case of Lech Wałęsa, the national president? Was it possible, or indeed desirable? Certainly, audiences no longer cared about the great ideological battles that had been fought on Polish screens in the 1970s and 1980s: they had more immediate practical concerns that films were ill-equipped to cater for at a time when these could now be openly discussed. Filmmakers, on the other hand, were suddenly forced to regard their audience much more than had been the case in the past, since funding in this brave new era was usually based on the assumption that the resulting film would attract a minimum level of popular support.

A NEW BEGINNING: POLAND, CZECH REPUBLIC, HUNGARY

The economic ruptures of the 1990s meant that film funding was increasingly difficult to obtain in Poland, and new commercial imperatives tended to favour either those filmmakers prepared to work in wholly commercial genres, or those who had already built considerable artistic reputations prior to 1989. From an international perspective, the highest-profile Polish filmmakers of the 1990s were familiar names: Agnieszka Holland,

Krzysztof Kieślowski, Andrzej Wajda and Krzysztof Zanussi. Most of their 1990s films were international co-productions of varying levels of "Polishness" – Holland had a big critical and commercial hit with the German-language co-production *Europa Europa* (1990) and the wholly French *Olivier, Olivier* (1991), after which she went to Hollywood. Kieślowski remained in Europe but worked mostly in French. Aside from the early scenes featuring the Polish character Weronika in *The Double Life of Véronique* (*La double vie de Véronique/Podwójne życie Weroniki*, 1991), Kieślowski's only culturally Polish film in this period was *Three Colours: White* (*Trois couleurs: blanc/Trzy kolory: Biały*, 1994), a mordant look at the dog-eat-dog capitalism of the early 1990s. Well before his premature death in 1996, Kieślowski was increasingly regarded as generically "European" rather than Polish.

Although already the most internationally-oriented of the quartet, having worked extensively in western Europe and America from the mid-1970s, Krzysztof Zanussi's output in the 1990s was much more rooted in the traditions of his native country – not just geographically but also spiritually. The English-language *The Silent Touch* (*Dotknięcie ręki*, 1993) was followed by the autobiographical *In Full Gallop* (*Cwał*, 1996), set in the early Stalinist period, and *Life as a Fatal Sexually Transmitted Disease* (*Życie jako śmiertelna choroba przenoszona drogą płciową*, 2000), the first in what became a series of films examining attitudes towards death. As for Wajda, he remained the most overtly Polish of the quartet, but the 1990s was a wayward, uncertain decade for him, as he acknowledged in a recent interview:

Squint Your Eyes, dir. Andrzej Jakimowski

> Shortly after Poland gained political freedom I made a few films from old scripts, which were previously restricted by censorship. Unfortunately it turned out that people in Poland were not interested in them, so I turned to more classical themes. Seven million Polish viewers watched *Pan Tadeusz* (1999), based on the 19th-century national poem, but the film was invisible elsewhere. It is not easy to be an old director, especially one with a long past.[8]

However, there were advantages to being an old director with a long past. Wajda was one of the few Poland-based directors to manage a consistent output throughout the 1990s, and he finished the decade with a huge domestic hit in the form of the *Titanic*-beating *Pan Tadeusz*, and an Oscar in 2000 for his entire body of work – the first Polish filmmaker to receive such high-profile recognition. In isolation, these would be triumphant achievements, but amongst his peers, especially those who graduated from the Łódź Film School in the late 1980s or 1990s and who had failed to progress their careers due to lack of funding, Wajda was one of the industry's most unpopular men. Ironically for someone who had championed many younger filmmakers, especially in the 1970s when the Wajda-run Film Group "X" helped nurture the early careers of Holland, Feliks Falk, Andrzej Żuławski and others, Wajda recognised that he had inadvertently helped create a serious generation gap within Polish cinema. To his credit, he recognised the problem and tried to resolve it by founding the Andrzej Wajda Master School of Directing in 2002, but the damage had been done – the previous decade had seen hardly any important films by new Polish filmmakers, and talented graduates like Wojciech Smarzowski and Andrzej Jakimowski (both born in 1963) had to wait until their thirties or even forties before making their feature *débuts* in the early 2000s.

By contrast, the Czech cinema of the 1990s was studded with high-profile first films, many of which were also distributed internationally. The most obviously successful of the younger generation of Czech filmmakers was Jan Svěrák (b. 1965). Although his

---

8 Brooke, M. and Kuc, K. (2008) 'Lest We Forget: an interview with Andrzej Wajda', *Sight & Sound*, June 2008, pp. 34-37.

domestic popularity was boosted by being the son of the popular actor/screenwriter Zdeněk Svěrák, this had no influence on three Oscar nominations (and two wins) for films made when he was still in his twenties.[9] In fact, *Kolya* (*Kolja*, 1996) may be the single most popular central-eastern European film of its decade, packaging a serious subject characteristic of the region (uneasy relations between Czechs and Russians towards the end of the Communist era) into a warm-hearted odd-couple scenario between a grouchy cellist (Svěrák *père*) and a cute Russian boy. But Svěrák was no isolated case – other outstanding new Czech directors of his generation who also emerged towards the end of the 1990s included Jan Hřebejk, Petr Zelenka (both b. 1967), David Ondříček (b. 1969) and Saša Gedeon (b. 1970), all several years younger than Jakimowski or Smarzowski.

Despite a decade dominated by privatisation (Václav Klaus, Czechoslovakia's finance minister from 1989–92 and prime minister of the newly independent Czech Republic from 1993–97, was an ardent disciple of Margaret Thatcher), a successful lobbying campaign spearheaded by the veteran director Věra Chytilová secured government subsidy for up to one-third of the production costs of domestic features. Although this wouldn't protect Czech films from the need for co-production deals and television funding, it helped maintain cultural continuity, with a younger generation effectively nurtured alongside an old guard that also continued to find work. In addition to Chytilová, whose *The Inheritance, or Fuckoffguysgoodbye* (*Dědictví aneb Kurvahošigutntag*, 1992) and *Traps* (*Pasti, pasti, pastičky*, 1998) offered memorably sour studies of post-velvet revolution capitalism, especially the latter, a jet-black radical feminist comedy that made effective if unsubtle symbolic use of explicit rape and castration motifs. Of her contemporaries, Jan Němec returned to both Czechoslovakia and feature films in 1990 after a 23-year break, but struggled to fit his brand of highly personal cinema into an increasingly commercialised landscape, and by the early 2000s he was shooting the explicitly autobiographical *Late Night Talks with Mother* (*Noční hovory s matkou*, 2001) and *Landscape of My Heart* (*Krajina mého srdce*, 2004) on video with tiny budgets. The surrealist short-film master Jan Švankmajer moved permanently into features after 1992, relying on substantial cult followings in Britain, France and Germany to assemble co-production deals that allowed him total creative freedom. Jiří Menzel began the decade with an unexpected Golden Bear at the 1990 Berlin Film Festival for his long-shelved *Larks on a String* (*Skřivanci na niti*, 1969), but he spent most of the following years working in the theatre, producing just one feature (*The Life and Extraordinary Adventures of Private Ivan Chonkin/Život a neobyčejná dobrodružství vojáka Ivana Čonkina*, 1994) and a lot of legal paperwork over the rights to Bohumil Hrabal's novel *I Served the King of England* (*Obsluhoval jsem anglického krále*), which he finally filmed in 2006.

9
The short film *The Oil Gobblers* (*Ropáci*, 1988) won a student Oscar, and the features *The Elementary School* (*Obecná škola*, 1991) and *Kolya* (*Kolja*, 1996) were both nominated for Best Foreign Film – *Kolya* going on to win.

Hungary also tempered its rapid transition to free-market capitalism with a film subsidy administered by the Hungarian Motion Picture Foundation (Magyar mozgókép alaptivány), established in 1991, alongside similar funding initiatives. Hungary's leading filmmaker of the time, István Szabó, had more experience of international co-production than most of his compatriots, though in 1992 he made his first culturally-Hungarian feature in over a decade on a much lower budget than his usual one, as he knew that one of the most uncompromisingly bleak films of its era would struggle at the box office. *Sweet Emma, Dear Böbe* (*Édes Emma, draga Böbe*, 1992) is a study of two women and the problems they face through being in the wrong profession (Russian teachers) at the wrong time (after 1989), marginalised by an economic system that treats them as an irrelevance – a theme that anyone working in the region's film industries would readily recognise. While not explicitly nostalgic for the Communist era, it's hard to miss Szabó's underlying message that the transition to capitalism was too rapid for comfort.

Fellow veteran Miklós Jansco was also forced by circumstance to find new modes of expression, though in his case this was because his previous large-scale projects with casts of hundreds (sometimes thousands) were no longer financially or logistically possible. After two features that explicitly tackled the realities of the early post-communist era, *God Walks Backwards* (*Isten hátrafelé megy*, 1990) and *Blue Danube Waltz* (*Kék Duna keringő*, 1991), he spent much of the 1990s working in television before reinventing himself in 1999 with *The Lord's Lantern in Budapest* (*Nekem lámpást adott kezembe as Úr Pesten*), the first in a series of eccentric comedies about two gravediggers, Pepe and Kapa, vehicles for dense, allusion-packed, often satirical examinations of aspects of Hungarian history and culture. In a 2008 interview,[10] the octogenarian filmmaker admitted that to the younger generation, he is no longer Miklós Jancsó the 1960s and 70s Hungarian film master, but "Uncle Miki", an onscreen supporting character in the Pepe and Kapa films.

Béla Tarr had initially made his reputation with a series of social-realist features reminiscent (at least to western audiences unfamiliar with the work of Tarr's mentor István Darday) of the work of Ken Loach. With *Autumn Almanac* (*Őszi almanach*, 1985) and especially *Damnation* (*Kárhozat*, 1988) he adopted a more stylised approach, which culminated in *Sátántangó* (1994), a film that seemed deliberately made to throw down the gauntlet for "art cinema" in an increasingly commercialised film world. Shot in black and white and running over seven hours (with many individual shots surpassing ten minutes in length), the latter factor in particular seriously restricted its distribution potential, and the majority of its few theatrical screenings has been at festivals and retrospectives.

10
Conducted by Tony Rayns, Curzon Mayfair Cinema, London, 14 March 2008.

Pigs 2:
The Last Blood,
dir. Władysław
Pasikowski

TOWARDS THE MASS-AUDIENCE

Few of the region's filmmakers were willing or able to go down the aggressively uncompromising route that Tarr was mapping, and the highest-profile Polish films at the time of *Sátántangó's* premiere were explicitly Hollywood-influenced action films, of which Władysław Pasikowski's *Pigs* (*Psy*, 1992) and *Pigs 2: The Last Blood* (*Psy 2: Ostatnia krew*, 1994) were the best known. The latter was one of the biggest domestic hits of the 1990s, alongside the similarly violent *Fast Lane* (*Młode wilki*, 1995) and *Night Graffiti* (*Nocne graffiti*, 1997). These films depict a post-Communist Poland that has fallen victim to ruthless gangsters, usually opposed by cops who are themselves morally ambiguous in a way unthinkable in Polish films of only a few years before. In particular, Bogusław Linda, who had initially made his name in several important 1980s films by Holland, Kieślowski and Wajda, was reinvented as the closest Polish equivalent to an American anti-hero, a character who didn't exist in Polish cinema prior to 1989 – smart, cool, sexy, a maverick rule-breaker. In mid-1990s Poland, crime thrillers offered the only serious box-office competition to imported American films despite widespread social concerns about sharply rising real-life crime and the inability of the authorities to do much about it – presumably because the characters played by Linda and his equivalents elsewhere offered a measure of wish-fulfilment fantasy.

Although it superficially belongs to the same gangster-thriller genre, Krzysztof Krauze's *The Debt* (*Dług*, 1999) has several marked differences from its predecessors, most notably an uncharacteristic empathy with the victims of organised crime and a despairing attitude towards the shortcomings of the legal system. Krauze's protagonists Adam and Stefan should by rights be model citizens, seeking to better themselves by becoming entrepreneurs in the brave new capitalist Poland – until a business deal arranged by an initially affable middleman goes nastily wrong, and the duo is faced with mounting debts backed by increasingly potent threats. Their ultimately murderous solution to their problem stems more from wholly plausible desperation than any desire to emulate action-film archetypes. As a result, *The Debt* is one of the first post-1989 Polish films that genuinely reflected the feelings and fears of the majority of the Polish population.

There were numerous equivalents of the Polish gangster cycle all over Europe,[11] but Alexei Balabanov's *Brother* (*Brat*, 1997) offers one of the more interesting case studies. This low-budget thriller was enough of a box-office phenomenon, especially with younger audiences, to establish it as a cultural rival to Russia's big-budget showcase film that year, Nikita Mikhalkov's *The Barber of Siberia* (*Sibirskiy tsiryulnik*, 1997). Not only did it offer a satirical portrait of the chaos and corruption that had engulfed Russia since the Soviet Union's collapse, but it also drew passing inspiration from one of the most serious conflicts to erupt in post-communist Europe since 1989: the wars in Chechnya. These were more directly explored by a number of distinguished Russian films, including Sergei Bodrov's *Prisoner of the Mountains* (*Kavkazskiy plennik*, 1996), Balabanov's ultra-cynical *War* (*Voyna*, 2002), Andrei Konchalovsky's *House of Fools* (*Dom durakov*, 2002) and Nikita Mikhalkov's courtroom drama *12* (2007).

The other major European conflict of the 1990s was the one that tore the former Yugoslavia apart. This understandably dominated the region's cinema, high-profile examples including Emir Kusturica's *Underground* (1994), Srđan Dragojević's *Pretty Village Pretty Flame*

11
Between 1999 and 2002, Britain's film industry saw a particularly virulent outbreak in the wake of the surprise success of Guy Ritchie's low-budget debut *Lock, Stock and Two Smoking Barrels* (1998).

(*Lepa sela lepo gore*, 1997), Goran Paskaljević's *Powder Keg* (*Bure baruta*, 1998), Danis Tanović's *No Man's Land* (2001) and Jasmila Žbanič's *Esma's Secret* (*Grbavica*, 2006). Even an ostensibly slick commercial thriller such as Dejan Zečević's *The Fourth Man* (*Četvrti čovjek*, 2007) included a subplot about its protagonist's complicity in wartime atrocities and his lasting guilt. Black comedy abounded, together with widespread cynicism about the effectiveness of United Nations "peacekeeping" forces – UN officials are unambiguous villains in *No Man's Land* and Jasmin Duraković's 2006 siege-of-Sarajevo drama *Nafaka*. The war in Bosnia also featured in films from other countries, including Britain (Michael Winterbottom's *Welcome to Sarajevo*, 1997; Jasmin Dizdar's *Beautiful People*, 1999), France (Michael Haneke's *Code Unknown/Code inconnu*, 2000) and even Poland, though Pasikowski's *Demons of War* (*Demony wojny według Goi*, 1998) essentially transplanted his successful gangster-antihero formula (plus lead actor Bogusław Linda) to a Bosnian war scenario, and the film was ultimately more interested in exploiting crude heroics than exploring the nature of the underlying conflict: the Bosnian characters barely registered except as convenient ciphers.

After the uncertainty of the 1990s, the following decade has seen far more positive developments for central-eastern European cinema. Poland was one of the most proactive countries in this respect, and the foundation of the Polish Film Institute (Polski Instytut Sztuki Filmowej, or PISF) in 2005 marked a significant turning point. Supporting the development, production, distribution and exhibition of culturally Polish films, it has subsidised many important recent productions, including Wajda's *Katyn* (2007) and *Sweet Rush* (*Tatarak*, 2008), Jakimowski's *Tricks* (*Sztuczki*, 2007) and

Katyn,
dir. Andrzej Wajda

Małgorzata Szumowska's *33 Scenes From Life* (*33 sceny z życia*, 2008). When coupled with eight regional film funds that support production around the country, and various other financial initiatives, it is safe to say that Polish film production is in a surprisingly healthy state, at least as far as the domestic market is concerned.

A LESSON FROM ROMANIANS

But how about internationally? The most encouraging development for central-eastern European cinema in recent years has been the emergence of what rapidly became known as the Romanian New Wave. This was especially surprising because, aside from animation by Ion Popescu-Gopo and features by Lucian Pintilie, Romanian cinema had previously made virtually no international impact. Although a National Centre of Cinematography (CNC) had been established in the early 2000s, it had no financial support from the government – its annual budget of 8 million euros, largely came from the leisure industry. More seriously, cinema exhibition had almost collapsed after 1989 – at one point there were just sixty-five screens in the whole country, and Romanians had one of the lowest cinema attendance rates in the developed world.[12] In other words, the conditions for nurturing a sustainable national film industry appeared far from propitious.

However, the early 2000s also saw the emergence of a number of young directors, mostly born between the mid-1960s and mid-1970, with teenage or young adult memories of life under the dictator Nicolae Ceaușescu, but also firmly part of the post-communist generation. Most of them had already made at least one feature before the international spotlight was turned onto their work, starting with the victory of Cristi Puiu's *The Death of Mr Lazarescu* (*Moartea domnului Lăzărescu*) in the Cannes Film Festival's *Un Certain Regard* competition in 2005. Possessing a universally accessible theme (the tortuous passage of a dying alcoholic through various understaffed and underfunded

---
[12] Roddick, N. (2007) 'Eastern Promise' *Sight & Sound*, October 2007, pp. 36–39.

hospitals), its appeal was helped by the fact that there was little that was especially "Romanian" about it, certainly in comparison with later films.

By contrast, 2006's outstanding Romanian films were explicitly about the 1989 revolution. Cătălin Mitulescu's *The Way I Spent the End of the World* (*Cum mi-am petrecut sfârşitul lumii*) looked at the last months of that year from the perspective of the inhabitants of a small village on the outskirts of Bucharest. Radu Muntean's *Paper Will Be Blue* (*Hîrtia va fi albastră*) focused on the events of the night of 22 December 1989 (the day Ceauşescu fled), with a young soldier going AWOL and encountering numerous diverse people with differing views on the revolution. Corneliu Porumboiu's comedy *12:08 East of Bucharest* (*A fost sau n-a fost?*) analysed the same day, this time from the perspective of an underfunded local television station broadcasting a phone-in programme inviting those with memories of the revolution to share them – which inevitably dissolves into a muddle of denunciations, recriminations, libel threats and the implicit point that great historical events from the perspective of people on the ground are rarely as neat as historians would like to pretend.

The year 2007 saw an even greater Romanian triumph, with the Palme d'Or awarded to Cristian Mungiu's *4 Months, 3 Weeks and 2 Days* (*4 luni, 3 săptămâni şi 2 zile*), a grimly gripping study of the terrifying logistics of obtaining an abortion in Ceauşescu's Romania that was worlds apart from more nostalgic dramatisations of recent history seen elsewhere in eastern Europe. As of late 2009, international interest in Romanian cinema shows little sign of abating, with Cristian Nemescu's sadly posthumous *California Dreamin'* (2007), Muntean's *Boogie* (2008), Porumboiu's *Police, Adjective* (*Politist, adjectiv*, 2009) and the portmanteau collection *Tales from the Golden Age* (*Amintiri din epoca de aur*, 2009) achieving widespread international arthouse releases in addition to festival acclaim.

Are there lessons here for Polish cinema? Although individual Romanian films could differ sharply in style, content and subject matter, they nonetheless have enough elements in common, notably a darkly sardonic sense of humour and a confidence in their attitude towards dramatising the Ceauşescu years, to allow the impression of a generic "Romanian film" to be created for marketing purposes (equivalent processes were at work in the 1960s, where a "Czech film" was seen as a quirky, low-key comedy and a "Hungarian film" was an abstract, often visually stunning quasi-western). Something similar was true of Polish cinema during the Polish Film School and "moral anxiety" periods of the late 1950s and 1970s/80s, but the international focus since then has been largely on individual auteurs. Whereas the Romanian films mentioned above had a shared sense of history, and the same is even more true of films from the former Yugoslav states, too many Polish films seem at pains to emphasise their commonality with films from western Europe or Hollywood at the expense of their own cultural or historical roots. Language and location aside, there's little that's especially "Polish" about *Testosterone* (*Testosteron*, 2007) or *Midnight Talks* (*Rozmowy nocą*, 2008). The fact that Wajda's *Katyn* has had the biggest international impact of any post-1989 Polish film may be at least as much to do with the reassuring familiarity of its ingredients: even as recently as 2009 (when the film belatedly opened in English-speaking countries), Wajda was still seen as the standard-bearer for Polish cinema. The challenge for the next decade is to break this cycle and allow a new but just as distinctively Polish cinema to flourish.

THE ARRIVAL OF THE NEW DOCUMENTARY
TWO DECADES 1989–2009

ANDRZEJ KOŁODYŃSKI

The date of the parliamentary election, 4 June 1989, is considered to be the day communist rule ended in Poland. This boundary was set rather arbitrarily, however. In fact, the process leading up to the change of political system began much earlier, and did not end so abruptly. Traces of this process, along with the remains of changing perceptions of reality, are particularly noticeable in documentary films that reflected society at the time, even if only indirectly. From this perspective, it is interesting to look back on the winners of the 29th Kraków Festival (or Polish Short Film Festival, as it was known at the time), held between May and June 1989. Of its ten prize-winning films, only a few are still mentioned today. Justly or unjustly, time has erased all memory of them. Unfortunately, such is the fate of films in this mostly utilitarian genre. Their artistic merits fade into the background, and once they have lost their social relevance, they are only of interest to historians.

ON THE EVE OF THE TRANSITION

Among the films of the 1989 festival was the winner of the Grand Prix (the Golden Lajkonik): *The Peasant's Fate – a Film Triptych* (*Chłopski los – tryptyk filmowy*) by Zygmunt Skonieczny, a hard-working, veteran educational film director from the Łódź Educational Film Production Company. This is a characteristic work of the transition period. Its shooting was completed in the summer of 1981, but the declaration of martial law meant that its production was suspended, and it only became possible to edit the 50-minute film in 1988. It was impressive in scope: the entire history of the Polish countryside from the 1944 agricultural reform up to the registration of the Rural Solidarity union on 12 May 1981. This film about the long, persistent process of developing self-awareness, the insurgency, and the fading hopes of peasants is both bitter and very personal. Equally consigned to oblivion after the festival was Andrzej Piekutowski's full-length, 99 min. documentary *Coal Miners '88* (*Górnicy '88*), which won a Polish Filmmakers Association Critics Award. The prize did not assure it commercial success, however. Based more on observations than comments for the camera, this was a report on the August strike by miners at the "July Manifesto" mine, who were demanding the re-registration of the free trade union Solidarity. The film's literally day-by-day coverage is in classical documentary style, and shows the defiance of blackmailed, frightened people who occasionally break down, but still find the strength to survive. More generally, it is a picture of a confrontation between society and authorities that do not want dialogue, but are unable to offer any alternative. This metaphor of the situation after martial law has a symbolic ending: the miners leave the mine with no guarantees or deals, and the film breaks off, leaving the symbolically-significant image of a banner slogan above the gates: "The Strike Is On".

Things panned out completely differently, however, for another full-length film that won the Special Prize at the same festival – *The Parade* (*Defilada*, 1989), made by Andrzej Fidyk during the 40th anniversary celebrations of the Democratic People's Republic of Korea. The deciding factors were the film's subject and unusual cinematography. Fidyk, an experienced television director, made a report on these propagandist festivities which had a clear political agenda: they were intended to eclipse the Olympics being held in Seoul. The method applied in the film relies on maintaining apparent impartiality: there is no commentary, just a record of the collective efforts and genuine enthusiasm of people who staunchly believe in what they are doing. But they are people who are unaware, and cut off from the rest of the world by the shackles of totalitarianism. Only a spectator from another country with a different political and cultural background may accurately assess the ambiguous significance of the events captured by the camera. It was a risky procedure which paid off in the end by winning other prestigious awards in Lipsk and Mannheim, as well as the Prix Italia. This film was the starting point in the career of a filmmaker who also became involved in television as an organiser.

If one examines Fidyk's film in purely stylistic terms, it showed a new trend in Polish documentaries – a shift away from the simple recording of events to less obvious, often ironic games with the audience. This was the outcome of changes taking place slowly but surely in people's perceptions. Since the number of cinemagoers began to drop suddenly at that time, it became necessary to overhaul the general structure of film screenings. The influence of television on social life was growing dynamically. In practice, this signified that audiences had more intimate contact with films via the small screen. Documentaries started to disappear from cinemas, where they had previously served as "extras" shown at the beginning of film-shows and, paradoxically, were often more interesting than the main feature. This was not enough to ensure their survival, as commercial advertising was making its way onto screens by then, requiring larger time-slots. The old-style film screenings stopped in the early 1990s. Documentaries were squeezed out of cinemas altogether and, in this new situation, television became their only outlet.

A different kind of documentary

Television was a receptive medium. The Act on Cinematography passed in July 1987 opened up opportunities to produce and distribute films outside the state system (although it

still required official ministerial permission). New technology also contributed greatly to a surge in quantity and quality. Documentaries that had been made since the war using heavy, silent 35mm cameras were already history in the rest of the world, and that soon became the case in Poland as well. New, lighter equipment and magnetic recording of pictures and sound on small cameras made it possible for films to penetrate previously-closed areas. People had to learn how to make the most of this opportunity, but in practice it turned out to be a rapid process, which even allowed Poland to skip certain stages that foreign documentary cinema had had to go through. Basically, it became possible to use other people's experience.

At the beginning, things were rather chaotic and amateurish. In the early 1990s, small, private firms making recordings and cassettes of family gatherings started to spring up like mushrooms. Also on the scene was the ambitious Video Studio Gdańsk, which originated within the Solidarity political movement when it needed film

Coal Miners 88,
dir. Andrzej
Piekutowski
↑

documentation. The specific Polish situation meant that support had to be sought from a Catholic organisation outside of state influence – the Gdańsk Pallottine Fathers, with whose help the studio was able to operate under the name of the Catholic Film and Programme Foundation after February 1992. The people involved played a pioneering role in applying new technology to the production of professional cinema.

When censorship was abolished in 1990, nothing could stop the mass development of audiovisual productions. Nothing but the limited sales market, that is. There were only two national television channels. Polsat, the first nationwide independent television station officially started broadcasting in 1993. Two years later, TV Wisła was licensed to transmit a supra-regional programme, but only in southern Poland, leaving the TVN group to cover central and northern Poland after March 1997. The two firms soon merged into one single nationwide channel when TV Wisła was incorporated by TVN 24 in January 2005.

The new market situation inevitably brought about a significant increase in documentary production, since they were relatively cheap to make, and were a quick, satisfactory solution to various thematic issues. Unfortunately, artistic merit was often sacrificed as a result. The state film studios also continued to operate: the Warsaw Documentary Film Studio (which added "and Feature" to its title to emphasise its broadened scope in June 1988); the Łódź Educational Film Production Company (which added "and Programme" in 1994 to underline its close collaborations with television); and the

Czołówka Film Studio which used to be part of the Polish Army's Main Political Administration (since May 2009, there have been plans to merge it with the Warsaw Documentary Film Studio). Other agencies were producing commissioned films and television programmes: Interpress-Film, which closed down in 1991, and the Poltel Central Television Programme and Film Studio (opened in 1974, but particularly active in the 1970s and 80s). All in all, these studios produced around 180 documentary films of varying lengths each year.

MISSING PIECES

Despite this seemingly large figure, these productions were not very thematically diverse. Everyday requirements were met by hastily-made reports for television programmes. On the other hand, films with larger budgets and production costs concentrated mostly on taboo topics that had been banned by censors in the past. These were the so-called "blank spots" that were being hurriedly filled in. Without attempting to list all the subjects covered, we should mention first and foremost the historical issue of the Polish-Bolshevik war. Well-documented films were made by Wincenty Ronisz, an experienced filmmaker from Czołówka (*The Polish-Bolshevik War 1918–1921* [*Wojna polsko-bolszewicka 1918–1921*], 1992); Zbigniew Kowalewski (*Everything for the Eaglets* [*Wszystko dla Orląt*], 1992, about the defence of Lvov in 1918); Krzysztof Nowak-Tyszowiecki (*A Miracle at the Vistula River* [*Cud nad Wisłą*], 2005); and Zbigniew Wawer (*Forgotten Prisoners-of-War* [*Zapomniani jeńcy*], 2005). Another subject was Poles exiled to Siberia. Credit for this must go to Józef Gębski, who was supposed to make a film about *perestroika* in the mid-1980s for the Warsaw Documentary Film Studio, but was more interested in tracing Polish exiles. The result of his first trip to the northern areas of the former Soviet Union was the documentary *Siberians* (*Sybiracy*, 1988). A year later, he made the full-length documentary *From the Gulag Archipelago* (*Z Archipelagu Gułag*, 1989), in which modern-day sequences are crossed with diligently-researched archive material that had often been discovered completely by accident. The full documentation available to the director was made into a three-part series entitled *Crimes in Kołyma* (*Zbrodnia w Kołymie*, 1993): *The Uranium Rush* (*Gorączka uranu*), *The Gold Rush* (*Gorączka złota*) and *The Bread Rush* (*Gorączka chleba*). In addition, he made the reportages *From the Gulag Archipelago to America* (*Z Archipelagu Gułag do Ameryki*) between 1999 and 2001, documenting the American emigration of former Siberian exiles who had managed to survive and escape.

Katyn Forest,
dir. Marcel Łoziński

Another painful blank spot was the massacre of Polish army and police officers in Katyn. On the initiative of Andrzej Wajda, who was emotionally attached to the subject (the director's father was killed in Katyn), Marcel Łoziński made the one-hour documentary *The Katyn Forest* (*Las katyński*, 1990), a reportage of a train journey to Kozelsk by members of the Katyn Families Society. It includes interviews with former prisoners from Kozelsk, Starobelsk and Ostashkov, from where the victims were brought to be executed in the Katyn forest. The subject was quickly adopted by others, including *The Katyn File: Mass Murder as a Propaganda Tool* (*Katyń. Ludobójstwo i propaganda*, 1993), a weighty, interview-filled two-part TV film made by three journalist filmmakers, Barbara Dyrschka, Marek Grzona and Ingo Bethke, in conjunction with Russia and Belgium. Similarly, Józef Gębski made *A Film Found in Katyn* (*Film znaleziony w Katyniu*) and *Do Not Kill* (*Nie zabijaj*) in 1992, concerning the exhumation of the mass graves, and used the footage again later for his television film *Katyn* (2007).

The 1990s also saw a reappraisal of the extremely dramatic and complex theme of the Holocaust on Polish soil. Of particular interest were films by Jolanta Dylewska, an esteemed camerawoman who also directed her own films, and Dariusz Jabłoński, the director, producer, and head of Apple Film Production Studios since 1990. Dylewska's *Chronicle of the Warsaw Ghetto Uprising According to Marek Edelman* (*Kronika powstania w getcie warszawskim według Marka Edelmana*, 1993) uses inventively sparse archive footage to show daily life in the Warsaw ghetto, then brings in Marek Edelman's account, which begins on 18 April 1943. That was the date the Jewish Combat Organisation (ZOB), having learned the Germans were planning to destroy the ghetto, decided to launch their armed uprising. Filmed in close-up in a dimly-lit room, Edelman, the ZOB's last leader, talks calmly and dispassionately about the subsequent days of the uprising until 9 May, when he managed to escape the ghetto with a group of twenty co-militants. The report ends with a series of photographs of young, heroic fighters who died in battle. Later, Dylewska showed the daily life of Polish Jews in her moving documentary *Po-Lin. Slivers of Memory* (*Po-lin. Okruchy pamięci*, 2008). This is a snapshot of small provincial towns on the eve of the war, reverently compiled from short amateur films made by family members who had come from America to visit their relatives in Poland. The visual layer shows day-to-day situations, friendly waves for the camera, and anonymous smiles embellished with recent recordings of their Polish neighbours reminiscing. This nostalgic, peaceful film avoids showing any conflicts. According to a 13th century

Po-Lin.
Slivers of Memory,
dir. Jolanta Dylewska

legend, the Hebrew name Po-Lin (Poland) meant "stay here" and was intended to draw Jewish refugees seeking to get out of Germany.

Astonishing material in the form of colour slides from the Litzmannstadt ghetto in Łódź are the core of Dariusz Jabłoński's *Amateur Photographer (Fotoamator*, 1988). These slides were found in Vienna, and had been taken by Walter Genewein, an Austrian accountant from the ghetto's Nazi administration. The film contrasts these colourful images (consciously stylised by the photographer) with the black-and-white reality of the story of Arnold Mostowicz, a doctor and writer who witnessed the extermination. The story gains even more distressing impact due to the visual contrast. We should also mention another unusual film that brought back images of the Łódź ghetto: Michał Bukojemski's and Marek Miller's *Liquidation 08.1944 (Likwidacja 08.1944*, 2009). The date in the title refers to one particular moment: 29 August, when the last transport left Radegast station for the Auschwitz camp, carrying people to their death. The film uses authentic photographs discovered in archives and private collections in Israel, Poland, Germany and America, juxtaposed with reconstructed scenes and enhanced by a multi-layered soundtrack. Most importantly, it converts flat photographs into three-dimensional images. It is the first Polish 3D documentary, and its impact relies on pulling the audience into the centre of the situations it shows, haunting them with feelings that affect all the senses. This may be a one-off experiment, but it is immensely effective.

Painful reconciliation

The theme of Polish-Jewish relations during the war returns in a lot of films from a journalistic and critical point of view, as well as in films that not only depict the martyrology of the Jews, but also expose tragic controversies. In his film *début Birthplace* (*Miejsce urodzenia*, 1992), Paweł Łoziński (Marcel's son, who worked on several of his father's films) follows Henryk Grynberg, an American writer of Jewish origin, as he travels around the places where he, his parents and his brother hid during the occupation, and tries to solve the mystery of his father's death. One is impressed not only by the drama of the hero, but also by the crushing, stifling atmosphere of this documentary record, in which one can sense the fear that still chokes people up with emotion, and prevents the truth from being told. The wartime past has never been forgotten, but is ever-present and still affects the lives of successive generations. This film is significant well beyond the boundaries of current affairs. Another film that should be mentioned is the bitter *The Carousel* (*Karuzela*, 1993), in which Michał Nekanda-Trepka comments on the shameful case of the merry-go-round which was set up next to one wall of the Warsaw ghetto. The issue of the Jews massacred by Poles in Jedwabne and near Łomża in July 1941 is revisited with dramatic impact in Agnieszka Arnold's two-part documentary *Neighbours* (*Sąsiedzi*, 2001). The director had previously made the documentary *Where Is My Elder Son Cain?* (*Gdzie mój starszy syn Kain?*, 1999) about wartime problems in relations between Jews and Poles, and the difficulties that arose from the idea of reconciliation. Against all odds, the idea is taken to heart by good-natured people, as represented on screen by an unusual couple: Ariel Chazan, who now lives in Israel, and Jadwiga Siekierska, whom he has invited to join him there. She was the daughter of a peasant who saved him from the Nazis. The story of these two characters is cautiously optimistic.

The aforementioned films mostly concern wartime history, but there was another dramatic chapter in the Polish-Jewish conflict following March 1968, when an anti-Semitic campaign by the communist authorities led to a mass emigration of Polish Jews. A multi-faceted view of the resulting problems comes across in Marcel Łoziński's documentary *Seven Jews from My Class* (*Siedmiu Żydów z mojej klasy*, 1991) filmed during a Warsaw secondary-school reunion. Łoziński invited his peers and friends to meet up again in Poland after many years, but the gathering is far from peaceful. It is the setting of animated discussions that raise the issue of identity – who they are and what price they had to pay to become self-aware. Their children's points of view are surprisingly different, however – as seen in *A Cupboard* (*Kredens*, 2007) by first-time Danish director Jacob Dammas, who studied at the Andrzej Wajda Master School of Film Directing. Distance and curiosity predominate this story seen through the eyes of a young hero tracing his *émigré* family history through the buildings of Wrocław. The elderly people who greet him hospitably react in the same way. It is hard to find another film that shows so suggestively the effects of time, erasing and softening the acuteness of issues that are still part of the collective memory.

Among the documentaries dealing with history produced between 1989 and 2009, one must include those concerning the communist Polish People's Republic period. They were numerous, and touched upon fairly basic issues using a variety of artistic forms. Most of them were reconstructions of past events based on recordings of people's memories, archive photos and documents. One synthesis of this type is Maciej J. Drygas' *One Day in People's Poland* (*Jeden dzień w PRL*, 2005). This is a film portrait of one specific day: 27 September 1962. A gloomy work-filled day, not just for ordinary workers, but also for the militia informants constantly observing suspicious "targets". The depressing absurdity of this film shot in grey tones means it is probably unfair, but it is hard to question the truth of its individual elements. However, the director consciously avoids the historical context which is the mainstay of other important films made in censorship-free conditions. Films that chronicle the key political events of the period are extremely dramatic. Another crucial date was June 1956 in Poznań (A. Marek Drążewski's *I'm Still Waiting* [*Jeszcze czekam ...*, 1982] about the death of 13-year-old Romek Strzałkowski in the streets of Poznań; and Michał J. Dudziewicz's *Conductor Paradox* [*Paradoks o konduktorze*, 1997] in which actor Zdzisław Wardejn describes a sequence of events he witnessed). Also under the spotlight was the workers' unrest of December 1970 in Gdańsk and Szczecin: two particularly valuable films use hidden camera footage and material that was confiscated and recovered from the militia archives years later – Aleksander Stokowski's *The Sczecin Album 17/12/70* (*Album szczeciński 17.XII.1970*, 1995) and Wojciech Jankowski's *The Gdańsk Tapes* (*Gdańskie taśmy*, 1990). There were also the events of June 1976, the Radom workers' protest, summarised in the story of Fr. Roman Kotlarz, which Wojciech Maciejewski filmed as *And the Body Lies Quietly in the Grave* (*I cicho ciało spocznie w grobie*, 1999). Amongst the wealth of film documentation from 1980 and the start of martial law, one of the best was Aleksandra Ciechanowicz-Sarata's 1994 television diptych *In Memory of the Dead* (*Umarłym ku pamięci*) and *A Warning to the Living* (*Żywym ku przestrodze*) about the strike at the Wujek coal mine, which ended in tragedy.

Each of these films concerned one important episode in history, whereas Marcel Łoziński made an interesting attempt to give a complete overview in his 1990 documentary series for French television (co-produced with Poland) entitled *Poland as it Has Never Been Seen in the West* (*La Pologne comme jamais vue à l'Ouest*), or *45–89* on Polish TV. Its four 52-minute episodes mostly contrasted *Polish Film Chronicle* propaganda footage with comments by Solidarity activists – workers' movement leaders Lechosław Goździk (from 1956) and Zbigniew Bujak (from 1980–81), and the intellectuals Jacek Kuroń and Jan Józef Lipski. This kind of counterpoint arrangement emphasised the contentious nature of the series, which was Łoziński's intention.

Important, fascinating shots were also interwoven into film portraits from that period – famous and anonymous people, political activists, and individuals tangled up in history. This incredibly rich genre requires a separate introduction for, among other things, its artistic merits. Here it is enough to mention one extremely characteristic example, Maciej J. Drygas' film *Hear My Cry* (*Usłyszcie mój krzyk*, 1991). Its subject was an event which was entirely covered-up at the time and not part of the social consciousness. On 8 September 1968, Ryszard Siwiec, a 60-year-old accountant, set himself on fire in protest at the Polish Army's invasion of Czechoslovakia and the communists' hypocritical distortion of reality. This dramatic act was inadvertently recorded on film. Siwiec committed self-immolation at Warsaw's Tenth-Anniversary Stadium during harvest festival celebrations. Years later, the filmmaker discovered a seven-second clip that had been accidentally filmed by Zbigniew Skoczek, a cameraman covering the festivities, and providentially stored in the Warsaw Documentary Film Studio archives. He filmed a commentary around it based on interviews with the family and eyewitnesses. The film shows us the figure of a typical Polish intellectual brought up before the war, living his life in communist Poland; a thinking man questioning the limits of social indifference.

ENTER TELEVISION

Although such films were respected and reviewed by the press, this does not mean that they were seen by a lot of people. Distribution made this very difficult, particularly in the early 1990s. At best, the Kraków Festival, the most important event in Polish documentary cinema, would offer several repeated screenings for limited audiences. There were also some smaller, local festivals, which grew slightly in number after the mid-1990s, but which by their very nature were not designed for the masses. The film club movement was also in steep decline towards the end of that period. In practice, television was all that remained as a means for one-off screenings on a scale larger than that possible in cinemas.

The director Andrzej Fidyk understood this perfectly and managed to use that knowledge when he was in charge of state channel TVP1's documentary film department from 1996 to 2004. He created the programmes *Time for a Documentary* (*Czas na dokument*) for Polish documentaries, *Keep Your Eyes Wide Open* (*Miej oczy szeroko otwarte*) for foreign documentaries, and *Time for a Controversial Documentary* (*Czas na kontrowersyjny dokument*), which achieved amazingly high ratings not only because they was on at

Hear My Cry,
dir. Maciej Drygas
←

prime-time, but mostly due to the debate-inspiring subjects of the films shown. Fidyk was accused of common sensation-seeking and consciously shocking viewers, but there is no doubt it was thanks to him that documentaries became such social phenomena. As a producer, he would also commission films and act as their artistic director.

From the outset, Ewa Borzęcka was one of the "Fidyk school", and had previously made a name for herself with the film *Sheriff Story* (*Sprawa szeryfa*, 1987) – a portrait of a self-proclaimed and brutal small-town law-enforcement officer. The first in her series of documentaries on sensitive topics, often made in a way that the critics saw as a direct violation of ethics, not to mention good taste, was the moving *The Thirteensome* (*Trzynastka*, 1996) about a single mother raising thirteen children in poverty, and struggling ruthlessly for her existence. Despite winning the Grand Prix at the Kraków Festival, her film *Arizona* (1997) stirred up a storm of criticism. It is a cruel study of people demoralised by poverty and aimlessness, who used to work on a state farm that was shut down in 1990. The title refers to a brand of cheap wine that they compulsively get drunk on. The director was accused of using drunkenness unethically in front of the camera, and of being unable to see any good side to the reality she was showing. Was she unable or unwilling? Borzęcka does not conceal the bias of her films. It was not surprising that there were also plenty of complaints when her hour-long film *Them* (*Oni*, 1999) was shown on television – a group portrait of Warsaw's tramps and homeless, filmed not just in the streets, but also in the places they camp out (it is difficult to use the word "live" in this case): canals, ruins, bins, as well as the infamous doss-house known as "The Bunker". In the same in-your-face style, the director shows us "full-timers" and mentally ill people, and obviously provokes certain situations or peeks in on others. This is a powerful, courageous film that breaks the ethical rules of the genre in order to indict the helplessness of the institutional system, and the indifference of society. However, Borzęcka never achieved such power in her later films, which were made as interventionist documentaries. Both *Beijing: Gold of '83* (*Pekin. Złota 83*, 2002) and *On the Other Side of the Vistula* (*Z tamtej strony Wisły*, 2008) are nothing more than colourful curiosities about people on the edge.

Such a Beautiful Son I Gave Birth To,
dir. Marcin Koszałka
→

The support of Andrzej Fidyk was undoubtedly behind the successful directorial *début* of Marcin Koszałka, a cameraman from the University of Silesia's Radio and TV department – *Such a Beautiful Son I Gave Birth To* (*Takiego pięknego syna urodziłam*, 1999). This is an almost model example of what can be done with a simple camera set up in a small room to record everything in its field of view, using the camera's omnipresence artistically in an improvised and consciously provocative situation. The result is a record of totally authentic behaviour and frankness verging on exhibitionism. In his cramped Kraków flat, Koszałka films himself and his parents, especially his mother's grouchy commentaries on everything going on. The fact that the camera is constantly visible and present provokes the action even more. The irrefutable virtue of this family psychodrama lies in its intense psychological and social veracity, which go beyond the daily life depicted on the screen. However, an attempt to continue with this method five years later – *Things'll Work Out* (*Jakoś to będzie*, 2004), a similarly-made film about married life under the eye of his still critical mother – is no longer so revealing. Nevertheless, as a director, Koszałka remained faithful to Fidyk's aesthetics by consistently searching for touchy subjects, although not always with satisfactory results, as can be seen from the films *Death with a Human Face* (*Śmierć z ludzką twarzą*, 2006) about crematorium workers, or *Existence* (*Istnienie*, 2007) about the cancer-stricken actor Jerzy Nowak preparing for his death.

In sharp contrast to the above type of documentaries, we have the work of Jacek Bławut, an experienced director who, like Fidyk and Marcel Łoziński, has played a significant role as an artistic advisor for films by young directors from the Andrzej Wajda Master School of Film Directing. One may consider the 2004 film *Born Dead* as a model example of his method. It was made over several months during an experiment called "Duet" taking place between a Kraków prison and a social welfare centre. Bławut observes a 24-year-old repeat offender who has agreed, as part of the programme, to take care of severely-handicapped children. The director does not interfere on screen, and limits himself to recording from a specific distance, but from his detached narration there emerges a moving impression of the emotional maturation of a young man who shows no feelings. One can feel his sympathy and brusque displays of warmth, and the comforting certainty he derives from being able to offer impartial assistance. This makes the hard-to-reach disabled children cling to him. In his film, Bławut demonstrates the art of the documentary in its purest form as a combination of objectivity and social conscience.

Born Dead,
dir. Jacek Bławut
↑

Commentaries with ironic overtones

Administrative reshuffles in Polish Television have led to documentaries finding themselves on the periphery again. However, they have begun to appear more often in cinemas at one-off screenings or as part of seasons aimed at wider audiences. In the autumn of 2006, the indefatigable Marcel Łoziński released the full-length film *How It's Done* (*Jak to się robi*), which was the most penetrating commentary so far about the Polish democratic model. Ironic and disturbing, it monitors an experiment carried out over three years by Piotr Tymochowicz, a political marketing specialist. The premise may seem cynical: Tymochowicz wanted to turn a nobody with no views or ideas into a political figure. This undertaking did not come out of nowhere, but was a reaction to the mood of social approval that appeared so shockingly and worryingly when people watched the television programme *Big Brother*. This reality show imported from a Dutch model relies on the mutual elimination of contestants, and ran for three seasons in Poland on TVN in 2001 and 2002. Following a break, seasons four and five were aired in 2007 and 2008 on TV 4, but aroused much less interest than before. Łoziński uses Tymochowicz's idea to show a situation in which socio-technical trickery turns out to be more effective than ideological platforms and party slogans. Without any scruples at all, the likeable Darek K. presents himself on screen first as a centre-right politician close to PIS (the Law and Justice Party), then becomes an active member of the youth wing of the post-communist SLD (Liberal Democratic Alliance), and finally takes his place alongside the controversial populist Andrzej Lepper. The immediacy of the political references, which lose their relevance so quickly, is not the point here: the main thing is the mechanism, and the mechanism requires Darek K. to do everything with equal commitment, from taking part in street demonstrations to behind-the-scenes political discussions, all under the motto "the dumb people will buy it". Łoziński's film is satirical, something rarely found in Polish documentaries.

Does the success of new documentaries imply there will be more changes to come? Bartosz Konopka's film *Rabbit à la Berlin* (*Królik po berlińsku*, 2009), which was even popular internationally, suggests there might be. This is almost lampooning political satire. Its starting point is the case of the rabbits that lived in the empty green zone between East and West Berlin, which came into being after the Wall was erected in 1961. The film is obviously a metaphor of society living under a totalitarian system, and the director shows footage of the wild rabbits' placid existence, interspersed with documentary

Rabbit à la Berlin
dir. Bartosz Konopka

sequences that illustrate the political changes in the world around them, up until 1989 when the Wall was destroyed. The "rabbits' point of view" clearly conveys an image of society imprisoned in a socialist trap. Its casual and basically poetic language, which moves away from the inherent limitations and explicitness of classical documentaries, seems to be a vital step in the evolution of the genre. It is also conducive to achieving an impact beyond that of a localised phenomenon. Indeed, Polish documentaries have never been a commercially-viable export and their marketing strengths are limited, but they have been regularly represented at almost all the European thematic festivals and events (particularly those on human rights and the environment), ranging from Amsterdam, the world's most important documentary festival, to Bornholm, where films from the Baltic countries are screened. They have also been shown at important screenings outside of Europe.

The diversity of films on offer proves that documentaries are not losing their significance, and are constantly evolving both artistically and technologically (which, after all, drives the former). Lightweight cameras, digital recording instead of tapes, and sensitive lenses have all revolutionised the status of the genre. One could risk saying that in Poland, documentaries have ended up in an exceptionally favourable situation nowadays, actively supported by new, energetic firms and festivals (including the specialised Planete Doc Review) that have begun to influence the DVD distribution market at last. Similar things are happening with competing television channels and the Arthouse Cinemas Network, who are now reviving the 50-year-old tradition by distributing documentaries together with feature films. All this bodes well for the future.

Translated by Mark Bence

CINEMA AND HISTORY

ANDRZEJ WERNER

What presents sufficient reason for dressing actors up in outmoded costumes, assembling props, building sets and so reconstituting the shadows of past events through a feature film? In the film industry the sufficient reason is potential viewer interest: a reason that cannot be gainsaid. But how is such interest to be gauged, how is risk-laden probability to be brought closer to certainty? Let us leave aside for the moment purely commercial ventures, cases in which an appropriately large dose of attractions – however loosely connected with the historical subject of the narrative – would be sufficient. Interest is increased by the cultural sensitivity of the story, linking bygone times with current day needs: debate upon the road we have taken, and questions about the road to be pursued. Where and how are they connected? Can a common direction be plotted for all the inevitable twists and turns – and, along with it, a meaning for the entire sequence of events? Where should that meaning be sought? The very value of memory justifies every documentary reconstruction of the past, but it does not do so for every feature exercise in dressing up, where the representation itself involves deceit, however innocent.

The deception of representation remains inevitable in this genre, though of course not all representations are alike. Factual truth, however, is achievable and tangibly within reach. Truth may be a perilous concept, as facts will always be bound with interpretations and may mean different things relatively; but deception involving facts and events is usually easy to detect and probity in this respect remains a *sine qua non* for the meaningfulness of the historical film within the cultural sphere.

Before 1989, within the People's Republic of Poland, historical fancy-dress was particularly attractive. Paradoxically, this was due to proscriptions and censorship. Every truth or half-truth had to be stamped with an official stamp of concurrence with, or at least non-contradiction of, the official version. That version changed along with the limits of tolerance, and sometimes more was permitted, sometimes less; all of which prompted curiosity concerning the percentage of truth squeezed through this time. It is thought, not without reason, that Poles plunge into the past with particular relish, mulling over wrongs suffered and sacrifices made, and even (as has happened, and still does) discerning a higher meaning to them. But Polish historical cinema of this period, particularly that dealing with the Second World War and the resistance to the Nazi occupation, was glaringly averse to such martyrological impulses and to the erection of shrines to heroic warriors. Reaching further back into historical and cultural traditions, it questioned the meaning of these efforts, tending not to flatter public opinion and its assiduously cherished recollections of faded glory, but rather to provoke it. This was the cultural sensitivity of the historical cinema of the "Polish School" of yore.

Returns and auto-corrections

When one considers the countless silences enforced by the censor during the period of the People's Poland, their weight, the whole archipelago of tragic and painful experiences that could not even be mentioned, the blank spaces, whose need for registration in the cultural memory was proportional to the resistance against filling them in; when one considers all this, the freedom that prevailed with regard to such subjects after 1989 might seem to have offered a heaven-sent opportunity for a whole wave of films discussing what had been important, but forbidden, in the past. Such things had been forbidden and mendacious, with entire areas after all declared completely off-limits (above all, those involving Soviet crimes), while others could only be nibbled at, and even there at no small cost. The cinema of the Polish School often moved within these regions, sometimes paying a price quite unconsciously.

Having encountered a cool reception with his *Ring with a Crowned Eagle* (*Pierścionek z orłem w koronie*, 1992), Andrzej Wajda made a statement to the effect that the youthful public is not interested in history but only in concentrating on the things happening around them – and those are things of significance and moment. That was true, but it was not the whole truth. In general, despite the logic that would suggest the attractiveness of subjects hitherto placed off-limits, or condemned to expression as half-truths, the interest in historical subjects, particularly among those self-same young people, did indeed shrink drastically. The events of yesterday, and first and foremost among them those of

→ *Ring with a Crowned Eagle*, dir. Andrzej Wajda

the Polish People's Republic, acquire the subtly contemptuous label of 'archaeology', and are consigned to eccentric maniacs, in other words, somewhat older people. Wajda (to continue along the line of his own statements) assumed that his *Ring with a Crowned Eagle* would be an extension of certain tendencies of the Polish School, above all of *Ashes and Diamonds* (*Popiół i diament*, 1958). If *Ashes and Diamonds* yielded the suggestion that nothing stood in the way of the Home Army generation assimilating itself into the trends of political change mapped out after the war, *Ring with a Crowned Eagle* dispelled all such illusions. Whether the message of *Ashes and Diamonds* represented a concession to the imposed rules of the game, or a joint delusion of the director and scriptwriter, remains a moot point. In any case, the perspective present in *Ring with a Crowned Eagle*, whereby the persecution of young members of the resistance meant that the only form of co-operation possible with the communists was open treachery, was hard to imagine during the immediate post-war years. This is shown after all by the censor's blocking of Aleksander Ścibor-Rylski's novel *The Horse-Hair Ring* (*Pierścionek z końskiego włosia*), which was the basis for the script of Wajda's film.

The correction Wajda made in his *Ring with a Crowned Eagle* to the view of history was in fact only an auto-correction. It cast off the illusions present in *Ashes and Diamonds* and showed the tragic fate of the Home Army generation of survivors of the war; but at the same time, at the level of historical knowledge, the mechanisms it depicted were generally well-known. More valuable in this respect is Ryszard Bugajski's new film *General Nil* (*Generał Nil*, 2009), as it is based on the particularly tragic experiences of the legendary leader of the KEDYW (the Diversionary Wing of the Home Army), General Fieldorf, who was condemned to death in 1952 after a rigged trial.

A comparison between *The Ring with a Crowned Eagle* and the films of the Polish School must seem inapposite inasmuch as this film's view of history is enclosed entirely within the confines of past time: it speaks only of what once was, and completely lacks that dramatic sensitivity which made it possible to bring the past into the future. In this respect the television film *The Condemnation of Franciszek Kłos* (*Wyrok na Franciszka Kłosa*, 2000), a screen adaptation of the novel of the same title by Stanisław Rembek, has more in common with the Polish School. The expectation that once again a story from the period of the occupation will present deeds of valour and glory is completely justified, not only by the natural desires of the public but also by the historical reality itself. Franciszek Kłos, however, a police "boy in blue" in the service of the German armies of occupation, is a pathetic creature. Given an alteration of history he would be merely a grey figure with no distinguishing features; here, however, he commits vile and criminal acts: such are his duties, which he labours with all his strength to fulfil. What can one say? The reality of those times included such figures, and they were not lone exceptions.

The collective consciousness expects historical films to provide confirmations of collective identity. All the same, here we are dealing with a shifting of attention to the ambiguous, the problematic, to that which disturbs with an undercurrent of a sense of shame, even of collective guilt. Since the police performed an auxiliary function during the exterminations, Kłos's victims included Jews.

Jews and Poles

It is indeed the subject of the Holocaust, which unfolded on Polish soil, together with that of the problem of Polish-Jewish relations, that constitutes probably the most powerful and pronounced problem for the historical reckonings of the last twenty years. The strong focus on this problem, after all, also carries out the programme of filling in the "blank spaces" on the culturally-inscribed historical map wrought by the politics of censorship. The subject lay under a strictly-guarded censorship taboo, and within the duration of the Polish People's Republic only a handful of filmmakers succeeded in breaching this barrier: Aleksander Ford in his early *Border Street* (*Ulica graniczna*, 1949), Andrzej Wajda in *Samson* (1961), Stanisław Różewicz (up to a point) in *Birth Certificate* (*Świadectwo urodzenia*, 1961), and Czesław and Ewa Petelski in *Manhunter* (*Naganiacz*, 1963), a film in which a Polish blackmailer of Jews appears, but as an outcast from the Polish community – and even he undergoes a kind of redemption. The most interesting of the films held up by the censor was Andrzej Brzozowski's short *Beside the Railway Line* (*Przy torze kolejowym*) of 1963. Beside the railway line a young Jewish woman is lying, having escaped from a transport, with a broken leg. The inhabitants of a neighbouring village gather around her. The only form of help they can think of giving is to shoot her.

The sensitivity of the censor may indubitably have been the most important reason for the sparse screen presence of this subject, and of Polish-Jewish relations, but was it the only one? The subject was certainly a difficult and uncomfortable one. There are matters one is happy to recall, and others one would prefer to forget immediately and forever. The latter include the attitudes no small portion of society adopted *vis-à-vis* the extermination of the Jewish people carried out on our soil: attitudes of passivity (I do not mean the passivity enforced by the occupier), indifference, and even (although among a far smaller group, it was nevertheless painfully evident) a satisfaction that was not necessarily silent, as well as (something already treated as a criminal activity) collaboration with the Nazis.

The proportions are obviously impossible to determine, but the heart of the controversy is what they are intuited to be. Once the barriers imposed by censorship had disappeared, writers and filmmakers entering this gloomy terrain confronted a dilemma that resisted resolution, two mutually-cancelling forces. On the one hand was a desire to take the measure of so dramatic a problem, in accordance not just with the traditions of the Polish School but also with the nineteenth century literary one that required one to confront even the most painful experiences, "to tear open wounds lest a membrane of meanness cover them". On the other hand was the awareness of the insulting stereotype of the Pole as someone who had "imbibed anti-Semitism with his mother's milk", an insult not just to the image of history but first and foremost to the uncounted thousands of silent heroes and heroines who, at the risk of their own lives (only in Poland and in Soviet Russia was there immediate execution of the entire family) concealed Jews in their homes and saved them from extermination.

Film too played a role in the circulation of this stereotype. If its presence in *Shoah* is moot, there is no denying that Lanzmann's film prompted a wave of ignorant statements, including ones by its author himself. They were clearly present in Spielberg's *Schindler's List*.

The only way out of this situation therefore seems to be a faithful and just determination of the proportions. Such a strategy is dangerous, however, and not just because it does not convince the proponents of the stereotype, who treat every divergence from the stereotype as an exception that proves the rule. The very principle of justice, conceived in these terms, smothers the passion of the artistic mission, one of whose pillars can be a purposive injustice.

Andrzej Wajda's *Korczak* (1990) made no attempt to judge the collective attitudes of Poles to the extermination of the Jewish ghetto. It showed the inhuman physical and moral challenges imposed by life in that accursed area. No-one from outside it is capable of determining who and what matches up to the reconfigured norms of an inferno – one clear indicator of this in the film being the suicide of Adam Czerniaków, the head of the Warsaw Judenrat. But then there is also Janusz Korczak, pedagogue, writer, educator of children and youth, a person whose memory is revered equally by Poles and Jews (as

Korczak,
dir. Andrzej Wajda

a child, I too was raised to revere him), a figure who exceeds the usual human dimensions and who thereby salvages a distinguished notion of humanity.

All the same, how powerful is the weight of stereotype! Wajda's film was criticised harshly by French critics and accused of appropriating a Jewish legend. The most heavily-debated scene (in Poland too) was the ending: the last carriage, containing Dr. Korczak and the children, becomes detached from the train heading for Treblinka, and children joyously emerge from its open door, into a flowery meadow … I personally found this scene very moving and took it as an expression of humane protest against something that was a fact but after all should by no measure have occurred. The critics, however, trained their attention on the metaphorical significance of the scene, which could be interpreted in terms of the dogma (myth) of the Ascension, and accused Wajda of "Christianising the Holocaust" (a term used at the time by Konstanty Gebert). Wajda resorted to a symbolic language native to his culture, and did so within the context of the most sublime symbols (those of faith). What was he supposed to do? To speak in

Just Beyond This Forest,
dir. Jan Łomnicki
↑

a language that was not his? Yes, just that! And, what is more, better not speak at all, for it's none of his business. The consequences of this kind of integrationist position – one of many, but one rendered particularly evident by the aggressiveness of its tone – are very far-reaching. "It was not humans who imposed this fate on other humans", ran the Polish writer Henryk Grynberg's travesty of Zofia Nałkowska's famous statement, "but humans who imposed it on Jews". There is surely no need to state how damaging it is to place a nation outside the circle of the human community. This is surely the last place where the danger of a hypertrophied nationalism ought to manifest itself. In comparison with this, the extreme statement that one can only write of the Holocaust in Yiddish or Hebrew becomes an innocent child's game.

Wajda felt these reproaches deeply, and this may have had an influence on the form taken by his next film about Polish-Jewish relations. He had planned to adapt Jerzy Andrzejewski's story *Holy Week* as early as 1968, though censorship had rendered this impossible. This story about a Polish-Jewish woman in hiding in the Aryan sector of Warsaw had to provide a cross-section of the attitudes of her environment, ranging from the devotion of those who shelter her to attitudes that are reluctant and hostile, partly because of fear but also due to the anti-Semitic prejudice that threatens her with denunciation. Andrzej Wajda weighed the proportions carefully, and no one could reproach him for presenting the issue one-sidedly or in a partisan manner. That virtue, however, caused a serious weakness: it seemed to paralyse the life of the protagonists. Figures represent attitudes, thereby becoming their prisoners, or at least hostages.

In Jan Łomnicki's film *Just Beyond This Forest* (*Jeszcze tylko ten las*, 1991) the washerwoman Kulgawcowa accompanies a young girl from the ghetto and travels outside Warsaw to place her in a village, with her family. An image of Polish solidarity with the Jews? She is doing it for the money, and ostentatiously declares her distaste for Jews. Anti-Semitic slogans are the order of the day here, and similar reactions are found among casual fellow travellers. Nevertheless, for all that, the proximity of the little girl prompts a self-sacrificing gesture that exceeds the common norms.

There is a tendency to treat the notion of anti-Semitism in a uniform fashion and to draw a direct parallel with Nazi anti-Semitism. Yet, all anti-Semitisms are not alike. Obviously, all are deplorable and each one is socially dangerous, but that does not mean dangerous to the same degree. Łomnicki's film is interesting in pointing out nuances of this kind.

The numerous feature films dealing with the fate of Polish Jewry under the occupation also include films in which one may indeed be able to discern a certain image of Polish-Jewish relations, but whose directors' central focus clearly concerns other issues. Roman Polański's *The Pianist* (*Pianista*, 2002) is definitely one such film. Albeit admittedly a big international production, it is one whose most significant participation involves many members of the Polish film community. It deserves a mention, though yet another discussion of this famous work here would doubtless be beside the point. Jan Kolski's *Far from the Window* (*Daleko od okna*, 2000), tells of a young Jewish woman hiding with a childless couple. The realities of the occupation play an important role here, but the central tragedy is that of the girl concealed in the wardrobe, who bears a child from her relationship with the host, but has to give it up to the man's wife. For understandable reasons, works about the extermination, be they features or documentaries, stress the threat to life. Here, too, the female protagonist's life hangs continually on a thread, but equal attention is devoted to her moral distress also. A dramatically intense erotic triangle had been presented earlier in Janusz Kijowski's *Warszawa. Année 5703* (*Tragarz puchu*, 1992). In this case, after fleeing the ghetto a young married couple finds shelter with a forty-year-old woman who lives alone near the ghetto wall. Soon, however, the price of survival becomes an erotic relationship between the man and the apartment owner, in the presence of the wife.

Amateur Photographer (*Fotoamator*, 1998), an hour-long documentary by Dariusz Jabłoński, depicts the Łódź (Litzmannstadt) ghetto: its daily life and its death. It does so in a way that is both unusual and fascinating, as the story is based on a collection of several hundred slides made by an Austrian employed as a bookkeeper in the ghetto. He was an exemplary bookkeeper, not just in his professional work (he rose rapidly in the ranks, right up to the position of head bookkeeper) but also as an eager amateur photographer. For him the ghetto was a large, exemplary factory producing – extremely economically – a plethora of goods for the Third Reich. Within this frightening place, his lens (that of a requisitioned camera) encounters nothing that provokes astonishment or personal discomfort in him. He conducts an expert correspondence with the producer of his light-sensitive colour film (Agfa) and documents, or rather makes an inventory of, the effects of all this productive labour. The film's director confronts this near-idyllic image with the photographs of another inhabitant of the ghetto, which served the purpose of reporting. The effect is as intellectually resonant as it is terrifying.

Nevertheless the dark side of memory returns, first and foremost in the documentaries about the events that unfortunately evoke those unwanted memories (though the pogroms in the Podlasie region during the German occupation were recalled first by a feature film, *In the Middle of Europe* (*W środku Europy*, 1990), by Piotr Łazarkiewicz. Its action unfolds in the 1950s: a young boy learns that his mother died while desperately trying

Amateur Photographer, dir. Dariusz Jabłoński

to defend some Jews being lynched by a mob). Even before the passing of the communist era, Marcel Łoziński made a thirty-minute documentary for a French TV channel entitled *The Witnesses* (*Świadkowie*, 1986), a reconstruction of the tragic events of the Kielce pogrom based on eye-witness statements and archival photographs from the Polish Film Newsreel. In 1992 his son Paweł Łoziński made *Birthplace* (*Miejsce urodzenia*), a shattering account of a journey in which the film-crew accompanied Henryk Grynberg on his first visit in many years to the area where his family had lived. This is no nostalgic trip, as it evokes the bitter memories that burden the neighbours, that is, Poles. One particularly powerful scene shows the discovery by the film's subject of the previously unknown burial site of his father, murdered by a Polish peasant – whose loot was a cow.

An event that impressed itself strongly on the Polish collective consciousness was one that had been veiled in willing oblivion: the massacre of the Jewish inhabitants of the small town of Jedwabne, carried out in 1941 by their Polish neighbours, albeit obviously at the behest of and in collaboration with the Germans. The immediate trigger for a widespread and vocal public debate was Jan Tomasz Gross's book *Neighbours* (*Sąsiedzi*), but its author had learned of the incident from the filmic documentation performed by Agnieszka Arnold, which culminated in her 2001 feature-length documentary of the same title.

Several important documentaries referred to the shameful anti-Semitic campaign provoked and orchestrated by the communist authorities in 1968, which caused the mass emigration of families of Jewish origin. Here one should mention above all others Marcel Łoziński's *Seven Jews from my Class* (*Siedmiu Żydów z mojej klasy*, 1992) and *Gdansk Station* (*Dworzec Gdański*, 2006) – that having been the site of many tragic farewells – by Maria Zmarz-Koczanowicz.

One noteworthy event, also in an artistic sense, was the première of Jolanta Dylewska's feature-length *Po-lin. Slivers of Memory* (2008), a montage of unique amateur photographs showing the life of pre-war Jewish shtetls within the Second Republic, supplemented with the recollections of Polish witnesses from their vicinity. What emerges from the film is a surprisingly warm image of a murdered world which no-one can ever restore, along with a sense of regret common to both the witnesses and the audience.

Thus the tragic intertwining of the fates of Jews and Poles during the Nazi occupation yielded an unusually rapid and intensive autotherapy through art. Immediately after the lifting

of the censor's proscriptions there appeared a large number of moving and important films on this painful subject. And yet the same moment saw the freeing of subjects that had been guarded even more strictly, where the Poles were incontestably only victims. To get ahead of myself – it suffices to recall that we had to wait twenty years for a film about Katyn. Is it not the case that the mourning role of memory nevertheless plays its part? Speaking out loud may have been forbidden, but the memory of the victims never faded. Areas of repressed memory demanded expression all the more insistently.

THE POLISH-SOVIET BLANK SPACES

The number of injuries accumulated over the years, the depth of the wounds and the absolute nature of the prohibition, of even the smallest allusion to this subject during the era of the Polish People's Republic, permit the assumption that the blank spaces in Polish-Russian and Polish-Soviet relations would come to the fore as filmic subjects following the re-establishment of independence. And yet few films took them as their subject. The majority of these were documentaries, some of them feature-length. There was quite a wealth of documentation on the beginnings of the Polish State following World War One, presented mendaciously hitherto, and in particular of the Polish-Bolshevik war of 1920 (as in films by Wincenty Ronisz and Krzysztof Nowak-Tyszowiecki). Józef Gębski made several films devoted to the fates of Polish deportees to Siberia and the camps of the Gulag Archipelago. Significantly, most of these films came into being during the first years after 1989.

Nineteen-ninety-two saw the release of the first large-scale feature film devoted to this issue: Robert Gliński's *All That Really Matters* (*Wszystko, co najważniejsze*, 1992). The screenplay was adapted from the memoirs of Ola Watowa, wife of the distinguished Polish poet Aleksander Wat, a pre-war communist. Following his arrest by the Soviet authorities in January 1940 his wife and young son were exiled to Kazakhstan, and his moving personal story is played out against an epic about the fates of Polish deportees to Central Asia.

The Gates of Europe (*Wrota Europy*, 1998), a film made by two distinguished cameramen, Jerzy Wójcik (who directed) and Witold Sobociński (camerawork) shows the dramatic encounter between three very young nurses in the Polish eastern borderlands and the units of the Red Army that occupy the hospital in 1918.

All That Really Matters,
dir. Robert Gliński
←

Of all the Polish-Soviet issues with which there had been no reckoning, and which were strictly taboo before 1989, the crime committed at Katyń had a special significance. This was not only due to the scale of the tragedy, and not just because it bore the hallmarks of genocide, but also because of the theft of memory, which as usual proved counterproductive. As early as 1990 Marcel Łoziński made the documentary *Katyn Forest (Las katyński)*, which was of particular interest in relation to memory as – as it were – a black hole into which the experiences of events fall, never to emerge. In this case that means the memories of the Russian witnesses living around the Katyn forest. Most are silent. One can see that they know and remember, but such memory is forbidden: it exists, but has no right to be.

The account of this crime given in Andrzej Wajda's personally-inflected *Katyn* (2008) also revolves around the issue of memory. More of the plot unfolds in Nazi-occupied, and then post-war, Kraków than in the camp in Kozielsk or at the site of the massacre. Anxious waiting, German reports of a Soviet crime, finally their post-war reversal in the official version, which no-one believes any longer. The unfortunate Antigones are unable to bury their husbands and brothers, and cannot even anticipate a time of relief. Only at the end does there come the devastating sequence showing the crime, without even resentment towards its perpetrators: it is simply the work of a soulless, equally captive machine.

The image of the Polish People's Republic

Such was 1989: everything that preceded it, even when it lay only a few months before, passed into history. Every film whose plot was set before then, in the Polish People's Republic, automatically became a history film, a variety of reckoning with a closed epoch. Only the customary continuity of life prevented every one being conceived thus. There had been earlier success in saying something critical, even about important, systemic characteristics of the society run by the communists: for instance, critical views of the period of "errors and distortions", i.e. of the 1948–1955 period had been permitted, and it had been easy to draw analogies with the present. All the same, there were vast stretches of unmentionable issues. Moreover, particular importance had been attached to adopting a tone not of outrage, protest or even criticism, but rather of persuasion.

Despite the removal of the barriers no avalanche came hurtling down. The decisive factors were the ones mentioned already, and above all else the abruptness of the change: the past became as it were enclosed within itself, cut off from the urgencies of the contemporary. Nevertheless, this cannot change the fact that this twenty-year period saw the emergence of a significant number of films on this subject.

The choice that imposed itself most frequently involved a reckoning with the wrongs suffered in compulsory silence: particular events ripped out of history, submerged under the sands of oblivion. Filp Bajon's *Poznan '56* (1996) recalls the workers' protests bloodily suppressed by the military in June 1956. The form of narration adopted by the filmmaker (events are viewed from the perspective of an adolescent boy) nevertheless deliberately rejects that of the reckoning, which to some extent is an objectifying formula. On the other hand, that very formula – one of a workers' epic – was adopted by Kazimierz Kutz in *Death as a Slice of Bread* (*Śmierć jak kromka chleba,* 1994), a film that commemorated the "Wujek" mine strike and its bloody suppression following the imposition of martial law in December 1981. As Tadeusz Lubelski rightly noted in his *History of Polish Film*, what is particularly original about this film is that the striking "Wujek" miners are more a part of Silesia, its history and its mythology (one largely shaped by Kutz himself) than of the national Solidarity movement: they are inheritors of the Basista family clan of *Salt of the Black Earth* (*Sól ziemi czarnej,* 1969), of the rebels of *Pearl in the Crown* (*Perła w koronie,* 1971) and of the later films in Kutz's Silesian series. The traditions of the Polish School manifest themselves however. Hot on the heels of the pathos-laden vision of history in *Death as a Slice of Bread* Kutz's next film appears in cinemas: *The Convert* (*Zawrócony*, 1994), an ironic version of the myth of the fighter for social justice. The hero's behaviour is ruled not by conviction, courage and unbending will but – on the contrary – inertia, chance and naïve simple-mindedness.

Several films tell of the dark pages of the Security Office (Urząd Bezpieczeństwa) and "the administration of so-called justice". Ryszard Bugajski's above-mentioned *General Nil* delves back into the 1950s. *Street Games* (*Gry uliczne*), by Krzysztof Krauze (1996) concerns the 1977 murder by the Security Office of the Kraków student Stanisław Pyjas, which was followed by a rigged investigation. This case is taken up again in the 2008 feature-length documentary *Three Buddies* (*Trzech kumpli*) directed by Ewa Stankiewicz and Anna Ferens, this time with regards to the role of a secret collaborator of the Security Office, a friend of Pyjas, the student Lesław Maleszka. Rafał Wieczyński's *Popiełuszko. Freedom is Within Us* (*Popiełuszko. Wolność jest w nas*, 2009) goes back to Father Jerzy Popiełuszko and his murder by officers of the security forces, while Teresa Kotlarczyk's *The Primate* (*Prymas. Trzy lata z tysiąca*, 2000), tells of the conflict between the communist state and the Church at a moment when that systemic clash reached its apogee in the imprisonment of the Primate of Poland, Cardinal Stefan Wyszyński, during the early 1950s.

All these choices of subject matter appear correct and justified. The films recount important events that clearly illustrate the oppressive character of the communists' rule. They point out that the evil that manifested itself in this area was systemic, not the result of criminal

tendencies in the officers serving the regime. And yet all of them, taken together, fail to measure up to the need for a reckoning with this epoch, for collective self-knowledge among the heirs to it. They apply a stark opposition between the authorities and society, us and them, which is partly justified, but does not answer questions concerning the mental consequences of prolonged life within this sphere, which was not necessarily a collaboration, but, as it were, an adaptation to defined rules: questions that go beyond that of responsibility but are prerequisites of a diagnosis, for the present-day and the future. What is more, questions of this kind can doubtless be found in films that can hardly be called historical, but which present the reality of that time in a plot set in the Poland of yesterday. One such film is Wojciech Marczewski's phantasmagoria *Escape from the Liberty Cinema* (*Ucieczka z Kina Wolność*, 1990), which was made just after the transformation. Its entire plot is a metaphor for the most keenly-felt feature of life in the People's Republic of Poland: unreality, life within an arbitrarily-created fiction. At the beginning the actors on the screen rebel against the poor, utterly false roles assigned them in a film and simply step down into the auditorium. However, a similar experience is undergone by the film's main protagonist, a high-ranking censor who previously had eliminated the politically undesirable lines of authors and actors.

Three Buddies,
dir. Anna Ferens,
Ewa Stankiewicz
↑

In the unusual psychodrama that plays out in Grzegorz Królikiewicz's exceptionally original *The Case of Pekosinski* (*Przypadek Pekosińskiego,* 1993), the protagonist tries to reconstruct his own unknown curriculum vitae. He is, as it were, suspended between two opposed forces that are alien to one another, and to him also: the communist authorities and the Church. In these circumstances his sole refuge becomes the world of chess, with its clear and incorruptible rules of play. The most complete synthesis of the socio-political phenomenon that was life in the Polish People's Republic may well be found primarily in documentaries. *Hear My Cry* (*Usłyszcie mój krzyk,* 1991) by Maciej Drygas, is also a film about a singular, nay unique, occurrence: Ryszard Siwiec's self-immolation at the Tenth Anniversary Stadium in Warsaw in 1968 in protest against the invasion of Czechoslovakia by Warsaw Pact forces. It happened in the presence of a hundred thousand spectators and the director is interested to an equal extent in the carefully prepared action of this desperate man, a father of three and a bookkeeper from Przemyśl, and in the silence of the witnesses, the many years of silence only interrupted by this very film. Another, later film by the same director, *One Day in People's Poland* (*Jeden dzień w PRL-u,* 2005), provides a splendid reconstruction of everyday life in the People's Republic. The author selected an unremarkable day in 1962 and sieved through hundreds of archives nationwide, police ones included, to obtain material about the various recorded (and filmed) events, illustrations not so much of life itself as of the bureaucracy's way of thinking about life, along with its vigilance, lest it overlook anything important for the state's functioning in the areas subject to it. The result is a somewhat absurd picture, but as a witness I can add that this absurdity is not one that has been invented and tendentiously put forward for belief. Working for one of the French TV stations Marcel Łoziński filmed an idiosyncratic synthesis of the history of the People's Republic: four episodes, each lasting just under an hour, whose French title was *La Pologne comme jamais vue a l'Ouest*, and whose Polish title was *45–89* (1990). The film comprises material shot over the years, mainly for the *Polish Film Chronicle*, and that official version of events is offset by statements by leaders of the democratic opposition – both those of 1956 and of the later Solidarity one.

A FEW SCHOOL SET BOOKS

A few years ago an intense political game involving history began in Poland. The so-called historical policy was intended to engender a self-creating political perspective, due to the care taken to propagate patriotic values, which it was assumed would raise society's morals and feelings of proud identification with one's own community and its laudable traditions. There was a competition to think up more and more new subjects to put before schoolchildren and force-feed cinemagoers. There is hardly any need to prove that history is not well-served by such a diet, and that schoolchildren, and possibly even the

→ *Pan Tadeusz*,
dir. Andrzej Wajda

mass public, are likely to lose the remnants of their attachment to the lofty watchwords and models – not to mention the artistic effects of such historical didacticism.

However, filmmakers found "social commissions" of this kind (when a commission is called "social", one can be sure that political mechanisms are behind it) somewhat tempting, as they were linked to extra funding for production, script competitions, and so on. Such competitions even took place, though in the process new restrictions were revealed. Fuelled by the media, the patriotic passions of compatriots compelled them to protest heatedly and influentially (for protests cause sponsors with an interest in the political game to suddenly lose enthusiasm and close their wallets): for instance that the heroes of Westerplatte drink vodka and use bad language, while the Warsaw insurgents lead sex-lives that are not necessarily restricted to the confines of matrimony. One large plus of the historical films of the last few years is that very few films bearing the traces of conjunctural commissions have come into being.

Not every film based upon a classic work of Polish literature was marked equally by such a conjunctural character, though the anticipated flocking to the cinema of organised groups of youths and schoolchildren could be an essential stimulus to production. These are not historical films *per se*, for they are dominated by literary fiction, despite being set in concrete historical periods. The immensely popular *Trilogy* of Henryk Sienkiewicz, whose action unfolds around Poland's eighteenth century history, had already seen screen versions of its second and third parts, *The Deluge (Potop,* 1974) and *Pan Wolodyjowski* (1969; both directed by Jerzy Hoffman). Only now could *With Fire and Sword (Ogniem i mieczem,* 1999) come into being, following the fall of the Soviet Union, within whose former borders the film's battles take place (in the eighteenth century, they were within the borders of the First Republic). The problem remained, albeit this time it had changed shape. In Sienkiewicz's novel the uprising of Bohdan Chmielnicki had been a rebellion within the confines of the Republic; from the Ukrainian perspective it was a war of national liberation. Sienkiewicz's somewhat condescending, not to say seigneurial attitude towards Ukrainians had to be decisively altered in the light of the present day context, and it is not surprising that Hoffman took this step. However, it

rendered the whole conflict less clear-cut and emotion-laden. Jerzy Kawalerowicz's *Quo Vadis* (2001), adapted from Sienkiewicz's novel, and Jerzy Hoffman's *An Ancient Tale* (*Stara Baśń*, 2003), adapted from a novel by Józef Ignacy Kraszewski, cannot justify their existence and large outlay of production resources except on the basis of their status as popular and widely-read novels, but they demand classification as historical films because of their setting in the past (Nero's Rome and the pre-Christian, prehistoric Polish lands respectively) and because of the painstaking reconstruction built into their sets, within the limits of imagination and what the production would sustain.

Matters are completely different with respect to *The Spring to Come* (*Przedwiośnie*), based upon the outstanding and conceptually tremendously important Stefan Żeromski novel of 1925. For many years Andrzej Wajda had cherished plans to adapt this novel to the screen. In the first instance, censorship made it difficult, if not downright impossible, to maintain a basic honesty *vis-à-vis* a text that was old but of tremendous ongoing import. After the breakthrough of 1989, Żeromski's novel became in certain respects as up-to-date as it had been at the moment of its emergence, for Żeromski had taken up, a few years after the recovery of independence, the most fundamental question posed a hundred years earlier by the Romantics: *Poland, Poland, but what kind of Poland?* He had done so by taking into account all of its complexity, both the dreams and the disappointments, the rift between a hundred years of dreams of re-establishing what had once been the gentry's Poland, on the one hand, and something that would meet the demands of social justice and rectify deep-seated wrongs: with a sense of the irresoluble conflict between the pragmatics of political action and a system of values crying out at that very moment for embodiment in reality.

It is a great shame that Wajda did not undertake this task as the ideal culmination of his creative ambitions, interests, literary tastes and instinctive understanding of the insolubility of conflicts. This was done by Filip Bajon in his *The Spring to Come* (2001); and for all the appeal of the narrative, he failed to meet the challenge of Żeromski's prose and the need of the moment.

Instead of *The Spring to Come*, Andrzej Wajda made two films based on Polish literary classics: *Pan Tadeusz* (1999), adapted from Adam Mickiewicz's epic poem; and *Revenge* (*Zemsta*, 2002), from another nineteenth century work, a comedy by Aleksander Fredro. There is no shortage of sarcasm in the depiction in *Revenge* of the mentality of the gentry protagonists, which may, to some extent, be a portrayal of the Polish national character. *Pan Tadeusz* unfolds in a specific time period, 1811–1812, with historic events as a backdrop. Everything is conceived as close to the Lithuanian reality of the time, but based not on "it was thus" but rather "such things occurred". The characters enunciate a classic verse of thirteen syllables and the wealth of genre scenes is dazzling; the founding events of the narrative, however, are a literary fiction. And yet in this case there can be no doubting the generalising intentions: *Pan Tadeusz*, as filmed by Wajda, is a semi-mythical distillation of Poland and Polishness, complete with all the complexity that had marked his films about recent and contemporary history, the sometimes harsh and painful criticism, but also the affection and even love that found their fullest expression within this mythical construct. Just like in Mickiewicz's original.

Translated by Paul Coates

CINEMA AND HISTORY

THE SECOND YOUTH OF A SIXTY YEAR OLD
POLISH ANIMATION AFTER 1989

MARIUSZ FRUKACZ

The starting point

When considering Polish animation cinema after the political transformation, we should begin with a brief description of what came to be known as the Polish Animation School. The term, along with the Zagreb School or Estonian School, is a result of multiple phenomena emerging in certain cultural areas that strive toward a common denominator. This simplification is justly denounced by both artists and critics, who see on the Polish Animation School map distinctive islands opposed to such simplification. Nonetheless, this "Polish trait" in animation has also been remarked upon by foreign critics.[1]

Can we, then, provide a valid description of the Polish Animation School, knowing that its "golden era" was in the 1960s? We can definitely speak of auteur animation cinema where the final work could be seen as individual artistic expression, that is, when one man was involved in the directing, use of plastic arts, and audio mastering of the final work. There would not have been a "golden era" without the strong artistic character of those times, namely: Witold Giersz, Mirosław Kijowicz, Daniel Szczechura *et al*. It is also recognised that the Polish Animation School was unique for its narratives set within a philosophical-meditative discourse. What made it distinctive and uniform was also the *douleur*, as Bendazzi explains, an "intense study of human nature and destiny".[2] A great asset of the animation produced at that time and in the subsequent decade (the so-called "silver age") was the exceptionally high level of plastic animation being used. Bearing in mind that, from 1957, animation was taught at academies of fine art (first in Kraków, then in Warsaw and Poznań), it is no surprise that the authors were receptive to trends in visual arts and prone to shifting the emphasis from the narrative layer to the formal one.

It was over the course of three decades that state patronage supported philosophical-meditative auteur animated productions and subsequent party leaderships gave it a free hand. The usually watchful censorship office was primarily interested in more socially influential art, such as literature and feature films. The influence of animation was much neglected, even though, like other short films, animation was available to the public alongside feature films. What made animation immune to censorship (except for only a few films) was its Aesopian language and the subject matter, which facilitated free

---

[1] Such is the opinion of distinguished critics of animation such as Giannalberto Bendazzi, who claims this in Preface I, in: *Polish Animated Film* (*Polski film animowany*), [eds.] Marcin Giżycki, Bogusław Zmudziński, Warsaw 2008.

---

[2] Ibid., p. 7

expression by a careful selection of colours as well as changing the characters' speed of motion. Thus, such artificial creations suited both sides well. The artists could freely and in favourable conditions create their works, and were even encouraged and required do to so under employment contracts. The state, in turn, could boast before western countries that there was artistic freedom and a plethora of prize-winning artists (every governmental power likes to boast of prize-winners). What is astonishing today is not the fact that this system lasted for so long (even today artistic animation is in receipt of state grants), but the sheer volume of production involved.

The dark decade (1989–2001)

After 1989 the situation changed for the worse: state grants were withheld and national broadcasters were slowly withdrawing from productions aimed at children. A rather ruthless avariciousness had begun, and not only in animation, as was well anticipated in *Race* (*Wyścig*, 1989) by Marek Serafiński. In the climate of this new free market economy, animation film studios began thinking of more commercially viable productions, such as TV programme credits, special effects and advertising. State owned and overgrown enterprises were unable to compete with emerging private studios and advertising agencies. The dismantling of the old system came to a symbolic end in 2001,

Hobby,
dir. Daniel Szczechura

when the last of the state-owned studios was declared bankrupt and was transformed into a civil partnership. As a result, the new economic reality made auteur animation almost completely obsolete. Marcin Giżycki remarks, "It is ironic that the art which for decades had specialised in subtle sabotage and perfected the implicit language of the regime's critique, was now crumbling itself after its demise".[3] The preferences of the audience changed respectively. The public, hungry for entertainment so far associated with western productions, seemed more appreciative of the lighter "made in Hollywood" repertoire. Artists were further detached from the audience with the disappearance of animated films on television and before feature screenings at cinemas. Film festivals were also reluctant to include animation in their programmes. It seemed that, apart from the "animation underground", metaphorical reflections on sombre reality were becoming less valid. A bitter commentary to the dark decade of Polish animation was the closing scene of the full feature animation *Hobby* by Daniel Szczechura (2002). The feature, comprising the ten most popular animated films by Szczechura tied together with shots of an auditorium, closed with a shot of the auditorium being empty, except for one last viewer – the director himself. The establishment of the Film Production Agency and the Script Agency in 1992 introduced new ways of financing film projects, which allowed private producers to apply for government grants. As a result, many private production companies flourished but most of them were short-lived (only a few of them survive today: the Longin Studio in Kraków, Anima-Pol in Łódź, and the J&P Studio Grafiki Filmowej in Warsaw). Braving the labyrinthine corridors and vague procedures of the Film Production Agency could assure only half of the production budget and other partners had to be found to shoulder the costs. Film producers tried to get assistance from Polish Television, at the time the largest co-producer, eager to contribute to productions intended for television broadcast – such as children's films, musicals and sometimes educational features.

In this milieu by far the best productions aimed at children and teenagers in the 1990s emerged from the Television Studio of Animation Films. In the twelve-film series, *Impressions*, next to almost textbook lessons of European painting, there appeared films which creatively and attractively interpreted painters' achievements. Among these, unquestionably belongs *Magritte* (1995), made by Hieronim Neumann and Maciej

---

3
Marcin Giżycki, *Not Only Disney. On Animated Film (Nie tylko Disney. Rzecz o filmie animowanym)*. Warsaw 2000, p. 127.

→
DIM.,
dir. Marek Skrobecki

Ćwiek, which takes the viewer on a fantastic space-time travel through the work of the Belgian surrealist. Also the second-bestselling Polish Television production series *Animation Films to Classical Music* (1989–1997)[4] was aimed at the popularisation of classical music among children and young people. Kazimierz Urbański referred to this work as "music making with pictures", meaning that the feature conveys European composers' works through plastic art, texture, editing, and motion. In addition to the many features made as mere illustrations of these works, which may seem a little outdated today, there have also been insightful and inventive short features providing original formal interpretations. Among these are animation films made by the aforementioned Kazimierz Urbański, as well as *Flight of the Bumble-Bee* (*Lot trzmiela*, 1993) by Hieronim Neumann, *Carmen Torrero* (1996) by Aleksandra Korejwo, *Rondo Alla Turca* (1993) by Witold Giersz and *Vibrating String* (*Drgająca struna*, 1995) by Rafał Bartkowicz. One of the studio's most exceptional works was a series *14 Tales from Lailonia Kingdom* based on Leszek Kołakowski's philosophical parables (1997–2000). The tales were made using various animation techniques and, in accordance with the intentions of the recently-deceased philosopher, were directed at both youngsters and adults. A couple of tales boasted a remarkable level of artistry, in addition to their educational value. *A Tale of Great Shame* (*O wielkim wstydzie*, 1998) by Jacek Adamczak, *Humps* (*Garby*) (1998) by Marek Serafiński, and the most interesting of the series, a Puppetoon animation *The Biggest Quarrel* (*O największej kłótni*, 1999) by Zbigniew Kotecki, all proved that great auteur animated films could find their way to television. Despite these successful and well recognised productions, the formula used by the studio for over twenty years within the organisational structure of Polish Television was eventually discarded. In 2001 it was transformed into a limited liability company, the TV Studio of Animation Films and 90 per cent of its shares were distributed among long-term employees of the studio and its partners.

The tradition of Puppetoon animation was continued at Łódź Film Studio Semafor where a few interesting series for children were made (*Little Penguin Pik-Pok, Maurycy and Hawranek, Mordziaki*). However, the most important production of that time was a thoughtful film by Marek Skrobecki, who made references to philosophical or even religious questions. In the film *DIM.* (1992), which set in motion his international career,

---

4
Just after *The Decalogue* by Krzysztof Kieślowski.

> *Tuning the Instruments*
> dir. Jerzy Kucia

he portrayed the zone between the world of dead objects enlivened by human action, and that of perishable and mortal biological existence. In *Fairy Tale Pictures* (*Märchenbilder*, 1998), Skrobecki told the story of genius and madness as the two interwoven and inseparable features of truly great artists. In 1999 the Łódź Film Studio Semafor went into liquidation, and a related group of producers established a company under a similar name: "Se-Ma-For" Film Production.

The Animation Films Studio in Kraków moved to the production of children films after initially producing films for adults. In effect, a couple of short and full features were produced (directed mainly by Krzysztof Kiwerski), but its steadily worsening financial situation led to a declaration of bankruptcy by the studio, much valued for its high level of artistry. Among the last auteur films produced there were two animation films by Ryszard Czekała, one of the founders of AFS in Kraków. A psychological drama *Human and Bread* (*Człowiek i chleb*, 1997) was made as a monochromatic cut-out animation and evoked the times of *Ancien Régime*, depicting a prison-set relationship between a warden and a prisoner. The prisoner's disobedience towards the warden, and the situation he is in, is manifested by him using bread to plug his peep-hole and the other numerous holes from which cockroaches emerge, which can be read as a reference to human existence. We may find a meaningful link between this

film and *The New Bell* (*Nowy dzwon*, 2001), the last of the director's work and the last in the history of the studio – namely, a reference to religious symbolism. In *Human and Bread* the prisoner draws The Eye of Providence suggesting the repressive character of religion. In *The New Bell* Czekała is more subtle – people inside the temple are vain, proud, and *nouveau riche*, thus, in the middle of the inauguration ceremony it gets destroyed by a falling bell.

The Animated Film Studio in Bielsko-Biała found it too difficult to adapt to the new situation. The 1990s output failed to meet expectations since only a few feature films and parts of a series were made. Previously, the studio was the proud producer of the highly popular *Reksio* and *Bolek and Lolek* (distributed in English as *Jym & Jam* and *Bennie and Lennie*). The Short Film Studio SFS in Warsaw did not undergo an organisational transformation at this time: despite facing the difficulties of this period, it managed to produce a couple of important auteur films alongside a children's feature production (the cult one being *Jacek and Placek*, 1992). We must mention films made by Marek Serafiński (*The Race* [*Wyścig*, 1989]; *Exam* [*Egzamin*, 1992]; *Birth* [*Narodziny*, 1995]), who successfully continued his ethos of a politically engaged cinema, trying to grasp the *Zeitgeist*. Mirosław Kijowicz, the master of meditative-philosophical cinema, was unsuccessful in his attempts to produce films of equal quality. The last of his works, *The Hen* (*Kura*, 1991), was nothing like the politically satirical works of past times, which relentlessly criticised the reality of the former regime. SFS also produced one last film by Jan Lenica, a pioneer of Polish art animation. His *R.O. Island* (*Wyspa R.O.*, 2002), recalled totalitarian times but provided an existential commentary to the contemporary situation in Poland.

The most important auteurs of not only this but also the last two decades were unquestionably Jerzy Kucia and Piotr Dumała – both receiving numerous awards at film festivals in Poland and abroad. Since his first film, *The Return* (*Powrót*, 1972), Jerzy Kucia, described as the "Bresson of Polish animated film", was consistently insightful in his analysis of the surrounding reality in which he employed the language of emotions and memories, and in his last two works he managed superbly to depict shifting "portraits of memory". *Across the Fields* (*Przez pole*, 1992) is a poetic journey through individual and collective memories which develops simultaneously with a harvester's work. Kucia, depicting life in the province, undertakes to save from oblivion the requisites of the past, while at the same time searching for elements of existential truth among people living away from the rush of civilisation. An even fuller and more universal example of Kucia's auteur cinéma is *Tuning the Instruments* (*Strojenie instrumentów*, 2000), one of the most renowned Polish animated films in history, encapsulating the creative work of the director. The film opens with the morning "tuning" of the main hero into the reality, a reality which at one point enters into a dialogue with the world of associations, memories and nostalgia during the hero's motorcycle journey. In a trance-like fashion, comes a stream of pictures and sounds revealing how the past is made from the present, and the road movie evolves into a journey into the internal. Despite being multilayered and full of lyrical associations and references to the subconscious, Kucia's films remain primarily coherent. The sounds, pictures and stories remain indivisible and supplementary, creating a synaesthetic masterpiece.[5]

Piotr Dumała invited viewers into the fantasy world of psychology and literature created with stills etched onto plaster plates. His award-winning *Franz Kafka* (1991) presented an exceptionally interesting narrative, with the formula of an "animated document" slipping into dream visions based on Kafka's prose. Scenes depicting Prague and the life of the writer, along with inspirations based on Kafka's own *Diaries* are embedded in a documentary form. However, Dumała includes in it oneiric references to Kafka's prose, creating a world of dreams from the imagination of the protagonist. The director opens up a discourse on the relativity of time and death, and returns to it once again in his follow up, the half-hour-long film entitled *Crime and Punishment* (*Zbrodnia i kara*, 2000). Dostoevsky's logic of events is replaced with a dream-like narrative, where story lines appear and return in seemingly accidental order and characters undergo transformations in ways which make a direct reference to their literary prototypes impossible. The numerous metamorphoses of humans into animals in both films allow Dumała to underline how strongly animation falls into a dream formula, but also allows him to depict the gloomy psyche of the human, which is driven by instincts and base desires. His psychological considerations, even though derived from literature, are perfectly decipherable thanks to the artistry of form. The picture is suggestive and possesses an unusual depth thanks to the mix of plaster technique with spatial animation.

Aside from auteur films and children's productions of the 1990s, animation made its way into short TV series and music videos. *Nervous Life* (*Nerwowe życie*, 1992) by Piotr Dumała, *An Old Lady Goes to See the Doctor* (*Przychodzi baba do doktora*, 1993)

5
Reflexes of Reality, Magda Lebecka's interview with Jerzy Kucia, in: *Filmo-TV Kamera*, 2/2009.

by Andrzej Czeczot, *Erotic Confessions* (*Erotyczne zwierzenia*, 1996) and *Szczepan and Irenka* (1998–99) by Janek Koza, are examples of funny, anecdotal short stories which received a cult following. The production of music videos revealed new talents and techniques of animation. Among these was Mariusz Wilczyński, who received an award at Yach Film Festival and today is one of the most distinguished Polish animators. Many more perfected directing music videos: Robert Turło, Łukasz Jankowski, Krzysztof Kokoryn and Adam Wyrwas. Polish animation artists contributed to the plastic, artificial interstices seen on MTV (Jerzy Kucia, Piotr Dumała). Animation was fast making its way to television and becoming visible in the credits of TV programmes, film series and TV shows.

Much worse in the free market economy was the plight of students and graduates of animation faculties. Limited budgets, antiquated equipment, reservations about computerisation, all these factors barred their films from the realm of animation. Among the few *études* worth a mention were *Stupajkop* (1993) by Andrzej Zaręba and *Masks* (*Maski*, 1998)

Franz Kafka,
dir. Piotr Dumała
↑

by Piotr Karwas. The former made ironic reference to the tradition of newsreels, and the latter perfectly depicted generational dilemmas and identity problems caused by the transformation. Both artists discontinued their auteur animation work, yet Karwas, after the great success of his diploma work, including a Golden Bear Award and an award at the Annecy film festival, made it to Hollywood and worked for the big animation studios.

The 1990s were lost to almost an entire generation of animation filmmakers, who at the time had little chance of any creative work. One exception was Tomasz Kozak who practised the so-called "phantasmal critique".[6] In his work he stayed away from politics and the public domain. His interest was the collective imagination and his goal was to reinterpret collective representations. He was brave enough to touch embarrassing subjects otherwise repressed in social discourse and explore present day issues he was uneasy about. Made while still a student, *Black Burlesque* (*Czarna burleska*, 1996) is a piercing analysis of shades cast by all kinds of symbols: national, religious and social. In *Salvation Opera* (*Opera ocalenia*, 1998), he criticised enslavement in a post-industrial society and underlined the liberating power of sensuality. In 2000 Kozak made his *début* with *A Gentleman's Romance* (*Romans dżentelmena*), where he explored obsessions relating to the demonic aspect of sexuality and homoerotism. Despite this success, much sought after by his peers, Kozak abandoned animation for found-footage films. As he explained, he preferred to choose another medium for artistic expression rather than struggle with funding for subsequent animation films.

RANK-AND-FILE MOVEMENTS (2002–2005)

In the twelve years following the transformation, spirits in the animation industry were at a low. In a discussion on the problems of animation at the Forum of the National Festival of Author's Animated Films OFAFA in Kraków (Ogólnopolski Festiwal Autorskich Filmów Animowanych OFAFA) the most optimistic remark came from one of the prize-winners, Robert Turło, "That which doesn't kill us makes us stronger". It was the swan song of a dying production model.

There began a new period in Polish animation, and the cards were now being dealt by young, often still studying creators. The changes which started at the turn of the century resulted directly from two factors. One was that digital imaging came into common usage. It allowed producers to abandon (in most cases) film reels and offload great costs and logistic effort (processing, editing). The second factor was the growing popularity

---

[6] Entrenched by Phantasms, conversation with Tomasz Kozak, in: Mariusz Frukacz, *24 Frames Per Second. Conversations on Animation* (*24 klatki na sekundę. Rozmowy o animacji*), Kraków 2008.

Fallen Art,
dir. Tomasz Bagiński

of computer techniques (including 3D) and the rejection of limitations imposed by the requirement of making auteur films. It is debatable as to when exactly the rank-and-file movement began. Could it have been the moment when the aforementioned *Masks* was made, or perhaps with the films of Wojciech Wawszczyk, descending from the spirit of the Polish School but perfectly modern and produced using 3D technique? To me, the breaking point came in 2002 with the first film of Tomasz Bagiński. The Oscar nominated *Cathedral* (*Katedra*) was described by the creator himself as "pop auteur film" intended to bring high art to a mass audience. This oxymoron is well justified; the film was screened in multiplex cinemas but drew its inspiration from painting, literature and architecture. Bagiński's success proved to doubtful artists that the production of such a film did not require gigantic financial resources. This was in part due to the fact that after the nomination, the history of Polish animation came to be widely discussed – there was a growing interest in this art form. New festivals emerged, amateur films were being made, and animation faculties were now besieged by candidates. Bagiński's success also proved that really impressive animation could be made without an education in film (Bagiński was not admitted to Łódź Film School) and that it was possible to reach a mass audience with an animated work.[7]

Ever since then, professionally-made entertainment films have become much acclaimed, with Tomasz Bagiński being one of its best recognised creators. His subsequent film, *Fallen Art* (*Sztuka spadania*, 2004) can be read as a popular lesson in fashioning animation, that

---

[7] Bagiński's film, like Paweł Borowski's *Love Gamestation* two years earlier, was screened before full feature films.

is, the art of enlivening still pictures and creating the illusion of movement. At the same time Bagiński strongly criticises the thoughtlessness of power and speaks of the absurdity of another art – the art of war. A man of "two professions" is Wojciech Wawszczyk who is both a director of auteur animation films targeted at a mass audience, and an animator working for pragmatic reasons. As director, he combines 3D with traditional techniques and bases his films on legible narration (stories of altruism, conformity and love) and strengthens it with technical solutions (colour operation, camera viewing angles). The success of his school films (*Headless*, 1999; *Mouse* [*Mysz*], 2001) and the privately produced *Penguin* (*Pingwin*, 2002) gave Wawszczyk a pass to Hollywood. However after two years of work there he resigned to make his own films. Izabela Plucińska does not distance herself from popular films and her clay animated stories won the hearts of audiences and critics alike. Her graduation film *Jam Session* (2005) was awarded the Silver Bear at the Berlinale and showed how great a combination spatial techniques with relief clay animation could be. Andrzej Gosieniecki and Joanna Jasińska-Koronkiewicz also produce, in addition to auteur films, films directed at a mass audience, mainly children. It is worth noting that films like *Sunny Town* (*Słoneczne miasteczko*, 2004) and *Flax* (*Len*, 2005) are strongly affected by the auteur's creative vision, which allows us to hope for a mix of good entertainment and stimulating plastic art. Let us bear in mind that most of the artists mentioned above are graduates of the Łódź Film School and thus are prone to put more emphasis on the narrative and directing, rather than visual art.

At the time of the new *fin de siècle*, changes came to animation schools. Here we should emphasise the extremely important contribution of great artists in the field, who as

Jam Session,
dir. Izabela Plucińska

pedagogues, helped educate the young generation of directors. Jerzy Kucia (Academy of Fine Arts in Kraków), Kazimierz Urbański (AFA in Poznań and the National Higher School of Film, Television and Theatre in Łódź), Daniel Szczechura (AFA in Warsaw), Hieronim Neumann (AFA in Poznań and Warsaw) and Piotr Dumała, Marek Skrobecki and Mariusz Wilczyński (the National Higher School of Film, Television and Theatre in Łódź) have all contributed to the education of artists who today are at the forefront of Polish animation. Better technical facilities, easier access to professional equipment, and cooperation with film studios made it possible to make school *études* and graduation works that could compete with professional films at all kinds of festivals. To the aforementioned list of students from Łódź school we should also add Maciej Majewski, who calls his works "surrealising animated documentaries". In a film made using comic book aesthetics *Beware of Fierce Dogs* (*Uwaga! Złe psy*, 2001), Majewski depicted in grotesque fashion the paradoxes of our times and criticised the bloodthirsty, ambulance-chasing news media. Artists from the Jerzy Kucia studio put more emphasis on the visual elements of their films. Highly critical towards everyday reality is Anna Pankiewicz, who condemns a world lacking values and immersed in consumption in her *There Will Always Be Tomorrow* (*Zawsze będzie jutro*, 2003) and *Happiness* (2005). One of the most disturbing and memorable student animated films of this period was the monochromatic reflection on loneliness and death entitled *TV-Set* (*Telewizor*, 2005) by Tomasz Siwiński. The director made a superb piece by connecting paint animation directly with film narrative (shot framing, panoramas). Siwiński also marks a strong connection between animated film and dreams, and he pursues meanings hidden just under the surface. Marta Pajek's films are in turn a journey to the other side of consciousness in search of the "eternal child". The restrained black-and-white world of a child's imagination in *After Apples* (*Po jabłkach*, 2004) is not as it might seem, a world of chaos – it is, in fact, ordered by strict rules of rhythm. Similar traits are to be found in *Next Door* (*Za ścianą*, 2005), where Pajek invites us to observe the spectacle of redefining subjectivity.

We should also spare a moment to discuss the work of three graduates of the Academy of Fine Arts in Kraków who had finished their education by the end of the 20th century.

All focused on auteur animation, based on perfect visual art backgrounds and had to search for their chance of a *début* outside of the existing structures. They established a cooperative and became producers of their own films, which, at the expense of a double work load gave them unlimited creative freedom. Although their early work appeared in the subsequent period of the history of Polish animation, they very much belong to the previous, being dynamic and replete with rank-and-file initiatives. In her animation work, Wiola Sowa is preoccupied with interpersonal relations and with the way they are portrayed. Both in her graduate work *Between Us* (*Pomiędzy nami*, 2000) and in her first film *Refrains* (*Refreny*, 2007) she subtly accentuated emotions and experiences by finding their visual, plastic art equivalent. It is best seen in *Refrains*, a film which brought her several awards at some of the most important festivals devoted to animation. The snowy and overexposed frames, with intriguing whispers and the contrasting music of Leszek Możdżer shape the unique ambience of this film. Edyta Turczanik is in turn fascinated by the function of memories and the issue of fading, which bears a resemblance to the works of her teacher, Jerzy Kucia. Woven with reflections of memories, *Shadows* (*Cienie*, 2000) shows the destructive mechanism present in the repression of reminiscences. Her next film *Everything Flows* (*Wszystko płynie*, 2007) is a painful metaphor of fading but also an affirmation of life, where all the paint blotches and every frame of movement seems to vibrate. Robert Sowa uses Puppetoon animation technique to speak of difficult experiences which shape our lives. Set in chambered, almost claustrophobic spaces, Sowa's dramas are touching studies on loneliness and longing. The bitterness of old age and the process of forgetting in *Hairdresser* (*Fryzjer*, 1997), the pain of unfulfilled love in *Interior Portrait* (*Portret we wnętrzu*, 1999), the unassuaged sorrow after a break up in *Sequence* (*Sekwens*, 2007); all Sowa's films refer to neuralgic and painful difficulties. In his very personal and uncompromising auteur films, Robert Sowa merges realistic observations of his environment with a depiction of the mental states of his protagonists, which he achieves by the employment of formal means.

Other already recognised artists also produced acclaimed films in the period under discussion. In *Professional* (*Zawodowiec*, 2003), Marek Serafiński criticises superficial political pseudo-élites dating back to former times and finds hope for changing the language of politics in a young generation not tainted by the past. In *Ichthys* (2005), Marek Skrobecki presents two attitudes towards religious truths while referring to Christian symbolism. On the one hand, he presents the impatient, doubtful and immediate-gratification-seeking guest of a restaurant (symbolising the church), and on the other, a patiently waiting and task-oriented waiter (symbolising the priest). Hieronim Neumann, a student and follower of Zbigniew Rybczyński's investigations, continued with experiments based on manipulating live-action sequences, which were not merely formal plays but also described a fraction of reality. Such was *Remote Control* (2002), where the director portrayed a collective portrait of tower-block folk who are linked with a constantly on and ever-present television set. In *Zoopraxiscope* (2005), Neumann pays tribute to Eadweard Muybridge. Referring to his series of photographs in motion, Neumann constructed a humorous story on the complexities of relations between men and women. The growing interest in abstract and experimental films is visible among his students in Poznań and Warsaw. Films by Natalia Wilkoszewska, Olga Wroniewicz and Joanna Polak daringly merge various techniques and alternative approaches with narrative structure.

Towards normalisation (2006–2009)

The rapid growth of interest in animation and the increased activity of young producers did not find an ally in the system of film financing. This situation vastly improved when the Cinematography Act of 30 June 2005 was passed, establishing The Polish Film Institute (PISF). Since its inception in 2006, one of its tasks has been to develop special operating programmes supporting the production and promotion of animation, with one of the priorities being to support directorial *débuts*. After a couple of years, it can be said that it definitely has changed the state of Polish animation for the better. The number of applications and the volume of grants are on the increase, coupled with a flood of new films (which are often delayed by a few years). The reception of animation films has changed as well: every year there are more festivals presenting animation; after thirty years even books on the subject have appeared, and enthusiasts can finally get the most interesting films on DVD. The crowning of this process was a celebration of the 60th anniversary of Polish animation in 2008.

Those studios which took legal form best coped with the new and difficult situation. Today, they find it easier to get funding (also internationally) and to attract young artists. The best example is "Se-Ma-For" studio. It managed to assemble one of the best teams in Puppetoon animation in the world. This was made evident when a Puppetoon screen version of Sergei Prokofiev's *Peter and the Wolf* (2006) was produced in cooperation with BreakThru from Great Britain. It was directed by Suzy Templeton, who among many awards, received an Academy Award for Best Animated Short in 2007. Audacious support of aspiring students gave way to many spectacular *débuts*, to name but two: *Joyets* (*Radostki*, 2008) by Magdalena Osińska, and *The City Sails On* (*Miasto płynie*, 2009) by Balbina Bruszewska. The TV Studio of Animated Films is also more open to young directors, as seen in their newly-invigorated series *Animation Films to Classical Music*. Among other productions were two series of Polish fairy tales, altogether 26 episodes, each sparkling with humour and acquiring contemporary meanings. Especially worthwhile were the episodes directed by Robert Tarło, who can surprise the audience with his artwork, animation techniques and a witty dialogue with popular culture. A few interesting productions came out of the Short Film Studio in Warsaw. We should mention here films based on the paintings of Edward Dwurnik *Cornerhouse 360 degrees* (*Warzywniak 360°*, 2006); *Oasis* (*Oaza*, 2009) by Andrzej Barański, the *début* of Maciej Majewski entitled *Krasicki Reactivation* (*Krasicki Reaktywacja*, 2007) and *Titanic World* (2008) by Hanna Margolis. Private studios have an even larger share of the productions being made. The Warsaw studio Platige Image presents an exceptionally high level of professionalism which is combined with amusing storylines in productions like *The Ark* (*Arka*, 2007) by Grzegorz Jonkajtys, *The Chick* (*Laska*, 2008) by Michał Socha, or *Cinematograph* (*Kinematograf*, 2009) by Tomasz Bagiński. The output of the Serafiński Studio in Warsaw and Studio Mansarda in Poznań is substantial. Despite the support of The Polish Film Institute, the explosion of first films in recent years would not have been possible were it not for the shift in attitude among young producers. Many of them did not simply wait around for offers from the existing film companies, but established their own companies and cooperatives in order to produce films. Others gathered resources thanks to international cooperation. Such was the case with the medium-length feature film *Splinter* (*Drzazga*, 2007) by Wojciech Wawszczyk, the films of Anna Błaszczyk as well as the first film by Kamil Polak. There are yet others who choose to work outside Poland. Berlin-based Izabela Plucińska produced the twenty-five minute long film *Esterhazy* (2009), which, from the perspective of rabbits inhabiting the space between the Berlin walls, tells a story of the changes taking place in 1989. Similar was the choice of Izabela Bartosik, who now lives in France. Many others, including Wojciech Bąkowski and Norman Leto, produce their films in home studios and cover the necessary expenses on their own.

The greatest asset of Polish animation today is the generation of twenty- and thirty-year-olds. However, it would be difficult to find a common denominator to jointly refer to their artistic output. Far easier is it to find differences. This great variety is due to the very individualistic approach to the subject matter of animated film and treating animation as a medium designed to express one's own personality. Another factor is the attitude towards the achievements of the past generation of animators and the new outlook on the future of animation. The heterogeneity of the young generation is also a sign of the times they live and create in. They need not fight for things their grandparents and parents struggled for, and there is no single meta-narrative which would be predominant in their

Peter and the Wolf,
dir. Suzy Templeton
→

Refrains,
Wiola Sowa
↓

works. Aesopian language utilised by older generations to speak about the absurdities of the former regime has now been replaced with the language of emotions and expression. The focus is now on the inside of man and interpersonal relations. Such is the auteur cinema of Wiola Sowa, Edyta Turczanik and Robert Sowa. Similar features can be found in the decade-older films of Mariusz Wilczyński, who is a self-taught auteur of animated films and the producer of the opening titles for TVP Kultura. Wilczyński developed his distinctively expressive style by merging suggestive and pulsating pencil animation with an oneiric narrative based on numerous repetitions and transformations. Using his favourite array of motifs (kings, hearts, fish, old men, birds) Wilczyński takes a closer look at strong interpersonal relations: an overprotective mother and her son in *For My Mother and Me* (*Mojej Mamie i sobie*, 2000), an old couple in love in *Unfortunately* (*Niestety*, 2004), a lonely woman in a double relationship in *Kizi Mizi* (2007). Numerous references to childhood and the recurring scenery of industrial city districts make Wilczyński's cinema extremely personal and allow the viewers to enter into the intimate world of the film. The originality of his work is confirmed by screenings at the most prestigious institutions all around the world (e.g. The Museum of Modern Art in Kraków) and at renowned festivals.

Contemporary Polish animation reflects not only interpersonal relations but also social and political transformations. The trend, drawing much inspiration from the achievements of the Polish Animation School, bears witness to the times we live in. *Safari* (2009)

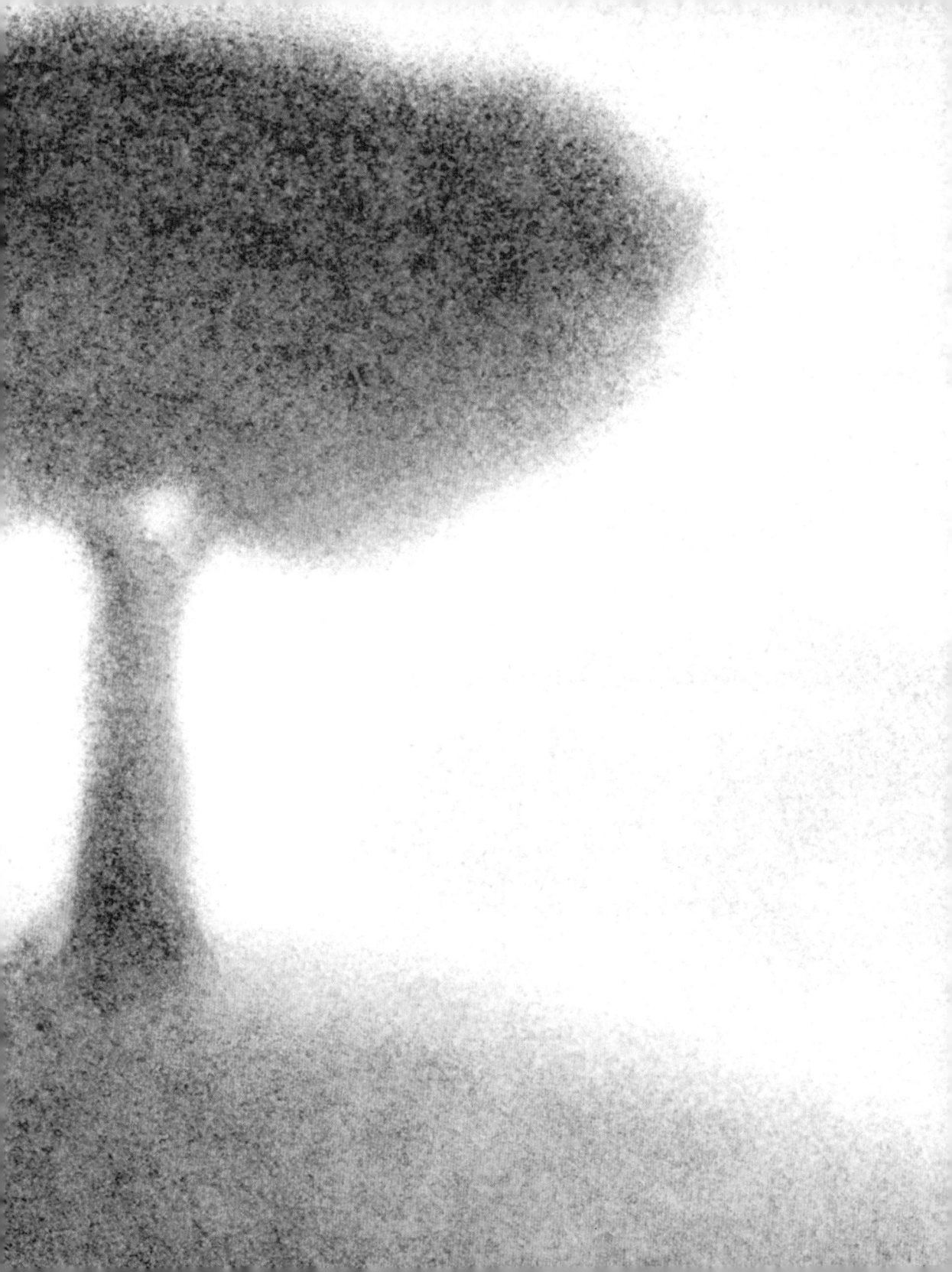

by Marek Serafiński is an epilogue to the two-decades older *Race* – this time however, the aim of the competition between its protagonists is not money but a labyrinthine "rat race" of emotions and interpersonal relations. In the feminist *Dokumanimo* (2006), Małgorzata Bosek presents a vivid tale of a housewife's life who fights the monotony of her duties with a specific art – she creates collages from labels, price tags and other waste. Krzysztof Kiwerski offers cinema of political and social references. Inspired by a Jacek Gaj's copperplate *Drabiny*, and directed together with Zbigniew Szymański, *Level* (2005) is the story of a ruthless and brutal way of pursuing one's goals. *Witness 1919–2004* (*Świadek 1919–2004*) is an animated lesson in Polish history shown from the perspective of a scarecrow. Marches by various armies, insurrections and political and social transformations are shown through the eyes of an atypical witness with the music of Zygmunt Konieczny. In turn, in his debut *Shadowland* (*Kraina cieni*, 2006), Tomasz Głodek speaks about saving one's identity during the Second World War. Głodek refers directly to current world events and cannot accept the violence of war promoted in the media.

Recently, we have witnessed a clear rejuvenation in the language of animated film and its responsiveness to events and problems characteristic to modern visual arts. Responsible for this process is a group of artists who find shopping centres more suitable for screenings than cinemas. The most distinctive representative of this movement and the entire young generation of artists is Wojciech Bąkowski. In his early work we can find traces of a critical trend in animation. It is particularly visible in *Mass* (*Masa*, 2003), where he undertook a broad critique of homogenisation, blaming the repressive character of all totalitarian and religious systems hidden under the cover of democracy. However, in his following films, most of which employ the 'non-camera' technique, Bąkowski abandons this approach in favour of overdrawn and over-expressive realism. His animated films are examples of vagrant art,[8] mixing subtlety with pungency. In the animated poetry of Bąkowski, and specifically in one of the most interesting series *Spoken Movie* [*Film mówiony*] (*Film mówiony 1*, 2007; *Film mówiony 2*, *Film mówiony 3*, 2008; *Film mówiony 4*, 2009), we encounter a sensitivity to the dirt and banality of every day life, and also to the omnipresent illness and the banality of death. Bąkowski's phenomenon proves also that auteur cinema can be produced in a home studio with the use of simple and inexpensive materials. What is important is that Bąkowski's achievements are valued not only in animation circles but also among art critics around the world, achieving nu-

---

[8] Vagrant art – in Poland also referred to as "new Poznanian expression" – is the work of young artists and is characterised by a "sensitive boorishness" and a vulgar but simultaneously delicate view of reality, penetrating the dark and repulsive aspects of reality with the use of intentionally minimised formal means.

merous awards and invitations to international exhibitions. The Poznań-based group Penerstwo cooperates with yet another well recognised visual artist, musician and producer of animated films, Piotr Bosacki. In his films he conducts logic experiments (*String Movie* [*Film sznurkowy*], 2005) and poses questions about the nature of things and human nature (*A Film About the Grim Reaper* [*Film o kostuchu*], 2008; *A Film with no Sound* [*Film bez dźwięku*], 2009). In the 3D films of Norman Leto, we see attempts to blur human boundaries and formal labels (he himself conceals his identity behind a pseudonym). The illusion of reality that he provides is full of intentional mistakes, loaned words and traces of foreign influence, and the advanced algorithms of artificial intelligence increase the confusion of the audience. Transformations and distortions of photography are the subject matter of Agnieszka Polska's plastic art. She is most interested in the way identity is shaped by ideology (*The Calendar* [*Kalendarz*], 2008). Polska is also fascinated by the movement itself: in *Medical Gymnastics* (*Ćwiczenia korekcyjne*, 2008) and *Militiamen and Thieves* (*Milicjanci i złodzieje*, 2009), she creates dance forms using films initially made with completely different intentions.

Future prospects

The presented overview of contemporary Polish animation now allows us to be more optimistic about the future than ten years ago. A regulated system of financing and production results in the creation of several short films a year, and a large proportion of *débuts* allows for generational continuity. Grants for schools providing education in animation have increased the number of these films from twenty to thirty. Amateur films are improving technically and often surprise us with new ideas, due to the fact that amateur artists often have similar equipment to that used in professional studios. New film clubs are flourishing where children and teenagers under supervision create exceptionally fresh and intriguing films (Dziecięca Wytwórnia Filmowa [Children's Movie Studio] in Wrocław, "Laterna Magica" in Legnica). The stabilisation of the market is seen via increased cooperation with foreign studios (the aforementioned *Peter and the Wolf*, and many others), and in some cases productions being relocated to Poland (as is the case of the renowned Brothers Quay, whose *Inventory of Traces* [*Inwentorium śladów*] was produced by Serafiński Studio). The growing number of awards at international festivals of animation and new media allows us to believe that both auteur films and professionally made digital productions for mass audiences are headed in the right direction. Every year there are more film festivals and publications on animation, which is evidence of the shrinking gap between artists and the audience. One of the weaknesses of Polish animation is the lack of support for the development of full feature productions. We may hope for some improvement as there already appear to be initiatives in place to change this situation (e.g. the cult comic book *George the Hedgehog* [*Jeż Jerzy*] is now in production).

Still, there is very little chance that the phenomenon of the Polish Animation School will be once again repeated. There is no meta-narrative to cement young creators and allow for such classification. Instead we see that new productions are extremely varied and polyphonic. Next to popular films, which are competing with the entertainment films of other countries, there are auteur films, boasting exceptional visual artistry and insightful reflections. It is still a cinema capable of breaking through the peals of laughter and of posing challenging questions. In this respect, what Bendazzi was quoted as saying is still valid.

Translated by Bartłomiej Reszuta

THE SECOND YOUTH OF A SIXTY YEAR OLD

IS POLAND A WOMAN?
FEMINIST AND HOMOSEXUAL THEMES IN POLISH FILM FROM 1989–2009

ANITA PIOTROWSKA

In Polish, the word Poland (Polska) is feminine. It is no coincidence that in classic Polish culture (particularly 19th-century romantic literature and painting, so dominated by patriotic and martyrological themes after the loss of independence), Poland was identified as a mother figure, a suffering mother, the Polish Mother (referring to Adam Mickiewicz's poem), or the *Polonia* (series of drawings) by Artur Grottger. Assigning femininity to the patriotic paradigm was preserved in culture throughout entire generations struggling with various threats to the state or national sovereignty. It is not surprising, therefore, that the issue of women, or gender identification issues *per se*, were only of secondary concern to Polish filmmakers. They were too busy settling scores with history (i.e. World War II, communism, the Solidarity phenomenon, or the traumas of martial law), and too devoted to their socio-political duties to make films pertaining to the most intimate recesses of human existence. In 1957, the incorrigible Witold Gombrowicz discussed this in his *Diaries* (*Dzienniki*) written abroad, urging his fellow countrymen to overcome their restrictive movements of "Polishness", and demanding that people be autonomous in expressing their identity to the fullest extent.

RELAXATION FOR THE WARRIORS

Before the crucial system-change of 1989, Polish cinema was bravely shouldering the burden of a socio-political mission. After World War II, together with advancing socialism and its related propaganda, Polish women began driving tractors and became "shock workers", which was immediately reflected in so-called "industrial" films. In 1960s cinema, the face and form of the imaginary Polish Woman were those of the iconic actresses of the period, such as Beata Tyszkiewicz, Pola Raksa, Kalina Jędrusik, Barbara Kwiatkowska or Elżbieta Czyżewska. Even then, however, some attempts were made to break this stereotype. Wojciech Jerzy Has' film *How To Be Loved* (*Jak być kochaną*, 1962), starring Barbara Krafftówna, gives an interesting view of the war and its heroic mythology from the point of view of a woman in love with a burned-out hero. However, unlike Zbigniew Cybulski, who died prematurely and was best remembered for playing Maciek Chełmicki in Andrzej Wajda's *Ashes and Diamonds* (*Popiół i diament*), no actresses ever became true symbols of the entire post-war generation by articulating its obsessions, fears and dreams.

In the historical-themed films of the "Polish School" of 1955–61, as well as the so-called "cinema of moral unrest" of the late 1970s (which anticipated the birth of Solidarity), women were mainly depicted as ornamental "relaxation for the warriors" – Polish men fighting "for the cause" and wrestling with the past and the present. Women had a similar status in the majority of films made during the communist Polish People's Republic period. In his films like *Salt of the Black Earth* (*Sól ziemi czarnej*, 1969) or

Pearl in the Crown (*Perła w koronie*, 1971), which mythologised the patriotic traditions of plebeian Silesia, Kazimierz Kutz portrayed women as mute guardians of home and hearth, full of plain homeliness. In *Mother of Kings* (*Matka Królów*, 1982), the story of a widow with four sons fighting to get by during World War II and the Stalinist era, Janusz Zaorski subscribed to that Polish Mother figure rooted in national martyrological tradition. Some films appeared which did try to break away from this image, however. In *Man of Marble* (*Człowiek z marmuru*, 1976) and *Man of Iron* (*Człowiek z żelaza*, 1981), Andrzej Wajda created the character of Agnieszka – "a woman with a camera", dynamic and determined in her search for the truth behind the abuses of the system. She was played by the then very young Krystyna Janda, who defined a new archetype of femininity in Polish cinema. Yet at that time of intense political change (the increasingly bold re-examination of communism during the so-called "carnival of Solidarity"), even such a distinct female identity receded into the background as it was overshadowed by important political messages. Indeed, only Agnieszka Holland opposed this trend in *A Lonely Woman* (*Kobieta samotna*, 1980), an unusually realistic and painfully intimate portrait of an unmarried postwoman left on the sidelines with an illegitimate child. The film's heroine is ignored by the authorities on every level: the social services, the ruling Communist Party, the trade unions, and ordinary people bereft of all feeling. The most important point, however, was not the political system or social backdrop, but the fact that it is a desperate, ageing "lonely woman" who takes centre stage in the film, seeking to escape her everyday hopelessness in the arms of a young disabled man. The uninhibited way in which Holland observes her heroine's fight for survival is striking and impressive even today. No other Polish People's Republic-era film depicted the fate of women so bravely and harshly. Similar interests may also be found in the work of Barbara Sass who, even in her early films like *Without Love* (*Bez miłości*, 1980) or *Debutante* (*Debiutantka*, 1981), scrutinised the situation of young women about to embark on professional careers, yet still at risk of becoming dependent and entangled in unequal relationships with men. Dorota Stalińska's roles were definitely the strongest point of these films – she used her acting abilities with defiance and bravado, whether playing an ambitious professional prepared for anything (*An Immoral Story* [*Historia niemoralna*], 1990), or a vulgar criminal who is sensitive at heart (*The Scream* [*Krzyk*], 1982).

The uncompromising films of Holland and Sass should be considered, however, as glorious exceptions from that bygone era. Gender-related themes (relating to sexual identity) were doomed to play a minor role in the Polish People's Republic-era cinema. To illustrate this phenomenon, let us mention the case of Juliusz Machulski's film *Sexmission* (*Seksmisja*, 1983), the most popular Polish comedy of the decade, which attracted 10 million viewers. Machulski created an anti-utopia about a world without men: after a nuclear war, all male genes have been destroyed, but in 2044, the last two specimens of that sex awake after many years in suspended animation. Instead of being an ideal system, the ruling matriarchy turns out to be a kingdom of absurdity and totalitarian violence. Self-sufficient in every way, women have rewritten the history of the world (e.g. the famous line "Copernicus was a woman!"), and are striving to eliminate the last traces of manhood. The finale leaves us with no illusions, however: the formerly "weaker sex" reveals its inherent frailty, and the perfect world without men turns out to be deeply flawed. In 1980s Poland, a large part of the adult audience had no doubt about the real message behind *Sexmission*: its mockery of radical feminism was seen as a metaphor for the communist system, disguised as science fiction, much less a story about the eternal battle of the sexes (the result of which was clearly not in favour of women in this case). Even today, Polish feminists view the film rather leniently, perceiving it above all to contain political references that were consistent with the period. Nevertheless, the term "sex mission" has entered the vernacular for good, and is used these days by adversaries of the feminist movement.

Women as pop-culture icons

Once the spectre of political censorship had vanished in 1989, Polish cinema also started to lose its former "politically-engaged" stance, which had required filmmakers and audiences alike to have a critical attitude to reality, and seek political allusions on the screen. One would have thought that this was the ideal moment to start tackling subjects that had been neglected by Polish filmmakers in the past. However, the anticipated changes did not occur immediately. After being starved for so long, Polish cinema of the 1990s was far too busy providing entertainment modelled on western popular cinema, and looking for its niche in the new politico-economic reality, to start reducing its backlog of behavioural issues, including ones directly connected with sexuality. In the tremendously popular so-called gangster genre (e.g. films by Władysław Pasikowski or Łukasz Wylężałek), women were mostly reduced to stereotypical sexy "gangster's molls" who were generally very young, calculating, loose, and changed hands willingly. The tough guy image in Pasikowski's *Kroll* (1991), set inside the Polish Army, was obtained at the expense of one-dimensional, marginalised female characters, who were devoid of any charisma and unlikely to please the audience. Polish cinemagoers particularly recall one cynical quote: "Because she was a bad woman …", uttered by the jaded ex-Secret Service officer Franz Maurer in Pasikowski's *Pigs* (*Psy*, 1992). By saying this, the hero (played by Bogusław Linda, with whom lots of young men identified in those days) was hinting that female nature is innately imperfect. In the films of Pasikowski and other directors of his ilk, women were often tokens of the venality and breakdown of ideals. This corresponded perfectly to the pessimistic mood of Poland's early transition years, when only a select few were able to benefit initially, and not always in accordance with

the letter of the law or the Ten Commandments. In the comedy-type Polish gangster movies (e.g. films by Olaf Lubaszenko or Witold Adamek), no-one even bothered to try to add ideology to the unambiguously crude image of women. Big boys' gangster exploits were accompanied by women reduced to mere sex objects by being labelled as "Cycofons" ("tits-on-legs"), after a character in Lubaszenko's *Boys Don't Cry* (*Chłopaki nie płaczą*, 2000).

At this stage, it is worth mentioning the main cult actress of the 1990s, namely the voluptuously-endowed Katarzyna Figura, whose changing image over the last two decades can basically be regarded as an example of how a woman's body may be used in a wide variety of film genres. Originally launched as a sex symbol in films by Piotr Szulkin, Radosław Piwowarski and Juliusz Machulski during the declining years of the Polish People's Republic, Figura dominated the next two decades of Polish cinema by playing over fifty different parts. Figura's "over-presence" on the screen (although she did gain some credibility with a minor role in Robert Altman's *Prêt-à-Porter*) was a phenomenon in itself: she found herself a place in Polish art-house cinema, as well as in comedies, which were very popular at the time. In the auteur films of Andrzej Kondratiuk (*The*

← *Boys Don't Cry*, dir. Olaf Lubaszenko

↓ *Killer*, dir. Juliusz Machulski

Spindle of Time [*Wrzeciono czasu*], 1995) and *The Sundial* [*Słoneczny zegar*], 1997) she embodied a life-giving force in the role of a Dionysian muse who satiates the senses of an ageing, cranky artist hiding away with his wife in a forest, miles from anywhere. But her image was hardly any different in the hit comedies of the time, such as *Killer* (*Kiler*, 1997) and *2 Killers* (*Kilerów 2-óch*, 1999) directed by Machulski, or *Happy New York* (*Szczęśliwego Nowego Jorku*, 1997) by Janusz Zaorski. Figura played almost the same character in almost all of these films: a mature, slightly infantile sex-bomb; a kind of poor man's Marilyn Monroe, all too willing to exhibit her physical charms. In time, however, everyone (audiences, filmmakers, and the actress herself) grew tired of this one-dimensional and admittedly sexist image. The first turning point came with *Sour Soup* (*Żurek*, 2003) by Ryszard Brylski, in which Figura, aged and stripped of all glamour, plays the part of an exhausted mother wronged by fate who seeks justice when her handicapped underage daughter gets pregnant. However, even here, despite her physical transformation, Figura still continues to act with her ample charms – this time for the "social cinema" genre. At the same time, the actress' mature sexuality was used in political cinema too: in Szulkin's *King Ubu* (*Ubu król*, 2003), she plays the caricatured Mama Ubu who, in one of the film's best scenes, suckles her husband with

Ladies,
dir. Tomasz Konecki, Andrzej Saramonowicz

her huge breast in order to galvanise him into carrying out a *coup d'état*. (Similar power was wielded in Polish cinema by another bust of impressive proportions, that of Renata Dancewicz: whenever it appeared on screen, it elicited tears of sheer emotion from the eponymous *Colonel Kwiatkowski* [*Pułkownik Kwiatkowski*] in Kazimierz Kutz's 1997 comedy.) The deconstruction of Figura's entire previous image was finally accomplished by Piotr Uklański in *Summer Love* (2006). Subverting the western genre, this esteemed photographer and performer dealt the *coup de grâce* to its iconography by including an image of a Sheriff's Woman, whose femininity is abused and scraped away in a shocking head-shaving scene. Here, Figura, often referred to as a "biological" or even an "organic" actress, reached the heights of her artistic courage. This extreme performance for Uklański was the symbolic termination of her on-screen "brief history of a body".

Another enclave of sexual stereotypes appeared in Polish cinema in the form of romantic comedies, which broke box-office records during the first decade of the 21st century. Cocky-sounding titles like *Never Ever!* (*Nigdy w życiu!*), *Why Not?!* (*Dlaczego nie!*) and *I'll Show You!* (*Ja wam pokażę!*) seemingly heralded a reassessment of the place of women in the new reality, but in fact only aped the tried-and-tested formula. What is interesting is that these comedies were all made by men – as if they knew best what women wanted. However, as it turned out, the male film-marketing specialists had hit the nail on the head with their diagnosis: millions of Polish women evidently did want

light-hearted plots, comforting tones that preserved the patriarchal model (despite the general liberalisation), and serial-style glamour which was supposed to offer them refuge from the stark reality outside their door. The perfect image that shone through in these films was one of women not subject to the ageing process, sexy, well-groomed, resourceful, living in the lap of middle-class luxury, seemingly liberated, but dreaming in their hearts of true love and settling down with a man. One can but wonder whether the feelings in these kind of naïve adult fairytales, and other similar mass cultural products (like television serials and women's literature presided over by the widely-read novelist Katarzyna Grochola), truly do reflect the prevailing mood, or whether they have in fact been skilfully created in order to get Polish audiences used to more easily-digestible, mass-produced fare. Around the same time, director/scriptwriter duo Tomasz Konecki and Andrzej Saramonowicz tried to rise above the level of these contemporary fairytales with their hit "hormonal comedies" *Testosterone* (*Testosteron*, 2007), *Ladies* (*Lejdis*, 2008) and *The Perfect Guy for My Girlfriend* (*Idealny facet dla mojej dziewczyny*, 2009). These films, which were advertised as the Polish answer to productions like *Sex and the City*, were intentionally provocative attacks on the sterile, false reality of romantic comedies and political correctness. Konecki and Saramonowicz's heroines represent a wide spectrum of women: from modern man-hunting "consumers" to the traditional style woman, daydreaming of ensnaring Mr. Right, having a baby, or getting some new silicon breasts. In their case, despite a bold breaking-down of various sexual taboos, the fight against sexual stereotypes actually turns out to be rather feigned, and is limited to risqué verbal sparring. For even in the lives of these seemingly liberated heroines, a man is always the centre of their interests and (to quote the well-known feminist Kazimiera Szczuka) he is intended to be their "prize for being emancipated". Therefore, feminism in its literal form, which had previously been so scarce on Polish screens, was simply being scoffed at here as incompatible with deep-seated, age-old female desires.

A peek beneath the lining

Looking back over the last twenty years of Polish cinema through the prism of a well-defined female presence, one can observe two completely different trends. Referring only to the aforementioned cases, pessimists would say that contemplation on the subject has hardly been inspiring, and they are backed up not just by examples from popular cinema. Indeed, in most acclaimed films from the period, women were given mainly supporting roles as "mothers, wives and lovers" (to quote the title of Juliusz Machulski's 1996

→ *Bellissima*,
dir. Artur Urbański

serial). Women as patient witnesses to masculine struggles with themselves and the world. Some Polish films were openly misogynistic, or even demonised female sexuality. An illustration of the first type is *Dad* (*Tato*, 1995) by Maciej Ślesicki, in which Bogusław Linda, the stock macho man of Polish cinema, engages in a single-handed and brave battle to be granted custody of his daughter. On the other side, the filmmaker inserts repulsive female stereotypes: the child is mentally ill and generally dangerous mother, and the hero's treacherous mother-in-law, stylised as a real broomstick-wielding witch. The film's character construction and emotional mood all encourage one to champion the brave hero in his war against destructive, irrational feminine elements in contemptuously-described "ovarian solidarity". Meanwhile, Andrzej Żuławski, who returned to Polish cinema after many years with the controversial *Chamanka* (*Szamanka*, 1996), scripted by the feminist-leaning writer Manuela Gretkowska, saw above all an uncontrollable, voracious sexuality in femininity. The hero of the film, a young anthropologist possessed by passion for a female student with unpredictable, truly bestial reactions, gradually loses his grip on reality and heads for a complete breakdown. The final scene, in which the eponymous "she-shaman" eats her lover's brains with a spoon, was interpreted as an exemplary illustration of the perennial male fear of a man-eating women. Then, in Radosław Piwowarski's characteristically-titled film *The Dark Side of Venus* (*Ciemna strona Wenus*, 1997), the hero's male nightmare is provided by the two women closest to him: his faithful, virtuous wife, who turns out to be not what she seems, and his licentious lover, the tellingly-named Suczka ("Little Bitch"). If cinema is the mirror of the collective or individual subconscious, the aforementioned films would supply abundant research material for a psychoanalyst.

Even today, in 2009, one can look at Polish cinema from a completely different point of view. During the absence of Agnieszka Holland, who has been making films abroad for the last two decades, several talented female and male directors have emerged who do speak up for women in the new Polish landscape. Although the feminist movement had been present in Poland since the early 19th century, it was only in the 1990s that it became a universally-recognisable force represented in the democratic media, and started to make its voice heard in Polish literature, film and the arts. The first reckless attempt to penetrate the subconscious of Polish women in cinema was made by Piotr Szulkin, formerly an excellent creator of political allegories in the guise of science fiction. Following several years of inactivity, he returned to the screen with *Femina* (1990), a film adaptation of Krystyna Kofta's novel *The Small Predators' Pavilion* (*Pawilon małych drapieżców*). Taking inspiration from Luis Buñuel's memorable *Belle de Jour*, Szulkin made a portrait of a 30-year-old Polish woman in search of erotic adventure, showing her as a victim of having grown up in a doubly-oppressive system. In a series of visual, sometimes grotesque flashbacks, *Femina* takes us back to the heroine's childhood in the 1950s – the dark days of the Stalinist era. At that time, two forces were battling for the girl's soul (and body): the totalitarian system personified by Iosif Vissarionovich Stalin, and the strict educational model imposed by the Catholic church. Although *Femina* ended up being a failure with audiences and critics, who saw first and foremost the director's private obsessions disguised in feminine form, it was one of Polish cinema's few attempts to treat feminism seriously.

Barbara Sass did not abandon women's themes, and entered the new era with the not entirely successful comedy *The Cat-Burglars* (*Pajęczarki*, 1993), a tale of two burglar sisters trying to outwit a male enemy. During the same period, she also made several other less ambitious films, such as *Nothing But Fear* (*Tylko strach*), starring the excellent Anna Dymna as a journalist grappling with alcoholism, and *Temptation* (*Pokuszenie*, 1995), in which Sass describes the drama of a young nun locked up in a Stalinist prison, torn between faith, forbidden emotions, and the underhand promptings of the communist authorities. It is also worth mentioning that it marked the screen *début* of one of Poland's most outstanding dramatic actresses, the intelligently blonde Magdalena Cielecka, whose brilliant theatre roles have often been deeper than those offered to her by Polish cinema. A lack of interestingly-written female characters has always been one of the weaknesses of Polish films, so we should list some exceptions to this rule. Breaking out of the usual mould were: resolute Aunt Idalia (Maja Komorowska) who refused to fear the communist system in Krzysztof Zanussi's film *In Full Gallop* (*Cwał*, 1995); the neurotic, morbidly-ambitious mother (Ewa Kasprzyk) from Artur Urbański's TV movie *Bellissima* (2001); and Maja Ostaszewska's numerous roles that demonstrate

Reverse,
dir. Borys Lankosz

both fragility and strength in young heroines. In recent years, this tendency has definitely started to change. It is enough to recall the dynamic film career of Krystyna Janda, once a star of politically-engaged cinema. Even though she was never off Polish screens, Janda only recently made a truly stunning comeback to the cinema in Andrzej Barański's film *A Few People, A Little Time (Parę osób, mały czas*, 2005). This story of the great Polish People's Republic-era poet Miron Białoszewski was filtered through the eyes of his blind female friend and guardian, Jadwiga Stańczakowa, and it is she who really stands out in the story (which was not the case in reality). Andrzej Wajda's *Sweet Rush (Tatarak*, 2008) is a moving psychodrama in which the actress builds on personal experiences following her husband's death, and it won the Alfred Bauer Prize at the Berlin International Film Festival. The film is based on a short story by Jarosław Iwaszkiewicz, a shrewd expert on female nature – as seen also in Jerzy Kawalerowicz's *Mother Joan of the Angels (Matka Joanna od Aniołów*, 1960) or Andrzej Wajda's *The Maids of Wilko (Panny z Wilka*, 1979). *Sweet Rush* combines a modern autobiographical theme, written by Janda, with Iwaszkiewicz's portrait of a woman living in the shadow of death who throws herself into the arms of a young lad, to have one last fling. In Borys Lankosz's *Reverse (Rewers*, 2009), winner of the Polish Feature Film Festival in Gdynia, we see Janda (together with Anna Polony and Agata Buzek) in a role that picks apart the post-war history of Poland with truly picaresque bravado – showing normal people fighting for survival during the hardest Stalinist period in ways that are not always straightforward or in accordance with widely-accepted models of heroism, particularly the male variety. In the last few years, Polish cinema has also begun to appreciate the older generation of actresses, who were usually most neglected in terms of interesting film offers. For instance, the grey-haired Danuta Szaflarska in Dorota Kędzierzawska's *Time to Die (Pora umierać*, 2007) creates a rebellious and fanciful portrait of old age, while Krystyna Feldman is almost unrecognisable in Krzysztof Krauze's *My Nikifor (Mój Nikifor*, 2004), as she transforms herself into the figure of a real-life (male!) primitivist painter; an eccentric, blessed simpleton who bucked all artistic trends in the early days of the Polish People's Republic.

A different view

There is still no cinema with a strictly feminist agenda in Poland. Instead, one can speak of "women's cinema", defined mainly by characteristic points of view most evident in

films by directors with their own clear hallmarks and sensitivity regarding truly intimate subjects. Dorota Kędzierzawska, whom we mentioned previously, and whose films mostly deal with the destiny of children maltreated and neglected by adults, touched openly on the issue of feminism in her film *Nothing* (*Nic*, 1998). This drama about female loneliness in the face of domestic violence and harsh anti-abortion laws stirred up mixed feelings among audiences. However, the film's refined artistic form, which made it closer to Greek tragedy, seemed incompatible with the contentious moral and legal issues of new Poland. Another director, Izabella Cywińska, who previously worked mostly in theatre, dared to show femininity that went against accepted standards for Polish serials in two seasons of *The Lining of God's Coat* (*Boża podszewka*, 1997 and 2005). Telling the story of successive generations of Polish women living in the provinces near Wilno in the first half of the 20th century, she repudiated old myths about those pastoral borderlands, favouring instead blunt naturalism in her description of human passions, sexuality and perversions. Her younger friend, Małgorzata Szumowska, born in 1973, had been consistently observing women placed in extreme existential situations. In her first film, *Happy Man* (*Szczęśliwy człowiek*, 2001), although the main protagonist is a young man who fears the challenges of adulthood, it is the vivid female characters (his over-protective, seriously-ill mother, and an older friend bringing up her child alone) who

Time To Die, dir. Dorota Kędzierzawska
↑

force the hero to define his own place. A woman's perspective completely dominates another of Szumowska's films, *Stranger* (*Ono*, 2005), in which a girl who finds herself with an unwanted pregnancy gradually begins to see the world through the eyes of her unborn child. The director's most prominent film so far, *33 Scenes from Life* (*33 sceny z życia*, 2008), which was awarded the Special Jury Prize at the Locarno International Film Festival, shows pitilessly and candidly (almost verging on exhibitionism) its young heroine's helplessness when faced with the death of close relatives. All of Szumowska's films have been artistically uncompromising, with a characteristic "woman's touch", which should be seen as a function of her particular sensitivity, rather than her gender alone. In this respect, Mariusz Grzegorzek has been a "woman's" director for years. His auteur films have fought with the demons of dysfunctional motherhood (*Conversation with a Cupboard Man* [*Rozmowa z człowiekiem z szafy*], 1993), exorcised the embarrassing fantasies and obsessions of both sexes (*The Queen of Angels* [*Królowa aniołów*], 1999), and performed a painful psychoanalysis of female-male relations under Polish capitalism (*I Am Yours* [*Jestem twój*], 2009). In recent years, one of the most original attempts to transfer female sensitivities to the screen (or perhaps "girly sensitivities" would be more apt, considering the age of the film's actresses and co-director) was made by the creative duo of Aleksandra Gowin and Ireneusz Grzyb in their unassuming, medium-length film *Filaments* (*Druciki*, 2009). This picture of a lazy summer in a city is saturated with magical realism, and is captivating thanks to the sensuality and fantasy radiating from the film's charming adolescent heroines, who create an intimate microcosm around themselves. In turn, Wiola Sowa's world-acclaimed animation *Refrains* (*Refreny*, 2007) captures the tangled fates of three generations (a girl, a mature woman and an old lady) in a very poetic and personal way.

The generational "changing of the guard" that has taken place in Polish cinema in recent years has been the factor which most favoured a more incisive approach towards dealing with women's issues. In the 20 years of the new political system, which has to a great extent re-evaluated the former roles of families and society, one can see more and more young female characters on screen who appear to be stronger than men of the same age (i.e. more determined to fight for what they want, both privately and socially). This particularly concerns films by directors (such as the aforementioned Szumowska) who became adults after the 1989 watershed, and made films in an entirely new reality less encumbered by memories and social obligations. Anna Jadowska's successful feature film *début It's Me Now* (*Teraz ja*, 2004) may be considered as a sort of manifesto for women's

33 Scenes from Life, dir. Małgorzata Szumowska

independence, in which the young heroine escapes her orderly life by setting off on an adventure-filled journey around Poland. Desperation coupled with admirable bravery can be seen in the struggles with Poland's aggressive, demanding new reality faced by the heroines of Iwona Siekierzyńska's *My Roast Chickens* (*Moje pieczone kurczaki*, 2002), Przemysław Wojcieszek's *Kill Them All* (*Zabij ich wszystkich*, 1999) and *Louder than Bombs* (*Głośniej od bomb*, 2001), or Łukasz Barczyk's *I'm Looking at You, Mary* (*Patrzę na ciebie, Marysiu*, 1999), in which the above-mentioned Maja Ostaszewska plays an outstanding part. Barczyk has specialised in making extremely powerful, multi-faceted portraits of women, especially in *Changes* (*Przemiany*, 2003), an oppressive, "Bergmanesque" drama about the strained relations between three sisters and their mother. In his latest film, the controversial *Unmoved Mover* (*Nieruchomy poruszyciel*, 2008), with its psychedelic atmosphere reminiscent of David Lynch, Barczyk shows us a woman degraded and subjugated by brutal male domination. Even though she has been raped and humiliated by her employer, the young female Silesian factory-worker instigates something like a perverse game with her torturer, but becomes its passive victim. Although the filmmaker's main interests are clearly the employer's (not her) psychopathic profile and his final transformation aimed at expiating his guilt, *Unmoved Mover* must be regarded as an unusually brave attempt to expose the sexist social pathologies which still persist in female-male relations in modern-day Poland.

FROM A DOCUMENTARY STANDPOINT

Documentary cinema since 1989 has also shown a marked shift in emphasis. The Polish People's Republic period was dominated by politically-engaged documentaries by masters like Marcel Łoziński, Krzysztof Kieślowski and Tomasz Zygadło, who set their sights on unmasking official reality by using metaphorical language freely, aiming for a more profound reflection about the world. However, this engagement did not extend to contemplating sexual identity. Maria Zmarz-Koczanowicz's short film *I'm a Man* (*Jestem mężczyzną*, 1985), was the first in which a critical view of reality revealed an unexpected gender dimension: the film's hero is a multi-tasking activist from near Wrocław who, apart from being in charge of a local branch of the Party, a social organisation and a choir, also holds an honourable position as head of the local Women's Club. Years later, Ewa Pięta debated the communist propaganda image of a woman in *Poster Girl* (*Dziewczyna z plakatu*, 2001), which rediscovers the Polish People's Republic's most prominent woman tractor-driver as a still zealous, yet grey-haired old lady, and confronts her with her former legend. The most brutal diagnosis of the 1989 transition period was made by Ewa Borzęcka, who has a reputation for highly controversial work. In her 1996 documentary *The Thirteensome* (*Trzynastka*), she lays bare the conditions in which a single woman is forced to bring up her thirteen children. A year later, in the highly contentious *Arizona*, Borzęcka filmed the moral decline and degradation of former state-farm workers left jobless and penniless by the new Poland. Later, in her *Female-Male Issues* (*Damsko-męskie sprawy*, 2001), she was brave enough to shatter the taboo surrounding the sex lives of elderly people who have not given up their search for a "better half". Although Borzęcka was accused of mocking her heroes and being too fond of social pathologies, her films remain as some of the sharpest documentary evidence recorded in post-1989 Poland. Maria Zmarz-Koczanowicz was another tireless chronicler of the period, and her films have documented social antagonism, frustration, extremism, exclusion, and phenomena like the early days of the sex business and *disco polo* music. The issue of religious fanaticism, so rarely touched upon in Polish cinema, became the focus for young Magdalena Piekorz who, in *Girls from Szymanów* (*Dziewczyny z Szymanowa*, 1997), filmed the day-to-day life of girls in a convent school. Although her film was not cuttingly iconoclastic, it was met with criticism from certain Catholic authorities, who saw Piekorz's documentary as a mockery condemning the austere living conditions and customs at the Sisters of the Immaculate Conception school.

Apart from auteur documentaries, Polish cinema also gave rise to documentaries (funded by both private investors and state television stations) that probed fields unexplored by contemporary Polish feature films. But let us avoid any illusions: by bringing audiences closer to phenomena such as the humiliation of Polish girls hired as dancers in "gentlemen's" clubs at home and abroad, filmmakers are more concerned with satisfying common curiosity, than diagnosing important social issues. This was the case in the highly popular documentary soap opera *Ballad of a Slightly Erotic Nature* (*Ballada o lekkim zabarwieniu erotycznym*, 2003) by Irena and Jerzy Morawski, or in Michał Rogalski's film *Silesian Business* (*Śląski interes*, 2006).

Documentaries about women over the last decade can hardly be accused of being predatory or courageous, but still the most-discussed portrait of a woman in a documentary was made by a man – Marcin Koszałka. His first film, *Such a Beautiful Son I Gave Birth To* (*Takiego pięknego syna urodziłam*, 1999), shook up public opinion when it was shown at prime-time by the most popular television channel of the period. Koszałka was

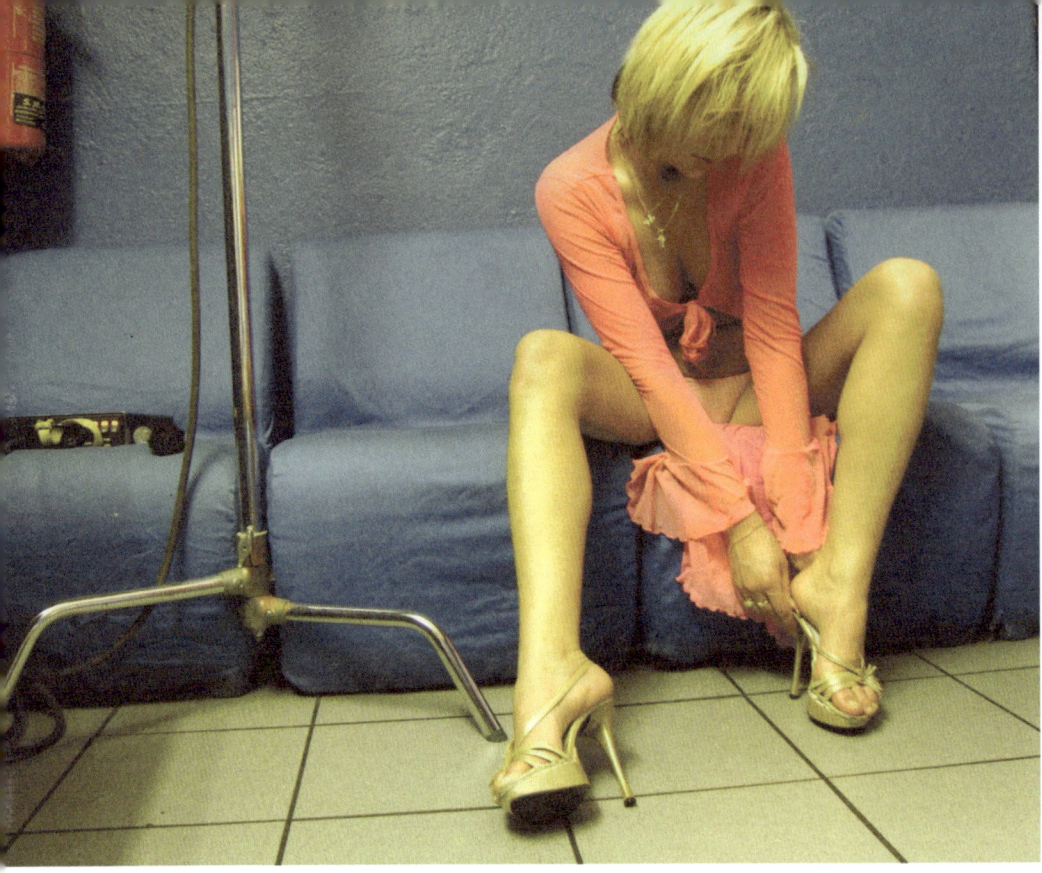

merciless in filming his own domestic hell, and the most dysfunctional character proved to be his mother, who put on a shameful show for the camera. For that, the filmmaker was criticised most of all: he was pardoned for his exhibitionism and for having provoked his own parents, but was not forgiven for having dishonoured what is still regarded as Poland's holiest of holies – motherhood.

Gays and lesbians – forbidden liaisons

Although homosexuality stopped being a criminal offence in Poland in 1932, homosexuals were almost absent from the Polish People's Republic-era cinema because they "threatened the healthy fabric of the nation". Even if they did make it onto the screen, it was merely as characters that were as irrelevant as they were shady and,

Silesian Business,
dir. Michał Rogalski

consequently, either comically "bent" or mentally degenerate, shamelessly exploitative, or leading astray minors. In short, gays under Polish communism were in the same grey area as prostitutes or black market money-changers, which is exactly how they were portrayed in Polish cinema. This made Marysia Lewandowska and Neil Cummings' project *Enthusiasts* (*Entuzjaści*) all the more surprising and interesting when it was shown at Warsaw's Centre for Contemporary Art, Ujazdowski Castle in 2004. It included a rich collection of amateur films from 1952–81, made with unbiased passion at film clubs that had been set up in socialist workplaces. These non-professional, completely independent films by Polish workers expressed many repressed yearnings, desires and fears, including ones concerning homoerotic relations. For example, Piotr Majdrowicz's *Misunderstanding* (*Nieporozumienie*) and *Depths* (*Toń*) by Jan Bujak, both from 1978.

Following the turning point of 1989 and the resulting lifting of censorship, the so-called "people who love differently", started to be represented in media and culture as part of an increased liberalisation and westernisation. Their presence, however, was often stigmatised as provocation or sensationalist attention-seeking intended to attract the maximum number of readers (in the case of the tabloid press) or viewers (in the case of commercial television). Homosexual themes even began to creep into popular family-orientated serials, although they were extremely watered-down, somewhere between political correctness and the conservative order glorified by long-running series. The same status was ascribed to almost caricatured bits of gay lore to be found in numerous Polish comedies made between 1989 and 2009. In Tomasz Drozdowicz's satire *Fur* (*Futro*, 2007), one of the biggest scandals to ruin the *nouveau riche* family's idyllic life during a First Communion party is the discovery that the host's son-in-law is gay. In Tomasz Konecki's comedy *Ladies* (*Lejdis*, 2008), the husband of one of the heroines, a respected member of the European Parliament, is compromised when it transpires that he is secretly indulging his homosexual tendencies somewhere in far-off Brussels. An even more stereotypical view of gays shows through in Krzysztof Zanussi's comedy *A Warm Heart* (*Serce na dłoni*, 2008), in which a cynical oligarch punishes his bodyguard, a die-hard homophobe, by sending him a gay prostitute with caricatured behaviour. Far from trying to get used to the idea, these examples rather attempt to reaffirm the belief that homosexuality is an exotic subculture. While trying to keep up with social transformations, Polish cinema still has to learn how to deal with minorities in earnest – not from a superficially judgemental or mocking

perspective, but through close identification with alternative sexualities. Sometimes this is limited to discreet, ambiguous suggestions, like in Izabella Cywińska's *The Lovers of Marona* (*Kochankowie z Marony*, 2005), a screen adaptation of a short story by Jarosław Iwaszkiewicz. The passion which erupts between a young village woman (who used to be a schoolmistress before the war) and a moribund young man with tuberculosis is intensified by a third character – the dying man's ex-boyfriend and lover. Cywińska was praised for not being too literal (the implied story of this love triangle leaves the film open to a variety of interpretations), as well as criticised for not addressing the homosexual theme clearly enough. Indeed, a more direct view of homosexuality characterises Mariusz Treliński's bold film *Farewell to Autumn* (*Pożegnanie jesieni*) from the late 1980s. It is an adaptation of a modernist novel by Witkacy (Stanisław Ignacy Witkiewicz) from 1925, in which the typical hero of that "age of exhaustion" willingly experiments with breaking various taboos, including sexual ones. Ten years later, Treliński returned to a similarly decadent atmosphere in *The Egoists* (*Egoiści*, 2000), this time set against the background of modern Warsaw. This is a very expressively-sketched collective portrait of the new élite revelling in easy money and hedonistic debauchery. The film's most tragic character is the architect Filip (a brave performance by Jan Frycz), an ageing gay whose young lover has left

The Lovers of Marona,
dir. Izabella Cywińska
↑

ANITA PIOTROWSKA **124**

him and who, after a night of excess, sets himself on fire in a spectacular finale. In Magdalena Piekorz's *Drowsiness* (*Senność*, 2008), the most convincing part of three interconnected episodes about modern single thirty-somethings happens to be a gay story. Defying everything (a traditional Catholic family, social status, and pressure from a council-estate environment), a young provincial doctor gets into a relationship with a boy from the skateboarding subculture. In Piekorz's film, one senses the authenticity of the homosexual heroes' intimate relations, and the dramatic alienation they experience in society. Newcomer Agnieszka Smoczyńska was also exceedingly subtle yet daring in her award-winning short film *Aria Diva* (2007), which shows the sudden awakening of a sedate, stay-at-home housewife, who decides to change her life under the influence of an intimate affair with an eccentric opera singer from her neighbourhood (played by Katarzyna Figura). Smoczyńska goes one step further than most of her older colleagues, showing lesbian love as a viable option and a mysterious feature of profound interpersonal relationships, which may appear unexpectedly, in complete defiance of one's previous life.

Since 1989, the most determined attempt to tame homosexuality, this time in Polish documentary cinema, was Robert Gliński's HBO-produced film *Homo.pl* (2007), in which gay and lesbian couples filmed mostly in the privacy of their homes, talk openly about their lives in modern Polish society. For many viewers, the topic itself was not shocking, but rather the way the subjects themselves were shown – as everyday people you pass on the streets, living in stable, long-term relationships. Speaking to the camera were a would-be priest, the owner of a hairdressing salon, and the manageress of a building firm. There was nothing radical or demonstrative about them being different; they were just dreaming of a quiet life alongside their partners. By showing their faces and airing their views, they broke the conspiracy of silence surrounding the group of anonymous, "grey" gays and lesbians who do not flaunt their orientation in public, or go wild at multi-coloured "Love Parades". A year later, Sławomir Grünberg made a similar attempt to bring Polish homosexuality out of its exotic ghetto in his short documentary *Coming Out Polish Style* (*Coming out po polsku*), which was produced in America. In turn, the pioneering *Trans-Mission* (*Trans-misja*, 2008) by two female directors, Julie Land and Justyna Struzik, explored the official trials and tribulations of its hero who has decided to have a sex-change. Apart from documentary filmmakers, the old enthusiasts' niche has now mostly been filled by underground filmmakers like Piotr Matwiejczyk who, in his medium-length film

Farewell to Autumn,
dir. Mariusz Treliński

Homo Father (2005), voted best independent film at the Polish Feature Film Festival in Gdynia, presents the highs and lows of a gay couple who must unexpectedly face up to the task of parenting – not because of the touchy issue of adoption, but when one of the heroes finds his heterosexual past has caught up with him. For a change, in *Seven Stations on the Way to Paradise* (*Siedem przystanków na drodze do raju,* 2003), Ryszard Maciej Nyczka, also part of the underground scene, tells an allegorical story of two intimately-involved lesbians going on a pilgrimage together. Consequently, for years there has been a small revolution of values taking place on the fringes of mainstream cinema, going against the tide of both conservative ideology and the libertarian pseudo-bravery of mass culture, which is poised to break many a taboo purely for shock value in order to serve the market.

For years, the film critics have accused contemporary Polish cinema of being burdened by its self-censorship and pursuit of ways to relate to its home audience, and also of being prudish and half-hearted in its treatment of gender issues. This is true: Poland has yet to produce any strongly-committed filmmakers with well-defined homosexual identities, like Britain's Derek Jarman, Germany's Rainer Werner Fassbinder, Spain's Pedro Almodóvar, or France's Patrice Chéreau. The same can be said of Polish women's cinema which, despite a number of positive signals, is still awaiting its own Agnès Varda or Ulrike Ottinger: directors who openly examine feminist themes in their films. However, it is only a matter of time before culture will work through the social transformations currently taking place. It should be emphasised that a similar process has already occurred in literature, theatre, and the new visual arts. The internationally-acclaimed artist Katarzyna Kozyra mainly creates video installations that use the medium of film to play controversially with widely-held views of femininity or gender in culture. In *Men's Bath-House* (*Łaźnia męska,* 1999), in which the artist pretends to be a man and enters strictly male territory with her camera, or *Cheerleader* (*Cheerleaderka,* 2006), a parody of modern music videos that perpetuate traditional views of masculinity and femininity, Kozyra dons a variety of costumes in order to subversively reveal the fluidity of identity and the conventional nature of social roles. In this respect, "classical" cinema is considerably more conservative and vulnerable to self-censorship than theatre and other

→ *Homo Father*, dir. Piotr Matwiejczyk

visual forms (particularly those emerging from critical art). This is due to its dependence on established production infrastructure, big budgets, and even greater reliance on institutions. As a result, it has developed its individual voice at a different pace. While reducing its aforementioned backlog, however, the most important thing is to ensure that Polish cinema does not become something decreed from the top down, trying to catch up with world trends at any cost, or attempting to pander to a public which craves superficial "transgressions". Instead, it ought to stem naturally from the sensitivity of Polish filmmakers. Thankfully, the first signs of a breakthrough are already visible.

Translated by Mark Bence

THE PHENOMENON OF POLISH INDEPENDENT CINEMA IN 1989–2009

JOANNA ROŻEN-WOJCIECHOWSKA

Independent movies are currently an integral part of the Polish film industry, and artistic endeavours pursued in this arena contribute substantially to shaping our culture. A great many independent films are produced not only by professional filmmakers, but also by artists not directly related to the world of cinema and by experimenting beginners. These movies can be seen at festivals, on the Internet, and on TV – both the public broadcasting network and commercial channels. They are usually low-budget shorts, representing the artistic – as opposed to popular – side of the cinematic spectrum. In this essay I will attempt to explain how it came to be that niche, independent films made by a group of enthusiasts became an important part of Polish audiovisual culture.

The boom of independent films in Poland over the past two decades can be attributed to the turbulent transformation of the private film industry after 1989. These last years were mostly devoted to developing modern institutional solutions to financing culture – including film – in the public, NGO, and private sectors. Finally, and what is probably most essential to this analysis – it was precisely in this period that the new crop of filmmakers born in the 1970s and 1980s finally came into their own.

I would first like to address some terminology issues. The terms *fringe* and *independent cinema* are currently used interchangeably in Poland, and usually refer to movies produced on a small budget, without the financial aid of the Polish Film Institute, or any public or commercial TV station. Their "independent" status is therefore not indicative of their artistry, message, or form of distribution.

Amateur cinema is in turn a term that is both somewhat pejorative, and outdated, and is therefore used less frequently these days, especially by the filmmakers themselves. Amateur equals bungling, juvenile and unprofessional. The term is sometimes used to refer to the work of amateur filmmakers and amateur film clubs from the communist times.

Amateur Cinema before 1989

The current authors of independent cinema did not emerge out of nowhere. Before 1989, there was in communist Poland an institutionalised hobby in the form of "movies for everyone". Amateur Film Clubs, following the official ideology, organised the factory workers' free time by providing equal access to culture. The tradition of Amateur Film Clubs operating at factories and community centres, often in small towns, created the archetype of an "amateur filmmaker", which resonates to this day. This is someone who is passionate about cinema, a romantic with a natural, untrained talent; a simple worker refusing to resign himself to his mundane life. One such character, at least to some degree, was Franciszek Dzida – the co-founder and leader of the Chybie Sugar

Plant Amateur Film Club, who served as inspiration for the character of Filip Mosz in Krzysztof Kieslowski's *Camera Buff* (*Amator*, 1979).

Amateur filmmakers from communist factories had nothing to do with professional art. Particularly in the 1970s, film clubs popped up in industrial plants all over the country. They were supplied with film equipment and tape by the central headquarters in Warsaw according to their needs – as requested by factory, or community centre managers. The clubs were united in the Federation of Amateur Film Clubs. This organisation, which survives to this day albeit under a different, updated name (Federation of Independent Filmmakers), was created in 1956. By 1974, 348 different film clubs were affiliated in the federation. The federation also organised film festivals, the most famous of which are held to this day – OKFA (The National Amateur Film Festival in Konin), Pol 8 (The Józef Mika Film Festival in Polanica Zdrój), Dozwolone do 21 (Allowed Under 21, a festival of children's and young people's movies), Publicystyka (Publicity, a documentary festival in Kędzierzyn Koźle), and Kochać człowieka (To Love a Human Being), in Oświęcim – and initiated thematic competitions, for example for the best maritime tourist movie.

Among the most famous amateur film clubs that existed in communist Poland were AFC "Chemik" from Oświęcim (a member of which was Henryk Lehnert, the creator of an original animation method called "jerky film", and Guinness record holder for most awards received for his work), AFC "Sawa" from Warsaw, AFC "Awa" from Poznań, AFC "Groteska" from Kędzierzyn Koźle, AFC "Klaps" from Chybie, or AFC "Nowa Huta", which was the site of the amateur *début* of Krzysztof Zanussi, as well as various other filmmakers (such as Jerzy Ridan) who are part of Nowa Huta's cultural landscape to this day.

A valuable description of the phenomenon of amateur film in socialist Poland was proposed by the artists and cultural researchers Marysia Lewandowska and Neil Cummings in their exhibition called "Enthusiasts", presented at the Centre for Contemporary Art in Warsaw in 2004. The authors claim that in socialist Poland, amateur film was paradoxically a haven of spontaneous, independent and unrestrained activity; paradoxically, because the film clubs were created by the government in order to control the free time of its citizens and plan their extracurricular activities for them. The government created the conditions for controlled artistic expression, but the control system proved to be insufficient, and in effect the AFC members enjoyed substantial liberty and could pursue relatively uncensored filmmaking. Contemporary analysis of their work proves that their movies display not only deliberate reflection about the world, but also signs of formally intriguing artistry. The exhibition is broken down into three themes: Love,

Longing, and Labour. The attitude of an amateur filmmaker, who is able to find the resources to make movies (independence), as well as an audience for his work (festivals) is proof of the existence of spontaneous culture animators. These clubs continued to operate after 1989. The most interesting discovery made in this microcosm of amateur filmmakers is, therefore, the realisation that communist Poland's amateur cinema laid the foundation for the contemporary independent film movement. It also explains why there are so many independent film festivals in Poland.

However, it should be clearly stated that under the authoritarian regime that ruled Poland before 1989, the existence of independent cinema in the current sense of the word was simply impossible. There could be no films independent of government funding or free of censorship. Therefore, we need to make a distinction between the enthusiasm of amateur filmmakers and the liberty of unrestrained artistic expression. The government carved them out a niche in which they could create their films without endangering the system. However, their actions had to be predictable and conform to its rules, and their films, just like any other form of artistic activity, were subject to oversight by GUKPPiW (The Polish Censorship Office). Illegal video recordings from the 1980s showing, for example, political riots, or documenting the lives of oppositionists are a completely different phenomenon, and belong in the realm of politics rather than art. Artistically, ideologically and institutionally, independent cinema was able to emerge only after the fall of communism.

The 1990s

In order to describe the landscape of independent film at the beginning of the 1990s, we should start with film clubs organised in community centres, which had hitherto created movies steeped in the tradition of the communist era, and were looking for new challenges. These clubs gave their members access to cameras and a platform for sharing their experiences. They were, however, seen by young people as completely inefficient relics of a previous age which stifled any sort of uninhibited creativity. Thus they were quickly fading into obscurity.

When at the dawn of the 1990s the first video players and VHS cameras appeared in Polish stores, thus becoming readily available for home use, local community centres ceased to be the only places where young people could record films. This also heralded the golden age of video shops. It was a time of frenzied catching up with cinematic pop culture from around the world. Young people played with movies and with making movies. The image of amateur filmmakers changed – now they were mostly kids from school who spent time together making movies. However, we would still have to wait half a decade for them to mature and for this activity to produce anything interesting from an artistic standpoint.

The first half of the 90s brought us films from the most famous filmmakers, often called the classics of Polish independent film. Amateur cinema of that time was dominated by pastiches and parodies of popular box office hits – usually American genre movies. These so-called "xeroxes" were short films made by groups of friends (usually playground friends at that), including the preeminent "indie" directors of the past two decades such as Grzegorz Lipiec and the Sky Piastowskie group, Piotr and Dominik Matwiejczyk, Piotr Krzywiec, the Cramp filmmakers, and even the artists from Spoon or Chilli.

FILM YOUTH

Grzegorz Lipiec, along with his – legendary at this point – Sky Piastowskie group was a child of the early 90s videomania. He obsessively watched VHS movies, learning them by heart. There were not a lot of them available, so one was forced to watch the same films over and over again. Lipiec reminisces in an interview with Piotr Marecki that he had memorised all the scenes and dialogues from Bruce Lee's *Enter the Dragon*.[1] Just like most kids from his neighbourhood, he started frequenting the now defunct community centre and signed up for all of its programmes – art, film and photography. He ran around with his tape recorder, recording scenes from life in his neighbourhood. Organised filming began with hiring (using his and his friends' pocket money) a camera operator who specialised in videotaping weddings and first communions. That is how, in Zielona Góra, a film group was born which in a few years' time would spearhead the Polish independent film movement. It was 1990, and the members were still teenagers. At first they did comedy sketches. When these got boring, they started recording mirror copies of the movies they knew from video stores. The first of them was a "xerox" of *The Terminator*. The films were edited on home video equipment with an insert function (copying sound and video separately from tape to tape in real time). Then came *Terminator II* and *Terminator III*. The films were shown during home screenings and became something of a sensation in the Piastowskie housing estate – kids would start quoting them, and the fever would spread. Lipiec recalls that during the filming of *Horizontal 8* (*8 w poziomie*, 2009) they had over five hundred extras. The next period of the group's work was devoted to pastiches of American box office hits, where half the protagonists would die in epic shoot-outs, spewing gallons of fake blood. Finally, the moment arrived for deliberate filmmaking, with actual scripts. Grzegorz started

---

[1] Piotr Marecki, *Independent Cinema in Poland 1989–2009. A Spoken History* (*Kino niezależne w Polsce 1989–2009. Historia mówiona*), Warsaw 2009.

sending his films to festivals and they began to get noticed. His *0.5l* (*0,5 litra*, 1996) was broadcast on Canal+. Along with his colleagues, he was invited to a popular talk show hosted by Piotr Najsztub and Jacek Żakowski, where he was noticed by Iwona Ziółkowska and a number of others from the film industry. Lipiec then became an assistant on Andrzej Wajda's *Pan Tadeusz*, where he learned the ropes by practicing the trade. He showed his next script to Wojciech Marczewski, who bluntly told him, "Don't make movies about New York – there are thousands of them already. Make one about Zielona Góra, and it will be truly unique". Lipiec started getting into socially-aware cinema, focusing on the life of young people at the dawn of the 1990s – the era of burgeoning capitalism, high unemployment rates, low standards of living, and a general sense of lack of prospects for the future, seasoned with drugs, dealers, and rising crime. Lipiec decides to make a movie about drugs, which posed the biggest threat to the emotionally and socially neglected youth of that era. That was how the feature film *That Life Makes Sense* (*Że życie ma sens*, 2000) came into being. It surprised viewers with its incredible aesthetics and the way it captured the elusive spirit of that time – so different from today's universe of Facebook and shopping malls.

There were no real drugs on the set of *That Life Makes Sense*, as Lipiec decreed that everything was to be make-believe. Members of the Sky Piastowskie group were not users themselves, but they lived in a housing estate of twenty thousand people that was relatively rife with junkies, and this movie was about them. The soundtrack featured socially aware songs from the legendary Kaliber 44. Grzegorz got part of the money for the film from his father, and the rest he earned working at the local cable company. The finished product made its way to some members of the film industry, was seen by someone at *Machina* – a popular alternative culture magazine – and finally landed on the desk of Stefan Laudyn, the director of the Warsaw Film Festival. The film was screened publicly and received a distribution deal from Best Film. In the wake of its success, the Zielona Góra city council presented the filmmakers with a digital camera, which the members used to shoot their next movie, *The Day I Die* (*Dzień, w którym umrę*, 2004) about a 30-year-old man having a crisis as he finds himself floundering in the soul-crushing aimlessness of adult life. It's a tale about the feeling of senselessness, being stuck in a rut and the lure of consumerism, laced with post-punk philosophy. The themes of Sky Piastowskie movies reflect the life experiences of their peers and Poland's changing social landscape post-2000. Things are seemingly getting better: there's more work for young people, we've achieved some basic economic stability, and live in the colourful *faux*-reality of shop windows, offices, computers and cell phones, but young Poles – especially outside Warsaw – still feel that they don't control their own fate.

The Day I Die was produced in 2004. Digital editing on home computers was commonplace by then and filmmakers had much greater access to technology than they did a decade earlier. The Sky Piastowskie group took full advantage of these opportunities. They bravely experimented with form, exploding traditional narrative and editing, and using the language of music videos instead. They edited the film emotionally, distorting the images in a flurry of quivering expression. They found the perfect means of expression for presenting a world sunk into chaos, and those who rail against it.

In 2009, Grzegorz Lipiec experienced another breakthrough in his career when his movie *Horizontal 8* won the Independent Cinema Competition at the Polish Film Festival in Gdynia. He got up to receive the award onstage along with a big group of the Sky Piastowskie filmmakers and delivered a manifesto in which he appealed to the film industry, journalists, and the Minister of Culture to free current and future film projects from the patronising tag of "indie cinema". Lipiec has proven that he knows how to make movies, that he has something to say, and most importantly that he is perfectly attuned to the spirit of his times and is a worthy representative of the 1970s generation. With his passion, charm and commitment, he has proven time after time that his films are worth watching. He has found his audience, and I'm very curious to see where he'll go from here.

The journey of Grzegorz Lipiec seems to be symptomatic of his generation. A similar pattern can be traced in the stories of other amateur filmmakers of the early 1990s: no artistic education, out of control videomania, learning the language of movies at the video store, spontaneous filmmaking and artistic exhilaration, followed by attempts at serious reflection on reality through cinema, coupled with a constant struggle with adversity and lack of funding, eventually the first breakthrough, generating interest in the artistic world, followed by more movies, awards, and finally an attempt to enter the mainstream on equal terms.

There are two other interesting directors who produced their first films around the same time as Lipiec: the Matwiejczyk brothers – the elder Dominik and the younger Piotr. They come from a small town near Wrocław and since the early 1990s they've been shooting films featuring the kids from their neighbourhood and their numerous cousins, using a camera borrowed from their aunt, as well as anything else they could get their hands on. Their favourite pastime during that initial stage was trying to mimic genre – especially horror – movies. Racing to top one another in inventive ways of filming severed limbs or geysers of blood spewing from eye sockets, the brothers gradually matured, as did their movies. At some point they decided to part ways, so that each could pursue their own artistic vision.

Both filmmakers are above all incredibly prolific. During the period of their mature, self-aware work – let us say from 2001, which was the year their production company Muflin Pictures was founded, to 2009 – Piotr wrote, directed, and in most cases produced (often he was also the director of photography) nearly thirty shorts and thirteen feature films. Meanwhile, between 2002 and 2009, Dominik Matwiejczyk directed and edited nine films, most of them feature-length.

Initially Piotr, called the *Wunderkind* of Polish indie cinema, continued to indulge in his favourite pastime, and kept shooting parodies of American movies, such as his *Chinacity* (2001), where he deftly used real-life locations to create the feel of a classic gangster movie. On top of that, he is a great actor with tremendous comedic talent, which he unfortunately rarely uses these days. Another skillful pastiche mimicking many B movie box office hits at once is *Nightmare of Last Winter* (*Koszmar minionej zimy*, 2002). However, after *Kneeling-Moaning* (*Klęcząc jęcząc*, 2001), Piotr changed his focus and started moving towards intimate psychological films dealing with difficult themes the likes of which mainstream productions usually steer clear of. Thus the movies *Homo Father* (2005, about raising children in a gay family), *Beautiful* (2006, about trafficking in unborn babies and infertility), *Shame* (*Wstyd*, 2006, about teenage rape, its psychological ramifications, and the erotic coming of age in an oppressive environment dominated by men), *Barefoot* (*Na boso*, 2007, about the suicide of a lost, lonely teenage girl), *Buy Now* (*Kup teraz*, 2008, about Internet human trafficking), or the still unreleased *Wistful* (*Smętna*). In his comedy *Emilia* (2005) he parodied the French *Amélie*, which had gathered a cult following among those of his generation. Piotr brought to Polish independent cinema the courage to cast professional, often recognisable actors, who not only bring substance to his characters, but also help his movies find distribution and festival success. Among his regulars are Mirosław Baka, Dorota Segda and Marcin Dorociński. He has also worked with Artur Barciś, Cezary Pazura and Jan Machulski. In interviews, the actors who have worked with him on numerous occasions often profess their trust in him and point out that at a time when ambitious scripts are few and far between and most of the offers they receive are bland and purely commercial, Piotr's characters never fail to intrigue them with their original attitude towards the problems of modern man. Piotr Matwiejczyk's films, though not devoid of moralising undertones, present an acute ethical diagnosis of contemporary Poles.

The mature work of Dominik Matwiejczyk is best exemplified by *Nosebleed* (*Krew z nosa*, 2004) – an urban tale of three friends, acted with phenomenal ease and comic talent by Bodo Kox (another independent filmmaker, actor and performer, born in 1977), Dawid Antkowiak and Radek Fijołek. This socially aware film, inspired by Mathieu Kassovitz's *La haine*, showed the gray, hopeless Wrocław housing estates and the burgeoning hip-hop culture in a slightly more humorous light than was the case in Grzegorz Lipiec's *oeuvre*. Matwiejczyk's movie dominated the independent cinema festivals of 2004/2005 – it received, among other trophies, two Offskars, the Grand Prix of the Toruń Film Festival TOFFI, the directing award at the Young and Film (Młodzi i Film) festival in Koszalin, and the main award of the New Polish Cinema festival in Wrocław. It was also recognised by Polish Television as the best film at the 3rd Polish Independent Film Festival.

Another of Matwiejczyk's films, *Fallow Land* (*Ugór*, 2005), dealt with a topic that was completely absent from the Polish silver screen: growing up in rural areas. The movie tells the story of two brothers in conflict who lie to their bedridden grandmother, keeping her convinced that they're taking care of the family farm. In reality, they're selling it bit by bit to pay off their debts. Scenes such as shooting up in the barn and the drug-induced vision of being chased around the dark farm by one of the brothers dressed in a Gestapo uniform will surely go down in the history of independent cinema. Naturally, the film was shot completely on location, in the area where Matwiejczyk grew up. I should point out here the phenomenon of Regina Grudzień, the Matwiejczyks' grandmother, who often does cameos in their movies, as she turned out be a very gifted actor. In 2006, due to his success, Dominik was able to produce a movie in what amounted to almost mainstream conditions. The result was *Short Hysteria of Time* (*Krótka histeria czasu*, 2005) – a romantic comedy starring popular actors of the young generation (Kamila Baar and Mateusz Damięcki). It was released cinematically, but did not meet box office expectations. In 2006, Dominik made *Slaughterhouse One* (*Rzeźnia nr 1*) – an analysis of young people's psyche set against the backdrop of the petty intrigues of the Polish provinces. Simultaneously, he entered the mainstream through a back door, by directing several TV series, among them *First Love* (*Pierwsza miłość*, 2004–2010), *Criminal Section* (*Biuro kryminalne*, 2005–2007), and *Pit Bull* (*Pitbull*, 2005–2008).

Cinema in the hands of scoffers – a spoonful of counterculture

An overview of the last decade of independent Polish cinema would be incomplete without mentioning a phenomenon which – while occupying the same niche as the abovementioned artists – is at the same time diametrically different from them. The artistic group Spoon or Chilli (Łyżka czyli Chilli), established in 1992, is composed of three friends: Waciak (Tomasz Wójcik), Mendyk (Michał Mendyk), and Trzos (Tomasz Trzos). They're

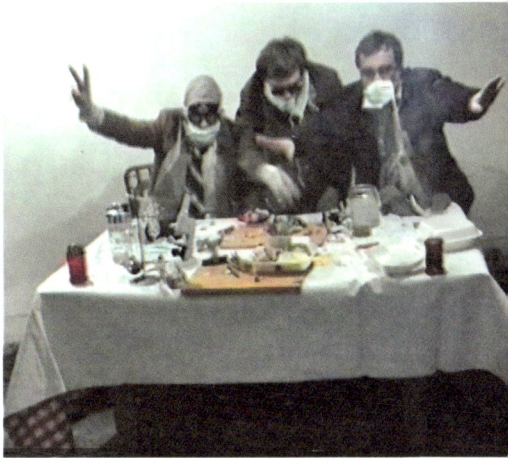

Rabolatory Or a Tribute to Science, Spoon or Chilli

all artists operating outside the mainstream, though born a decade before most of the other independent filmmakers, at the turn of the 1960s and 70s. They share with their younger peers the same maniacal attitude towards watching American movies - they consciously participated in the videomania that swept the nation in the 1990s, which urged them to pursue artistic goals. Their other main motivation was - as they declared in an interview with Piotr Marecki – the need to ridicule the boredom, aimlessness and charlatanism which permeated the video-art scene of that period.[2] Tomasz Wójcik, the only one in the group with an art diploma, while watching the video-art creations at the famous WRO, felt compelled to shatter the petrified definition of art proposed in gallery movies. He declared outright that what was presented by the so-called anointed artists did nothing to expand the medium – despite their own claims to the contrary. Video-art in that shape said nothing about the world. Therefore, the initial motivation for this original group – now considered to be legendary in their field – was a need to ironically debunk various fetishes of mainstream culture coupled with a childish delight in ridicule. Their peculiar narrative style, breaking and poking fun at conventions,

---

2 Ibid.

winking at the audience, and specific, original formal solutions have now entered the mainstream vernacular and are often, sometimes unconsciously, copied. These traits can be seen, for example, though in a toned-down version, devoid of the spontaneity and unexpectedness, in the delivery styles of today's satire programme hosts on TV and radio.

What was so characteristic about Spoon or Chilli movies? They were often simply the recordings of various improvised scenes. The viewer's surprise and delight was derived from observing how spontaneously and deftly they juggled conventions, entering a dialogue with their audience through meta-narrative – that is consciously altering meaning through a shift in the context. They would start improvising a scene by adopting the jargon and attire of a particular social or professional group. The setting is late 1970s. The decor – full-on Gierek,[3] with floral curtains and potted palms galore. The government is deep in debt, and Poles spend their nights dreaming about Fiat cars and apartments in prefabricated concrete housing estates. A group of scientists is sent to a conference. It takes place in a different city, so the gentlemen are to stay overnight at a workers' hotel. In the evening, after rather mediocre – just like everything else in communist Poland – presentations and gallons of strong tea, the obligatory liquor finally arrives and the inevitable bonding commences. The scientists wear 1970s suits which the Spoon artists are very fond of – with wide lapels, and short, broad ties in all the dazzling shades of socialist brown. Against *faux*-marble walls and potted ferns, in a cafeteria straight out of a communist TV series, the actors begin improvising. The dramatic trajectory of such a scene can be compared to a tightly wound spiral, which will at some point uncoil and explode, destroying everything in sight. After the initial exchange of pleasantries, as the alcohol gradually clouds their minds, the scientists start testing the limits of *savoir vivre*. The dismantling of stereotypes begins. Eventually, the movie exposes the true faces of the communist misers, nonentities, and self-interested, petty academics. The liquor loosens tongues, and the protagonists start breaking various rules on a multitude of levels – not only breaching cultural norms and protocol, but also deconstructing the conventions of the movie itself. The Spoon artists extend their spontaneous improvisation to the formal layer – actors not only perform their particular scenes, but also start mimicking specific film clichés, often drawing on the highly recognisable stylistic vocabulary of genre movies. Suddenly, a crack appears in the seemingly highly organised composition, and each new, tiny transgression against the rules of the scene spurs the artists on to take another step, which snowballs into a flurry of unpredictable actions, mutual verbal and physical aggression, and eventually – all-out havoc. The same mechanism is triggered on the narrative level, destroying the entire structure

---

3 Edward Gierek was a First Secretary of the Polish Communist Party from 1970 to 1980.

of the story.[4] Another of their movies, *Rabolatory Or a Tribute to Science* (*Rabolatorium czyli w hołdzie nauce*, 2001), begins with a scientific experiment. The film resembles a communist educational TV programme, except the experiments consist of totally absurd attempts to contradict the laws of physics. Checking how various objects will react when subjected to various treatment – for example, will a sausage stuffed with firecrackers and tossed into a kitchen blender explode? Naturally, it does. Eventually, entropy takes hold not only of the objects in question and the conventions of the story, but also – which is what makes the art of Spoon or Chilli so valuable – the preconceptions that we, as viewers, have become slaves to.

The group was unique in that it was never its goal to advance its members' careers, or give them professional filmmaking credentials. The film and theatre activity of Spoon or Chilli to this day seems to spring from a selfless need to express themselves and to analyse the communist legacy. The Spoon artists – much like many of their generation – still have one foot planted in communist Poland. They draw on these experiences to ridicule the relics of that era, many of which are still present in the thought and behaviour patterns of *homo sovieticus* Poles.

The movies of Spoon or Chilli place Polish independent cinema of the past two decades in the sphere of counterculture, fulfilling its obligation to be critical of the system. However, artists such as Spoon or Chilli – even though they have many fans and followers – constitute but a fraction of Polish independent film. Most of the indie scene is made up of young people trying to find a place in the industry through casual, creative, grassroots artistic endeavours, the closer to film the better – in a way personifying the romantic 1970s myth of artists expressing themselves through movies.

FROM FILM SCHOOL TO INDEPENDENT CINEMA

Independent, low-budget films were also the only way into the film industry for young filmmakers anxious to make their first film after graduating from film school. The movie business stagnation of that period left the new crop of filmmakers with no outlet for their creative energies. The indie scene, with its cheap, digital format allowed them to begin immediately, rather than wait for the situation to improve.

One of the artists who picked this route was Dariusz Gajewski, born in 1964 – a seasoned director with experience in documentary features, produced mostly for TV, who

---
[4] This description combines two different films: *Ty tani K. Or Personal Selection* (*Ty tani K. czyli wybór własny*, 2000) and *The Convention: Behind the Scenes Or the Power of the Tape* (*Kulisy zjazdu czyli siał taśmy*, 1999).

graduated from the Łódź Film School in 1993. After seven years of waiting for a chance to make his first feature, in 2001 he decided to produce it independently. The result was *AlaRm*, a formally interesting thriller based on the play *Leatherface* by Helmut Krausser. Around the same time, Polish public television took notice of indie cinema's potential, and organised an independent film festival, broadcast on TVP2 (2003). The event introduced independent filmmakers and their works to mainstream audiences, as the competition was interactive, and viewers were allowed to vote for their favourite movie via text message. The screening of *AlaRm* allowed Gajewski to pursue a career in feature film. His next film, *Warsaw* (*Warszawa*, 2003) received the main award at the Polish Film Festival in Gdynia and heralded a generational change of the guard.

Another Łódź Film School alumnus, Anna Jadowska, followed a similar path. In 2003, she made her film feature – with the directorial aid of Ewa Stankiewicz – called *Touch Me* (*Dotknij mnie*) – a brutal look at her generation, exposing its moral decay while at the same time underscoring man's need for love and closeness. Formally difficult, shot jerkily with a handheld camera, it was painfully honest and uncompromising. The movie presented the world of the homeless, as seen through the eyes of twenty-somethings, highlighting a part of Poland that was omitted in mainstream productions. *Touch Me* won the Independent Film Competition at the Polish Film Festival in Gdynia in 2003, opening everyone's eyes to the potential lying in independent productions, and giving its director a good start in the film industry.

Other middle-generation filmmakers currently working on the forefront of Polish cinema who also made their *début* in independent film are Jacek Borcuch (born in 1970) with his *Cauliflower* (*Kalafiorr*, 1999), Konrad Niewolski (b. 1972) with *D.I.L.* (2002), his brutal tale about drug dealers, and Andrzej Jakimowski (b. 1963) with his *Squint Your Eyes* (*Zmruż oczy*, 2003).

THE FESTIVAL REVOLUTION

According to a Polish Film Institute bulletin published in August 2009, of the sixty-six film events financed by the institution, over thirty are independent film festivals. Indie films posted on the Internet often get the same amount of hits as music videos from major record labels. Since 2002, a separate competition for independent movies has been held at the Polish Film Festival in Gdynia. The deluge of indie movies had to find its audience

↑
AlaRm,
dir. Dariusz Gajewski

↓
Touch Me,
dir. Anna Jadowska,
Ewa Stankiewicz

somewhere. Their authors' need to screen them outside their circle of friends resulted in the creation of numerous film festivals, which today serve as the main platform for independent productions: OFF CINEMA in Poznań, Camera Off in Cracow, KAN in Wrocław, OFFensiwa in Wrocław, TOFFI in Toruń, Oskariada in Warsaw, and many others.

One of the turning points in the history of this movement was the premiere of the Jutro Filmu (Future of the Cinema) festival – one of the first such events organised by someone other than the established movers and shakers of the scene. The festival was created by a group of Warsaw students, who set up the foundation ProVarsovia. From the start it was meant to be organised *for* young people *by* young people, and became incredibly popular almost overnight. The packed auditoriums and the dozens of movies submitted from all over Poland took even the organisers by surprise. At the same time, heated discussions conducted after screenings showed that a completely new sort of city culture was being born, devoid of the separation between artist and audience – one where everyone was able to share their self-produced art, bypassing the established structures and institutions. This assumption seems to lie at the core of the independent film movement, which is why I want to emphasise the tremendous role that the Independent Film Competition in Gdynia, and the festival of independent movies broadcast on national television played in this process. These two events liberated independent films from their niche, urging other young people to reach for their cameras and start making their own movies.

The breeding grounds for new talent

In the 1990s, Polish film hit a rough patch. Funding became so poor that even big name directors had problems with seeing their movies through. Filmmakers still fought for new legislation regarding cinema, securing the financial interests of the movie industry, and creating a legal framework for government subsidies. During that period, the bulk of film production consisted of low-budget indies and TV movies. Once the new Act on Cinematography came into force in 2005, bringing with it the creation of the Polish Film Institute, things started looking up. Today, the institute supports young filmmakers on a multitude of levels. All you have to do is access the "First Take" ("Pierwsze ujęcie") webpage to instantly learn how you can obtain funding for your film, how to write scripts under the guidance of professionals, as well as how and where to best present your work.

This leads me to anticipate a rift in the Polish independent cinema movement. Young filmmakers who will want to use their first DIY movies to get into the industry will find support and emerge from the underground, which will be reserved for those who choose this path consciously, either by experimenting with form, or by dealing with controversial subjects – like the abovementioned Spoon or Chilli group.

Manna, dir. Hubert Gotkowski
↑

What else has changed in the cultural landscape of young cinema over the second half of the decade? First of all, there are now enough private film schools for them to start competing with each other. In November 2001, the Andrzej Wajda Master School of Film Directing first opened its doors, under the honorary auspices of the European Film Academy. The founders and patrons of this venture were Andrzej Wajda and Wojciech Marczewski, though it also received support from donors.

> The decision to create this school was based on our conviction that the difficult situation in which Polish culture seems to have currently found itself calls for radical action. Our cinema, pushed to the sidelines by the economic transformation and lack of funding, disregarded by politicians and the administration, and threatened by a deluge of mass-market trash and poor taste, was on the brink of self-destruction. Meanwhile, an important sociological and cultural breakthrough was transpiring before our very eyes, and we felt we could not ignore it. Thousands of young people reached for digital cameras; directing ceased to be an élite profession. Hundreds of amateur movies are being shot, some of which successfully make it into cinemas. Many of these films offer a refreshingly new perspective on topics which were previously neglected, such as the reality of provincial life. Their authors are young, sometimes very much so. Though they may lack professional skills, they possess abundant talent and imagination. We want to help them by sharing our experience – to seek out young, talented people and educate, nurture, and aid them in making their first steps in the film industry, as well as bring them together with their European colleagues.

With these words Andrzej Wajda and Wojciech Marczewski announced the creation of their new school in the autumn of 2001. They weren't the only ones to notice the new generation's potential. In 2004, another new institution was created to compete with Wajda's and the two "established" film schools (the National Higher School of Film, Television and Theatre in Łódź and the Department of Radio and Television at the University of Silesia in Katowice) – Bogusław Linda and Maciej Ślesicki's Warsaw Film School. Ślesicki too saw the opportunity to tap the creative forces of independent filmmakers, launching the "Time for Youth" ("Czas na młodych") project. This was a turning point, which opened a new chapter in the history of young Polish cinema. At one of the independent festivals (Skoffka 2006), Maciej Ślesicki as the head of the jury offered the Grand Prix winner Hubert Gotkowski an opportunity to remake his feature film *Manna* – produced on a shoestring budget by him and his friends from

Rzeszów – with studio-calibre funding. Gotkowski, a self-taught talent, 10 years younger than Grzegorz Lipiec, took the challenge and rewrote *Manna*, which was then shot and produced by a professional crew – much like in some sort of Hollywood fairytale. *Manna* was an hour-long grotesque comedy filled with absurd humour – a *Waiting for Godot* meets *Clerks*, structured like *Cube* and set in a boring provincial town in the south of Poland. It starred the exceptional Marcin Kabaj – an amateur who showed true comedic talent. Much like Jerzy Stuhr in the 1970s, Marcin seemed like the archetypical teenager of his era: slightly overweight, bored, with a beer in one hand and a cigarette butt in the other, dejectedly offering highly quotable one-liners. That was how Hubert Gotkowski from Rzeszów, born in 1981, holder of a Master's degree in IT, and discovered at KinOFFteka 2006, became a true filmmaker. Just a year earlier, nobody had heard of him or his friends from the DDN group. He was interested in film from early on, shooting funny videos as early as high school. Along with his friends, he recorded everything: school excursions, pranks, you name it. Then, out of boredom, they decided to string those clips into stories and create real films. Such was the case of *Stiudent* – a humorous tale about flying grade books, the tribulations of the exam session, and the growing price of the students' beverage of choice. The film received ten awards at various festivals, and was broadcast by Kino Polska TV. But it was only in 2006 that DDN really made their mark on the scene. Their next film, *The Envelope (Koperta)*, won the grand prize at the BAREJADA festival. It is true that the artists from DDN have a knack for fishing out "Barejaisms"[5] from the surrounding reality and sculpting them into comic sequences. The group continued growing in fame. Their next movie, *Excuse Me (Przepraszam)*, received the main award at the Konin Film Festival and the Grand Prix in Łódź. Their films focus on the themes they know best – university life in a mid-sized city, exams, girls – but show them in a distorted fashion. In an interview for Kino Polska they declared,

> Professional filmmakers often make boring movies. We have no film background, so maybe that's the key? I'm serious – maybe our amateurism really is an asset. None of us was ever taught how to make movies, so we make them however we want to, as opposed to how they "should" be made. How is it possible that *Manna* actually grips you? When we were shooting it, we sequestered ourselves for a week in a forest with twenty cases of beer. Maybe the tension we felt on the set was translated into the movie.

By 2006, the independent film scene had matured. When in September 2006, during an interview with Feliks Falk, one of the jurors of the Independent Film Competition at the Polish Film Festival in Gdynia, I asked him about the direction of Polish independent cinema, he replied:

---

5 "Barejaisms" – expressions or scenes using a specific kind of humour invented by Stanisław Bareja (1929–1987), the director of extremely popular comedies such as *Teddy Bear* (*Miś*, 1980).

I think the indie movement is on the right track, it is shedding the stigma of amateurship. We're no longer dealing with clumsy tales told by beginners. Independent movies are slowly emerging from the catacombs of the underground movement, where they were only shown to small groups of friends. I see a bright future for the indie scene, mostly because it is shaping up to be the main venue for Polish auteurship. That's where the really ambitious projects will emerge from – ones that can't find governmental or TV funding because their creators are unwilling to succumb to commercialization.

The changes which have been taking place over the course of the last decade are not limited to the industry side of things, but also affect the type of stories today's filmmakers want to tell. These artists are inspired by different elements of the mainstream, and have new, distinct generational experiences. Their world is governed by the Internet, with instant distribution via YouTube, and the constant emotional exchange of Facebook. I eagerly await independent movies that will critically portray this reality. The road was already paved to a degree by the award-winning *Mall Girls* (*Galerianki*) by Katarzyna Rosłaniec – a young debutante of the 2009 Polish Film Festival in Gdynia who, it should be pointed out, is one of the first of the new crop of young filmmakers to completely bypass the independent route into mainstream.

Translated by Wojciech Góralczyk

POLISH CINEMA — A RETURN TO MARKET ECONOMY

JERZY PŁAŻEWSKI

Ahead of the pack

The tale of the development of the Polish film industry over the past 20 years can be of interest to a foreign reader for a number of reasons. Our cinema went through not one, but two revolutionary changes in the 20th century: after the communists took over in 1945 it lost its capitalist profile and was transformed to fit the Soviet mould; 44 years later, in August 1989, when Tadeusz Mazowiecki formed the first non-communist government in eastern Europe, the reverse process took place, and our film industry once again became governed by the rules of the free market. No one had attempted such an experiment before, and in that respect the systemic changes of Polish cinema were of a completely novel nature. Since there was no precedent for such a transformation, the evolution – which continues to this day – was something of a "trial and error". There was no lack of misguided predictions and failed solutions – abandoned immediately, or not quite so. But after two decades of debate, reform, and comparing experiences with other post-communist countries, it has become clear that there was simply no other way.

We should start by stating that in 1989 our filmmakers had a difficult time drawing on early 20th century standards, because our commercial, pre-communist film industry had little to show for itself. Lacking funds and rolling out movies at the behest of cinema owners who pandered to an unsophisticated mass audience, it failed to produce any significant works of art, or gain recognition on the international stage. To top it off, government support for Polish films was purely symbolic.

To even attempt to explain this state of affairs (which hardly anyone has even attempted) we have to go back further, to the dawn of the 20th century, when, following the Lumière brothers' invention, countries around the globe began laying the foundations for their national film industries. This process wasn't limited to the trailblazing France and United States of America, but also included nations with a big potential audience, such as Germany or Russia, and even small, but economically capable and export-oriented states, the likes of Sweden or Denmark. During that crucial, initial stage, the Polish state simply did not exist, having been partitioned over 100 years earlier by its three neighbours – Germany, Russia and Austria-Hungary. Polish movies started appearing much later than those of the three partitioners. The first Polish film was developed only in 1909 – 14 years after the Lumière brothers first demonstrated the Cinematograph at the Grand Café in Paris. The few scattered film producers were underfunded, and their productions encountered additional roadblocks, as Polish movies produced in one partition area had a hard time reaching the other two.

Not quite Soviet

When the Polish film industry began rebuilding itself after 1945, it had to start from scratch. The entire pre-war industry had been located in Warsaw, which was razed to the ground by the Nazi occupiers, its 1.5 million population reduced to zero. It should then come as no surprise that the Soviet model of managing the industry hastily imposed by Poland's new overlords was greeted by both artists and film-lovers with a big dose of hopefulness. It doesn't take a communist (and in the film industry, as well as in other artistic circles, they were few and far between) to be optimistic about the state taking over film production. Such a solution did, after all, present some very real perspectives for funding. At the same time, freeing cinema from the profit-oriented paradigm gave hope that these new films wouldn't pander to the lowest common denominator or promote kitsch.

In all fairness, one should note that not all of these hopes were dashed. The Polish film industry was reshaped in a relatively modern form, and our desperate lack of professionals was remedied by the establishment of a film school. Its alumni (Wajda, Munk) showed the world what the "Polish Film School" was all about. Following the brief period of Stalinist dictatorship, several ambitious Polish productions reached the heights of world-class art, granting our directors a margin of creative freedom that was unheard of in neighbouring countries. This was thanks to the creation of Film Groups, starting from 1955 (the year of the first political "thaw") – an institution so successful, it was soon copied by other members of the eastern bloc. Riding the wave of momentary liberalisation, the government – which had a monopoly on film production and distribution – sanctioned the creation of relatively autonomous production groups with a wide array of competences. Each group was helmed by an outstanding director, designated by the Polish Filmmakers Association. This model had its ups and downs, depending on the political course of the Communist Party, until the adoption in 1987 – during the communist regime's swan song – of the Act on Cinematography. Obviously, it was an inadequate and fearful half-measure, but at least it formally abolished the state monopoly on film production. Only one private company – ITI – was able to take advantage of the new law, foraying into video and advertising. To this day the ITI Group (International Trading and Investments Holdings S.A.) remains one of the biggest players in the Polish film and media market.

After the fall of communism

At the beginning of 1989, during the "round table" negotiations between the communists and the democratic opposition, the Polish Filmmakers Association proposed some radical changes. They postulated that the government relinquish its pivotal role in film production and distribution, while at the same time calling on it to subsidise films, create a tax system that would nourish the domestic film industry, and guarantee that Polish film culture would be shaped by the artists themselves. This issue was tackled by the Cinema Committee – a government agency established back in 1987 by the aforementioned, imperfect parliamentary act (of all the art disciplines, only film got its own agency, as if to accentuate its importance). Initially merely an advisory body, the Committee soon became the managing institution of the entire film industry when in June 1989 the eastern bloc's first non-communist government came into power. The Polish Filmmakers Association democratically elected the director Juliusz Burski to act as the Committee's chair. Its main task became to decentralise and privatise the Polish film industry in accordance with the tenets of market economy. Burski divided the funds assigned to the Committee between three newly created bodies: the Script, Production and Distribution Agencies (with production receiving the lion's share). Two solutions were being considered. The first one was to sell the entire industry to unrelated individual private entities. This option carried a certain risk, as there was no way of knowing the number of potential buyers, or how much capital they would have at their disposal, and how quickly they would be able to come up with it. The second, cooperative option had a bit more history as it had been in consideration even before the war, as well as after 1945, before the blind adoption of the Soviet model.

The Committee leaned towards the second solution, which was reflected in the way it dealt with cinemas. Previously the sole domain of the central government, they were swiftly handed over – free of charge – to local governments. In Burski's opinion, it was an ideal solution – after all, who knows better than local activists how much people need entertainment, and who will be quicker to ensure that they're not denied it? Unfortunately, it turned out to be an idealist delusion. The local governments often found it more beneficial to turn an unprofitable cinema into a supermarket, or even the proverbial car dealership. In 1990, there were 1549 cinemas in urban and rural areas of Poland, with 14.1 seats per 1000 people. Just two years later, there were only 772 left, with 8.9 seats per 1000 people. Theoretically, any interested party could attempt to purchase a cinema, but their chances were pretty slim compared to those of a Ford or Mercedes dealer – especially since the fluctuating tax law rendered cinemas unprofitable. Those venues which survived the carnage – the bigger, wealthier ones – ended up in the possession of seven private entities, which divided the market among themselves. It would be several years before the first wave of reactivations brought on by changes in the tax system. The construction of the first multiplexes began only in 1996.

Production is the slowest to privatise

Things couldn't have been more different in the most important area – national film production. For years to come it would remain mostly centralized. It was still the province of the seven Film Groups – quickly renamed "Studios" – which drew only on their own funds, and government subsidies. While in 1987–1989 there were around 35–40 domestic feature film premieres annually, and in the threshold year of 1990–28, that number dropped to 14 in 1991 and 1992. What's more, the fall of communism made Polish cinema so attractive to western producers, that half of those premieres were co-productions (Kieślowski's *Three Colours*, Costa-Gavras' *Small Apocalypse*, Spielberg's *Schindler's List*).

Additional producers were slow to arrive. The first one on the scene was public television. Alongside its own medium-length TV movies, it began producing films meant for cinematic distribution, which appeared on TV only after they had made the rounds on the silver screen (Filip Bajon's *Sauna*, 1992; Andrzej Barański's *A Bachelor's Life Abroad* [*Kawalerskie życie na obczyźnie*, 1992]). The government also tried using various restrictions and incentives to encourage the bigger privately-owned TV networks (Canal+, Polsat) to get into film production – which they did, though without much enthusiasm.

It was only in the mid 1990s that more private initiatives started popping up. Gradually, professional film producers – virtually unknown during the communist regime – began to emerge. This was brought on by a significant change in how the government subsidies were distributed. Initially, the Committee was supposed to provide simply money to the Film Studios (previously Film Groups), and left it to them to distribute the funds among the various productions as they saw fit. Soon though, it switched to funding specific scripts, presented along with a complete cost calculation to a panel of experts. The projects started being judged on two merits: artistic and/or commercial, as well as the legitimacy of the requested amounts. Projects from the Film Studios and those presented by private entities were given equal opportunity. All forms of political censorship were pointedly eradicated. The final say belonged to the Chairman of the Committee, who could go against the experts' opinion.

Schindler's List,
dir. Steven Spielberg
→

Unlike production, distribution was privatised rather quickly and far more radically. The seven old national distributors (Silesia, Max, Apollo, Helios, Odra, Film-Art, Neptun) quickly turned into four, and were subsequently marginalised by twenty newly-formed private companies. Of course starting a distribution company didn't require the same amount of capital as launching a production studio, especially since many of them were simply Polish branches of foreign consortia (Warner Bros, UIP, 20th Century Fox, SPI International). But what sort of repertoire did these distributors feed Polish audiences? With a comparable amount of around 130 premieres a year, in 1984 we screened 14 (9 per cent of the total amount) American movies, while in 1991 that number rose to 88 (77 per cent), which left nearly all domestic filmmakers without a way to get their movies into cinemas.

The dynamic but tumultuous development of the Polish market economy, coupled with a string of governments with conflicting economic policies, lent itself to fluctuations in the national debt. Year after year, budgets were adopted in the atmosphere of a tense tug-of-war. Obviously, budget shortages often result in reduced funds for culture. The Cinema Committee, and then the Ministry of Culture's Film Department (which became its successor), provided less and less subsidy to the three national film agencies: the Script Agency, which signed around fifty contracts with screenwriters annually; the Distribution Agency, which was rapidly losing significance; and, most importantly, the Production Agency. The last served as the system's main intermediary, feeding government funds into the film industry. Unfortunately, not only were the new grants getting smaller and smaller but the amounts which had already been allocated suffered from delays, which hindered the release of even the all-but-completed movies. The

situation got so bad that by 2005, the government owed producers PLN 35 million (with the production cost of an average movie amounting to 1–3 million).

This collapse wasn't stalled even by the intensifying cooperation between Poland and the European Union, initiated a long time before Poland's official accession to the EU in May 2004. Joining the EU Media Plus programme in 2002 did however – to some degree – help distributors and film schools, and made it easier for Polish films to participate in international festivals.

Time for reform

Though there was a consensus that national cinema was gravely underfunded, the legislative work was proceeding at a snail's pace. The opinion prevailed that new funding should be obtained not from the budget – i.e. the taxpayer – but from the entities which drew their profits from the audiovisual market. However, various potential sponsors did everything to ensure that their particular share in this expense was as small as possible – if not outright nonexistent. The biggest resistance came from the cable networks.

Meanwhile, government funds were running dry. Finally, Minister of Culture Waldemar Dąbrowski managed to merge two – or perhaps even three – bills that would ensure the proper development of the Polish film industry. As his deputy he appointed Agnieszka Odorowicz, who was supported by film circles (Wajda, Zanussi), as well as by the Polish Filmmakers Association. She took it upon herself to convince the various parties

represented in parliament to support this new bill, which was finally passed on 30 June 2005. It created a new entity – the Polish Film Institute – which would receive not only government subsidies, but also 1.5 per cent of all profits generated by TV stations, DVD and video producers, cable networks, cinemas, and film distributors. However, the fight did not end there. The cable networks challenged the law in the courts, the Constitutional Tribunal, and even the European Commission, claiming that the Ministry of Culture had exceeded its competence by submitting an actual bill. However, all of these bodies have confirmed the act's full compliance with the law.

Four years of the Institute

The Institute has been active for 4 years now, which allows us to perform a fairly accurate examination of its influence on Polish cinema. Its main function was naturally to nourish promising projects, especially feature films. However, the Institute became involved in all aspects of the Polish film industry.

First, I would like to present some basic statistical data regarding the production of feature films. This value determines the condition of cinema in any given country – after all, a handful of movies produced annually hardly constitute a national cinema. The quality of these productions is also related to their quantity: it's much easier to find noteworthy works in countries with a robust and prolific film industry. And so, though immediately after the fall of communism film production rapidly decreased by half (in 1992–16; 1995–12; 1997–14; 2000–20; 2003–21), by the year 2008 it returned to the previous level of forty-two movies per year, and in 2009 we had as many as sixty.

The best way to see how the Institute distributes governmental resources is to study its expenditures (in this case, for the year 2008). Its fundamental activity – i.e. film production – takes up a little over 50 per cent of its finances. The EUR 38 million budget was spent in the following fashion (bearing in mind that the production of a feature-length movie costs about EUR 1 million, some first films cost only EUR 300–400,000, epic costume dramas can consume as much as EUR 5 million, and the average Institute grant amounts to EUR 1.2 million):

A Bachelor's Life Abroad,
dir. Andrzej Barański
←

Aria Diva,
dir. Agnieszka Smoczyńska

Purchase of scripts and grants for screenwriters	3%
Production of feature films	32%
Production of debuts	14%
Production of films with big box office potential	9%
Production of documentaries	5%
Production of animated films	5%
Film industry subsidies	4%
Development of the cinema network	5%
Film distribution and marketing	5%
Promoting film culture	11%
Promoting Polish movies abroad	4%
Professional workshops	2%
Competitions, awards	1%

The grants offered to film producers are governed by the rule that the Institute itself does not produce movies, but merely provides financial aid. All applicants are required to have had already come up with no less than 50 per cent of the film's budget. Sometimes, however, exceptions are made for creators of low-budget films – especially highly ambitious or experimental ventures.

The photograph on the opposite page comes from the movie *Aria Diva* (2007) directed by Agnieszka Smoczyńska, which was produced as part of the "30 Minutes Programme" created jointly by the Institute and the Polish Filmmakers Association. It is a project with its own, separate budget, which aims to improve the quality of first films. All applicants are provided with artistic mentorship and offered a chance to shoot their own 30-minute movie. It is the best, quickest, and ultimately cheapest way of discovering true talent.

Since we now know that the government subsidises the film industry with a sum of EUR 38 million annually, we should next determine what part of this amount is shouldered by the tax-payer, and how much of it comes from the 1.5 per cent deducted from the revenue of audiovisual companies.

Government subsidies	10%
Funds for culture promotion	7%
TV broadcasters	36%
Digital platforms	17%
Cable networks	9%
Cinemas	4%
Distributors	1%
Other revenues	16%

Recently, a new way of securing additional capital for film production has emerged in the form of developing projects in cooperation with the Regional Film Funds. These funds are pretty commonplace in the European Union (there are currently 36 in France alone). Nine such funds, created by local governments, offer financial help by way of tender. In order to be eligible, a movie has to be related to the history of the region, and either be produced locally, or have most of its production budget spent in that region. The size of these grants varies from EUR 500 to 125,000.

How did the new film legislation influence audiences? After 2000, cinema attendance in Europe dropped, especially during the deepening economic crisis. Poland was very acutely affected by this decline. In legendary 1967, 160 million people visited Polish cinemas. By the mid-90s, attendance dropped to nearly 20 million, which meant the average Pole went to the movies once in two years! In 2008, that number increased to 34 million.

Since the government sold all its cinemas, relinquishing direct influence on repertoire and ticket prices, its attendance-boosting activities were limited to promoting good Polish movies with the potential to attract moviegoers. And that is exactly what happened. The distinct jump in attendance in 1999 was evidently caused by the success of two Polish epics: Hoffman's *With Fire and Sword* (*Ogniem i mieczem*), and Wajda's *Pan Tadeusz*. The statistical 0.89 tickets sold annually per capita still place us well below the 2.5 tickets average of the European Union, but as many as 25 per cent of Polish viewers buy tickets to family movies, which is something of a European phenomenon. The unquestioned favourites of Polish audiences are adaptations of national literature and romantic comedies – which comes as no surprise – but also movies touching on the metaphysical.

CINEMAS AND THEIR REPERTOIRES

New channels of distributing Polish movies appeared with the resurgence of art house cinemas. They played a big role in the development of Polish cinema during the boom of movie discussion clubs in 1960–1980. However, after the fall of communism, the market was flooded with Hollywood productions of questionable quality, and the so-called studio cinemas all but ceased to exist. Beginning in 1993, an effort was made to resurrect them, starting with thirty cinemas in university towns. These became the Studio Cinema Network. Since 2005 they have been under the financial and administrative stewardship of the National Film Archive, and their current name is the Local and Studio Cinemas Network. The first adjective refers to the sole cinemas in smaller towns, whose liquidation would deprive these communities of one of their main cultural centres. Today, there are 109 such cinemas, and their number is rapidly swelling. All are bound by law to screen a certain percentage of Polish productions.

Distributors now have the option of approaching the Institute with a film they have purchased and deem as having high artistic value. Should the Institute experts agree, the distributor receives funding for additional screening copies, posters, and advertising for this – usually much more difficult to market – movie. Initially, this procedure was supposed to apply only to "Polish and European" productions, but that restriction met with criticism, and was eventually abolished – after all, why shouldn't excellent Iranian or Mexican movies be able to take advantage of these funds? Were it not for this system, many movies would never have been screened in Poland.

There is also a more general, systemic problem related to the Local and Studio Cinemas Network. At the dawn of the 1960s, French film critics declared that "the repertoire of Polish cinemas is the best in the world, because it is shaped not by politicians or merchants, but by film critics". They based this statement on – among other things – the presence of movies awarded at the Cannes festival, noting that nearly 100 per cent of them were distributed in Poland. Following the political transformation, this share dropped to 20–25 per cent. This sad state of affairs has somewhat improved over the years, but over half of such movies are still unable to find a Polish distributor. The abovementioned procedure of "certifying" artistic value serves to remedy this problem, but it's not enough. It is applicable only if the distributor has already tracked down such a film, purchased the distribution rights, and prepared screening copies – risking losses. Unfortunately, the system doesn't remedy the two decades of backlogs, or prevent new spectacular but ambitious works from falling through the cracks. There is a need for a list of movies – prepared by film experts, and made available to the distributors – which would receive guaranteed financial aid if purchased for the Polish market.

Another new experiment – the results of which still remain to be seen – is the gigantic Institute project modestly named the School Film Archive. Fourteen thousand high schools all over Poland received a pack of fifty-five Polish feature, documentary, and animated films. They will serve as a basis for Polish, history and civics teachers to organise extra-curricular activities and school discussion clubs. The aim is not only to teach students about the history of Polish cinema, but also to familiarise them with the language of film, its role in the national culture, and provide them with a set of critical tools for analysing the cinematic experience.

The project was prepared by a team of forty film experts and educationalists, and is accompanied by a set of textbooks, addressed to both teachers and students. Special workshops for teachers participating in the programme have also been organised. The films, provided free of charge, have been grouped into twenty-six themes, for example "Contemporary Anxieties", or "National Stereotypes". Work is currently underway on a second series of the School Film Archive, addressing a new set of themes. Therefore, the decades-old idea of making film studies an element of the curriculum has finally resulted in a radical, comprehensive, and nation-wide response.

What will we send to the festivals?

Among the issues still waiting to be optimally resolved is having the presence of Polish cinema at international film festivals reflect its true standing in the world. This is not the place for a critical assessment of Polish film's artistic achievements over the past two

Three Colours: Blue,
dir. Krzysztof
Kieślowski

*Four Nights
with Anna*,
dir. Jerzy
Skolimowski

decades. Let's just say that our film industry has seen much more robust periods. The fall of communism deprived Polish filmmakers of their chief antagonist, whose money they used to fight for liberty and democracy, even if they had to do so using Aesopian language. In a way, this victory limited their horizons, concluding their righteous crusade against tyranny. However, even in the transitional period, we have received a number of prestigious international awards, which I will now present chronologically:

> An acting award in Cannes for Krzysztof Kieślowski's *The Double Life of Veronique* (*Podwójne życie Weroniki*, 1991), a Golden Lion in Venice for his *Three Colours: Blue* (*Niebieski*, 1993) a Silver Bear in Berlin for Andrzej Wajda's *Holy Week* (*Wielki tydzień*, 1995), another Silver Bear for his *Miss Nobody* (*Panna Nikt*, 1996) as well as a lifetime achievement Silver Bear and US Academy Award. A Grand Prix in Moscow for Krzysztof Zanussi's *Life as a Fatal Sexually Transmitted Disease* (*Życie jako śmiertelna choroba przenoszona drogą płciową*, 2000), a Palme d'Or in Cannes for Roman Polanski's *The Pianist*, and a Golden Globe in Karlovy Vary for Krzysztof Krauze's *My Nikifor* (*Mój Nikifor*, 2004).

However, it is also difficult to avoid reflecting on how many potential awards we've lost due to our own negligence, for example by not securing a spot at prominent festivals for Zanussi's *The Silent Touch* (*Dotknięcie ręki*, 1992) Wojciech Smarzowski's *The Wedding* (*Wesele*, 2004), or by moving Skolimowski's *Four Nights with Anna* (*Cztery noce z Anną*, 2008) to the non-competition section of Cannes, which isn't frequented by international critics.

The shortcomings in this regard were easy to anticipate. In communist times, the state monopoly maintained a special institution, which was in constant contact with the biggest festivals and was perfectly aware of what we had to show to the world at any

given moment. It was that institution that decided if film X was the perfect candidate for Cannes, whether A and B should be submitted to Venice, and Y be sent to Karlovy Vary if it doesn't get into Berlin. The system operated quite efficiently – as long as the work in question or its author did not stir up any political controversy. At the same time, efforts were made to ensure the adequate presence of Poles on international festival juries.

Once the number of production studios jumped to several dozen, each of them started acting of their own accord – as opposed to coordinating efforts with their colleagues. Given that the average producer has only occasional contact with individual festivals, and is usually poorly versed in their regulations, customs and procedures, achieving an optimal use of our resources is nigh on impossible. In order to guarantee a consistent festival policy and make the best possible decisions, the Polish Filmmakers Association has set up an impartial Festival Advisory Commission. Though greeted with enthusiasm by film festivals, and even by producers, it fell apart after six months, when the public television network scrapped its, already miniscule, budget.

These painful festival absences are only partially made up for by retrospectives of Polish cinema presented abroad – both in countries which are relatively steady importers of our movies, and those where our works are considered exotic. Thankfully, the Institute is working to organise more and more such presentations, often supplementing them with professional documentation.

Festivals made in Poland

Of course, there is no shortage of festivals in Poland itself (though some local reviews abuse this name despite having no jury or prizes). There are several dozen of them, even in small townships such as Ińsko, Niepokalanów, or Zwierzyniec, which most Poles wouldn't be able to find on a map. Their existence is validated by their financial results. A certain difficult Iranian film, when screened in metropolitan Wrocław, attracted ten to twelve audience members over the course of three days. Two months later, it was shown during a local festival, and the 700-seat auditorium was full.

Endeavours in this field came pretty late though, as it was generally felt that Europe already had too many feature film festivals. That is why in 1961, in Krakow, a short film festival was launched instead. It's still going strong to this day, and is now ranked among the top three such events in the world. The next big one, Camerimage (first organised in Toruń, then moved to Łódź), was named a Cinematographers' Art Festival. Movies from Cannes or Berlin can freely enter its competition section, since they are judged by a different set of criteria – therefore, there's no risk of the event having to satisfy itself with third-rate productions. The Warsaw Film Festival – recently having celebrated its 25th anniversary – has also earned its reputation and was just promoted by the International Federation of Producers Associations to the "A" section for presenting young filmmakers from countries with a low cinematic output. Finally, growing in prominence over the last decade, there's the Era New Horizons festival, organised in Wrocław by the accomplished distribution company Gutek Film. ENH's programme is usually based around a central, controversial, and discussion-worthy subject.

For nearly thirty-four years, a national festival has been organised in the seaside city of Gdynia, to take stock of the latest crop of domestic productions and recognise some of them with awards (including specialist categories such as editing or make-up). In 2009, the festival noted an astounding success, at least quantity-wise: twenty-four feature films were submitted for the main competition (including eleven first films!), seventeen for the independent film section, and ten for the Panorama, for a grand total of fifty-one productions. And several already completed movies weren't even sent in! It is rather perplexing that having for so many years organised such a specialised review of Polish productions, we've never attempted to invite top critics from around the world to attend it.

Film criticism and film studies

Whilst we are on the subject of film critics, it should be noted that Polish representatives of that profession have significantly contributed to the success of Polish films, as well as guaranteed the artistic freedom of our top artists and a high percentage of ambitious productions. They have always played a significant role in the FIPRESCI International Federation of Critics (of which a Pole, Bolesław Michałek, became honorary chairman). Recently, they have put forth the "Best Books" project, arguing that film critics should ensure that not only the best movies, but also the best books about film find their way into their country. The critics objectively select the publications which a foreign reader would find most interesting, and inform foreign publishers about them. It is only through this process that one could hope for an excellent Greek book to be published in Australia, or China. Of the several dozen Polish film magazines, one should point out *Cinema* (*Kino*) and *Film*, as well as the more theoretical *Film Quarterly* (*Kwartalnik Filmowy*).

A significant portion of the Polish film audience was accounted for by members of film discussion clubs, which have been popping up since 1955, and which were true oases of freedom of speech, remaining largely out of the party censorship's reach. Their goal was to broaden moviegoers' knowledge and awareness by screening masterpieces of world cinema, as well as organising meetings with artists, critics and historians. Following the fall of communism, their popularity rapidly declined – their number shrinking from 500 to 100. On the one hand, suddenly there was this assumption that access to movies would now be automatically guaranteed – and not necessarily by cinemas. On the other, the rapidly changing economic conditions caused many sponsors to withdraw their support, which in turn led to the closing down of small cinemas which housed the clubs. This tendency found its culmination in the years 1993–2005, when government funding for the clubs was completely scrapped, and local governments were only beginning to treat them as valued allies. However, recently the interest in such clubs seems to be on the rise, and the Polish Federation of Film Discussion Clubs submitted 129 initiatives to the FFCC World Federation. Its periodical, *Film Around the World* (*Film na świecie*) was reactivated, and club members have once again been granted access to a pool of artistic movies purchased especially for the network of studio cinemas, and unavailable in general distribution.

Around forty books on film are published annually in Poland, and two thirds of them are original works. This is related to the current state of film studies in our country. The more practical approach, focused on educating a new generation of filmmakers, is represented by two universities. The first of these is the National Higher School of Film, Television and Theatre in Łódź, which boasts directing, cinematographic, acting, producing and scriptwriting faculties. Among its alumni are most contemporary Polish filmmakers, many of whom in turn later became its professors. The university's reputation is such that nearly half of its students come from abroad, often from faraway countries such as Australia, or Singapore. Another slightly younger institution is the

Department of Radio and Television at the University of Silesia in Katowice – though it is geared more towards television. These two schools are in a way complemented by the Andrzej Wajda Master School of Film Directing. It has two faculties – feature film and documentary – and is more workshop-based, admitting only professional filmmakers with certain experience who want to hone their craft. There are also a dozen or so smaller directing and acting schools, and six universities maintain film studies departments educating film academics and students.

The Act of 2005 finally put an end to the financial problems of the National Film Archive – the biggest of Poland's film libraries. The NFA is engaged in fruitful cooperation with its equivalents in other countries through its association in the FIAF International Federation of Film Archives. It also protects cultural works from the realm of film, focusing on archiving Polish movies (it has archived 75 per cent of Polish movies produced since the dawn of cinema), and offers access to its extensive collection (spanning 15,000 titles) to scientists and film clubs. The NFA-owned Iluzjon Cinema screens the finest works of world cinema, and its library houses the biggest collection of film books in the country. Aside from literary works, it also boasts a unique collection of 60,000 movie posters – all the more impressive since many Polish graphic artists have garnered worldwide acclaim in the field of poster design.

The protection of classic national and foreign films, preserved in varying technical states, requires significant funds, which the National Film Archive alone is not able to generate. Though plans are already being made for digitising the archives, some of the movies are still stored on flammable film. Another costly venture is the restoration of outstanding works of film to their initial form.

How do we digitise?

As for the future, it seems that the next step will be digital cinemas. Currently in Poland there are eighty cinemas equipped with digital projectors. The Polish Filmmakers Association, along with the National Chamber of Audiovisual Producers has created the National Programme of Cinema Digitalization, which is supposed to double that number, and eventually raise it to 350.

Progress in that field will result in improving the cinematic experience: increasing sharpness, improving colour and sound, eliminating graininess, and maintaining those qualities despite repeated use of the media. However, the chief benefit – especially for smaller cinemas outside of big agglomerations – will be the increased availability of the latest movies (without the need to wait for them to finish their run in major cities), and cheaper access to the films desired in a given region, as well as various classics. In extreme situations, this could prevent the closing down of struggling cinemas by improving their movie selection, and perhaps even bolster the faith of Polish distributors in the profitability of promoting high art.

In September 2009, the Congress of Polish Culture took place in Krakow. Its participants debated the attitude of the government towards all spheres of cultural activity, from literature to opera and ballet. In their concluding statements, representatives of nearly all art disciplines declared wistfully, *Oh, if only the state developed such successful support mechanisms in our field as it did in cinema!*

Translated by Wojciech Góralczyk

POLISH CINEMA
SUCCESS STORIES

**JANUSZ
WRÓBLEWSKI**

THE FLAVOUR OF SUCCESS

Looking at the past twenty years from a modern-day perspective, one can clearly see it was a pretty good time for Polish cinema, despite the complaints of local critics who were often too harsh in their judgements. However, it must be said that things did not seem too encouraging at the beginning. For cinema, the transition from socialism to the free market was not an easy one. Organisational chaos reigned, fierce battles were fought over small state subsidies, and the lack of legal regulation incapacitated the divided film community. Considering the difficult conditions, probably the greatest achievement at the initial stage of the political system-change was that continuity was maintained for productions at risk of imminent collapse. In the 1990s, the situation in Poland was still not as bad as in the Czech Republic, for example, where barely one film a year was being released, or Romania, where film production had stopped altogether. Nevertheless, the number of films being made was in steady decline until the start of the 21st century, when the former average annual output of twenty-five to thirty films had dropped to less than ten. Only when the Polish Film Institute was set up in 2005 did the situation stabilise and, thanks to a comprehensive reform of the funding system, it was able to bounce back.

Despite the demanding conditions, quite a lot of films produced in the 1990s did not differ much from the European standard. In many cases, their technical maturity was quite astonishing, but unfortunately this could not always be said of their artistic values. This critical moment for Polish cinema prevented many talented filmmakers from establishing a career and becoming known outside their home country. On the whole, guaranteed success was only achieved by experienced directors who had emigrated, and managed to prove their worth in co-productions. For instance, after receiving an Oscar nomination for *Angry Harvest* (*Bittere Ernte*, 1985), which was shot in France, Agnieszka Holland went on to film the well received and ironic *Europa Europa* in Germany, for which she won a Golden Globe in 1992. Krzysztof Kieślowski is another fine example.

THE MASTER AND HIS ACOLYTES

The director of *The Double Life of Veronique* (*La Double Vie de Véronique*, 1991) and the *Three Colours* (*Trois Couleurs*) trilogy became the Polish filmmaker to be fully appreciated worldwide after the fall of the Iron Curtain. Even in the declining years of communism, while making his famous television series *The Decalogue* (*Dekalog*), instead of producing patriotic, pro-opposition symbolism in support of the Solidarity movement, he offered an entirely new vision of reality, aimed directly at the very heart of western European controversy over religion and the foundations of faith after long decades of

intense secularism. By asking seemingly naïve questions about Judeo-Christian traditions (e.g. Have the ten commandments lost their relevance in the post-modern era? By what criteria do we judge people's mistakes and faults? Can civilisation be built on the basis of secular ethics?), Kieślowski went far beyond the prevailing conservative-Catholic intellectual horizon, but paid for it by being misunderstood. Wisely escaping jealousies in Polish cinematic circles, he filmed his next projects outside his homeland, particularly in France, thanks to the generous support of his foreign producer Marin Karmitz.

His films were full of metaphysical turmoil, with a patently agnostic dimension. They raised the issues of responsibility, loneliness, loving in a place where God is "dead", epistemological chaos, and the reassessment of values. Their inscribed liberal points of view were deemed offensive in Poland (where he was accused of being preoccupied with increasingly outlandish and unreal issues and forms), but they were considered fascinating elsewhere. This Pole, who was praised for his free-thinking and later compared to Antonioni, eventually became the object of high hopes in Poland too. His sudden death in 1996 cut short a career that had been flourishing brilliantly. Despite his fatigue, discouragement and regularly-repeated threats to quit the film business altogether, he left behind several rough drafts, which were later expanded by his closest collaborator, the scriptwriter Krzysztof Piesiewicz. Works based on his ideas include *Heaven*, an interesting drama about terrorism by Tom Tykwer from Germany, and the Bosnian

← *Europa Europa*, dir. Agnieszka Holland

↓ *Love Stories*, dir. Jerzy Stuhr

director Danis Tanović's touching family tragedy *Hell* (*L'Enfer*). In principle, every single Kieślowski film made in Poland or abroad has won some kind of prize. Irene Jacob won Best Actress in Cannes for her excellent performance in *The Double Life of Veronique*. *Blue* (*Bleu*, 1993) won the Venice Film Festival, *White* (*Blanc*, 1993) was awarded a Silver Bear in Berlin, and *Red* (*Rouge*, 1994) was nominated for Oscars in three categories: for its screenplay, directing and cinematography.

Jerzy Stuhr, an eminent actor and director well-known in Italy, has attempted to fill the gap Kieślowski left behind. He is clearly a devotee of the traditions of conscience-stirring intellectual cinema. Stuhr's *début*, *The List of Adulteresses* (*Spis cudzołożnic*, 1995), surprised audiences with its story about a helpless intellectual who realises the full untranslatability of Polish experience and history. The mocking tone of the film superbly reflected the Polish state of mind at the time, when people found themselves bewildered by their sudden access to the outside world, still unable to shake off their complexes about the past. Two years later, the director's *Love Stories* (*Historie miłosne*, 1997) was well-received abroad (winning a European Film Award and a FIPRESCI Prize in Venice), and discreetly followed in the footsteps of Kieślowski's *Blind Chance*

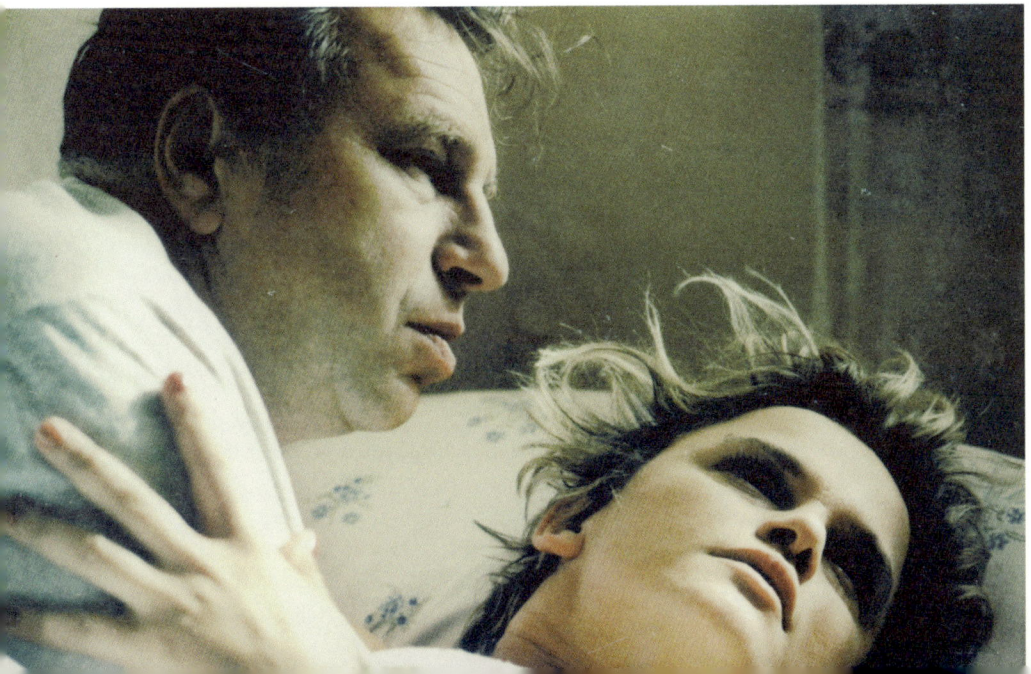

(*Przypadek*, 1981). It presented four variations of life. The excellent storyline is conceived for four characters (all played mesmerisingly by Jerzy Stuhr), and concerns the choices that determine whether a person is loved, and why: career, loyalty, tranquillity and family life as opposed to choices of the heart. In his next film, the allegorical *The Big Animal* (*Duże zwierzę*, 2000), which was based on a script written by the young Kieślowski (and won the Special Jury Prize in Karlovy Vary), Stuhr raised issues of intolerance and social exclusion. However, this story of a family keeping a camel in a small town was rather unconvincing.

SQUARING UP WITH THE WAR

Roman Polański was the first to show the world the new face of Polish cinema with *The Pianist* in 2002. This adaptation of Władysław Szpilman's bestseller about his life under the occupation, which won the Palme d'Or at Cannes and three Oscars, was reminiscent of the Polish School's best achievements, and justly deserved the title of the most outstanding Polish film of the past twenty years. *The Pianist* entered the Cannes race under the French flag, but when collecting his prize, the director only thanked his Polish actors and colleagues. How could a film depicting so crucial a period of Polish history have been funded abroad? This is how international co-productions work, in this case involving France, Germany, Britain and Poland. Each country is entitled to consider the film their own, and Poland was privileged in this respect, for obvious reasons.

Polański had managed to do something incredible. Half a century after the war, and several years after *Schindler's List* (which won three "Polish Oscars" for Allan Starski's scenography, Ewa Braun's costumes and Janusz Kamiński's camerawork), he filmed a masterpiece combining the experiences of Poles, Jews and Germans during World War II. This subject is still relevant in Poland, as proven by Jan Tomasz Gross' accusatory book, *Neighbours*, about the crimes committed by Poles against Polish Jews in Jedwabne, which were covered up so shamefully during the communist Polish People's Republic period. Polański described the suffering of the Jews in few words, but with poetic intensity. The film's restraint and the melancholy distance invoked by Paweł Edelman's newsreel-like photography (in keeping with the cinematic poetry of Wajda and Kawalerowicz) let one observe the tragedy from close range, but not gratuitously. The film gives us a wider perspective. It does not just discuss the fate of the eminent Polish composer of Jewish descent who survived the destruction of the ghetto, and miraculously made it through the horrors of the Warsaw Uprising in one piece by hiding in the ruins of the capital so devastated by the Germans. Szpilman's diaries, which were published (in heavily-censored form) for the first time in Poland in 1946, also contained numerous inconvenient truths about Russian, Polish, Ukrainian, Lithuanian and Jewish collaborators. Although Polański did raise this issue, he accentuated the reconciliation between torturers and victims.

There have already been many films that shatter stereotypes without seeking vengeance and just focus on being candid about complicated relations in the shadow of the Holocaust. Some of them were directed by Poles, for example Andrzej Wajda's *Holy Week* (*Wielki Tydzień*, 1995). What makes *The Pianist* so different in this context? The film is a testimony to human endurance in the face of death, portraying the triumph of an artist and his art over the absurdity of the world. It also pays tribute to humanity's vitality and solidarity on the brink of extermination.

The collapse of communism, the abolition of censorship, the opening of historical archives, and the breakaway from Moscow's sphere of influence all induced Andrzej Wajda to pursue his accounts of Poland's tragic fate. Eight years after receiving an honorary Oscar for his lifetime achievement, Wajda gained more major international success in 2008. This time he shocked public opinion with a reminder of a World War II incident that was little-known in the west, yet vital for comprehending the Polish mentality. The Oscar-nominated *Katyn* broke the most strictly-guarded taboo of communist times surrounding the Soviet genocide of imprisoned Polish officers. Following the annexation of eastern Poland according to a secret pact Stalin and Hitler concluded in 1939, the Soviets assassinated more than 22,000 prisoners-of-war with shots to the back of the head. The blame was placed on the Germans. For over 50 years, it was impossible to speak publicly about the lies surrounding the Katyn massacre, and anyone who sought to reveal the true perpetrators faced a long jail sentence. Wajda's epic gives a powerful account of this atrocious crime, while relating the history of the Katyn victims' families who fought for the historical truth to be respected. The result is an essential, outstanding film about the darkest chapter of Polish-Russian history and it functions as both a commentary and an appendix to previous works by Wajda and the Polish School. *Katyn* has been shown in Italy, Germany and France, and was seen by 2.7 million cinemagoers in Poland. Unfortunately, it could not be distributed in Russia because the licence was acquired by a certain company specifically to prevent it from being released into cinemas, and Wajda came up against similar obstacles in Ukraine (finally, Wajda's *Katyn* premiered on the Russian TV channel Kultura on 2 April 2010).

EXPERIENCE VERSUS YOUTH

One should also mention the widespread acclaim and high standards of several other veterans of auteur cinema, including Krzysztof Zanussi, who revisited the abominations of the Stalinist era in his intelligently ironic comedy *In Full Gallop* (*Cwał*, 1995). Five years later, he returned to his favourite themes of the roots of evil and the miracle of moral

The Pianist,
dir. Roman Polański

reconciliation in the splendid morality play *Life as a Fatal Sexually Transmitted Disease* (*Życie jako śmiertelna choroba przenoszona drogą płciową*, 2000), which won the Grand Prix in Moscow in 2000. Jerzy Skolimowski also distinguished himself with unexpected flair. In 2008, 17 years after the premiere of his rather unsuccessful *Ferdydurke* (1991), this Polish emigrant who had been working successfully in America and Europe, secretly filmed the poetic drama *Four Nights with Anna* (*Cztery noce z Anną*, 2008) instead of his planned Hollywood adaptation of Susan Sontag's *In America*, a novel about Helena Modrzejewska. This is an intimate story about the loneliness of a disabled man incapable of expressing his emotions. It received an ovation at its premiere in Cannes, and was invited for inclusion in several festivals, including Toronto, Sydney, Mar del Plata and Tokyo, where it won the Special Jury Prize.

Four Nights with Anna is a minimalist poem that is almost a museum-piece, from a formal point of view, as if recently unearthed from a film archive. Its monochromesque cinematography with no visual time-cues, its modest acting and bitter, surreal metaphors recall the spirit of the sixties. Such *nouvelle vague*, existentially-symbolic aesthetics were at their most striking in those days but, paradoxically, this is a justified return to that look. Just like Andrzej Leszczyc in *Identification Marks: None* (*Rysopis*, 1964) and *Walkover* (*Walkower*, 1965), the hero of *Four Nights with Anna* seeks to give his life some meaning, but does not know how. He runs away from himself, wanders, and rejects maturity. He makes mistakes, and because he is shy and hung-up, he sneaks in through a window to spy on the woman he has fallen in love with, but is then accused of rape.

The younger generation of directors, who are in fierce yet rather unsuccessful competition with their older colleagues, have won fewer international awards. Unfortunately, the 1990s failed to bring us many major revelations, but things became more positive around the turn of the century. The manifesto for the revival of young cinema was *The Debt* (*Dług*, 1999) by Krzysztof Krauze, an incredibly talented artist who, following an unsuccessful commercial *début*, spent a long time searching for a suitable subject. He found it among reportages and documentaries, from which he drew a tale of determined businessmen engaged in a life-or-death struggle with a mafioso debt-collector. This was not just a superb crime movie with a serious sociological bent; it also revealed and named the chief sore point of the transition period – it was impossible to get rich quickly. Krauze's film created a new type of hero – a businessman obsessed with a colour-brochure vision of reality and consumed by a desire to be successful. A well-qualified, inexperienced entrepreneur's lust for wealth at any price leads to his own downfall: a macabre scene in which he metamorphoses into a killer by desperately decapitating his persecutor, thus denoting the end of an intellectual ethos, and the breakdown of a system of values for an entire generation of 40-year-olds – the main beneficiaries of the changes that came after 1989. *The Debt* went virtually unnoticed in the west (it was only shown in the Panorama section of the Berlin International Film Festival), but in Poland, it is regarded as one of the decade's foremost achievements. Krauze was acclaimed abroad only five years later for his poetic drama *My Nikifor* (*Mój Nikifor*, 2004), which won the Best Director prize in Karlovy Vary. The title role in this soulful portrait of primitivist painter Nikifor Krynicki (who has been compared to Séraphine de Senlis and Henri "le Douanier" Rousseau) was played by the brilliant actress Krystyna Feldman.

Wronged simpletons

One more important discovery ranking high among the decadent films of the decade was Robert Gliński's *Hi, Tereska* (*Cześć Tereska*, 2001), which was evidently influenced by the "New Brutalists" such as Sarah Kane and Mark Ravenhill. This dark vision of humanity, which borders on the pathological, clearly sowed the seeds of unrest in the Slavonic soul. The film shows several days in the life of an average city-dwelling teenage girl from a block of flats who, while searching for warmth and love, collides with the cynicism of her peers and the heartlessness of the world. The 15-year-old takes out her frustration on the wheelchair-bound cripple who loves her. In revenge for being raped and humiliated, powerless to improve her own fate, helpless, grief-stricken, ashamed and disappointed, she cracks his head with a stick.

Krauze and Gliński's pessimism were not mere exceptions. At the turn of the century, an entire wave of works washed over Polish cinema, gloomily laying bare the problems involved in making a life in the inhuman new realities of capitalism. Important examples of this tendency, which were well-received by the critics, are two intimate dramas made in 2002: Piotr Trzaskalski's first film *Edi* and Marek Koterski's *Day of the Wacko* (*Dzień świra*, 2002). Despite being very different in formal terms, both films wonderfully capture the feelings of hypersensitive people on the margins of society, living with a sense of isolation and the impression of being permanently wronged.

↓
Edi,
dir. Piotr Trzaskalski

→
Hi, Tereska,
dir. Robert Gliński

The hero of *Edi* is an alcoholic scrap-metal collector from Łódź, who mostly lives off what he is given by others. Even though he is poor and homeless, he does not beg or steal. He is, as the reviews emphasised, as gentle as St. Francis. In his spare time, Edi looks at books he has dug out of bins and reads Shakespeare. Finally, he is hired by gangsters to watch over a teenage girl, but it ends in tragedy for him when he is accused of rape and castrated. On top of that, he also "inherits" the girl's baby and tries to take care of it. However, his refuge in the countryside, where he ends up after running away from the city, turns out to be a trap.

Trzaskalski recounts this simple parable of a drunk, a victim, and his destiny in a very subtle way. There are more references to mythological situations than to the mouldy, dark reality of the Łódź suburbs. However, in spite of its fairytale ambience, the film does not feel false. Why did this poetic picture floating somewhere between realism and magic become a symbol of contemporary cinema, capturing the spirit of modernity? American moviegoers

presumably asked themselves similar questions while watching *Scarecrow*, *Midnight Cowboy* and *The Panic In Needle Park*. *Edi* is in the same vein as those road mo-vies which reflect the atmosphere of life in the streets. Its discussion of the debasement of kindness defends those values that were most sorely lacking at the time. Trzaskalski's film, which avoids all political allusions, historical controversies and re-evaluations of current events, wins through with its moral aspect. It serves up a therapeutic fairytale which allows people to find their conscience and sense of measure in a time of poverty, depravity and the rat-race.

Humiliated intellectuals

Day of the Wacko makes a similar diagnosis, but offers no easy consolation. This uncompromising psychological drama, which changes smoothly from a farce into something grotesque, shows the creative suffering of a would-be writer and former Polish teacher who curses everyone and everything for the fact that his life has been a failure. This two-hour production is the prolonged lamentation of an outsider (named Miauczyński, [which implies "meowing" and "whining"]), who is about to turn 50 and moans at his own feebleness, how cruel fate is, and the stupidity of Polish society. The plot is confined to a description of ritualistic daily activities carried out mechanically (e.g. getting out of bed, brewing tea, going to the toilet, having lunch, walking around the housing estate) which then expand into acute, existential problems. By analysing them in depth, the hero drives himself into neurosis, considering suicide as the best way to get rid of his obsessions. *Day of the Wacko* ends at dusk, with a pious choir from his entire block of flats singing a prayer to request that their neighbour fall ill with cancer and AIDS.

The romantic Miauczyński's defeat is the defeat of the Polish intelligentsia. From the time of the partitions to the fall of communism, they ruled the people as a "government of souls" who had no power or means. They used to be intellectual and moral leaders, but this is no longer true. At least that would seem to be Koterski's conclusion as, with Gombrowicz-like fury, he exposes the complexes, inhibitions and incurable pessimism of a Polish intellectual despairing over his general impotence, low wages, and lack of prospects. Many people could see their own fates and everyday lives reflected in Koterski's tale of a modest day of a very modest man. Delighted critics exchanged compliments about the director, saying the film came close to true greatness, that it really represented the Poland of the time, and emphasised all the Polish national traits.

The psychological drama *The Collector* (*Komornik*, 2005) offered a rather different view of the problem of alienation. It was the work of Feliks Falk, one of the co-founders of the "cinema of moral unrest" (a group that criticised the actions of the communist authorities and anticipated the Solidarity workers' protests of the late 1970s). The veteran director was able to combine accurate social diagnosis with an attempt at analysing an ambiguous state official who does something evil (destroys people) in the name of the common good (by collecting debts). The lead role, played by the outstanding middle-aged actor Andrzej Chyra, paints an astonishingly realistic portrait of the fanatical debt-collector in whom humanity finally begins to awaken. Falk's *The Collector* has been compared to his first film *Top Dog* (*Wodzirej*, 1977), made in the 1970s; an indictment of the hypocrisy of the Polish People's Republic-era apparatchiks who had no scruples about getting into power. In many respects, Chyra's character (Lucek) is reminiscent of *Top Dog's* hero, Lutek Danielak (played by Jerzy Stuhr), even though the films were set in different circumstances and had entirely different aims.

FAMILY DISASTERS AND A RAY OF HOPE

Heavy pessimism was a particular characteristic of the middle-aged generation. They criticised inequality and the lack of prospects or state protection, focused on mechanisms of social depravity which left people with no chance in life, and this coincided with no less depressing visions of failed private lives, weakened family ties, marital crises, etc.

This trend increased towards the end of the first decade of the 21st century: Andrzej Jakimowski's *Tricks* (*Sztuczki*, 2007), an intimate story of a broken, fatherless home which verges on the metaphysical with its Silesian realism, became popular thanks to the Europa Cinemas Label it won in Venice; Krzysztof Krauze's *Saviour Square* (*Plac Zbawiciela*, 2006) caused reverberations with its story of an infanticidal mother. Małgorzata Szumowska gained even greater prominence by winning a Silver Leopard in Locarno for *33 Scenes from Life* (*33 sceny z życia*, 2008), the portrait of a mature woman whose parents die. This moving film which records her painful, personal experiences is no conventional elegy that dwells on the agony of losing loved ones. It is more of an admission of emotional helplessness when faced with familiar forms of expressing one's grief, fear, solitude and bereavement. The trauma following the tragedy proves so strong that it gives a grotesque feeling of being involved in some unwanted, absurd show, in which stupid rituals offer no help at all in dealing with misfortune. Quite the opposite, in fact – they elicit detachment and even laughter. Another phenomenon noticed and promoted by the critics is the work of 30-year-old Przemysław Wojcieszek, a director

Day of the Wacko,
dir. Marek Koterski
↑

The Collector,
dir. Feliks Falk
↓

183 POLISH CINEMA SUCCESS STORIES

so different from the rest of his young peers that, in his case, it is impossible to speak of any generational ties or common ideological bonds. Wojcieszek's defiance amounts to his rejection of pessimism, and his acknowledgment that films' heroes are entitled to their own little existence in Poland. This shockingly optimistic suggestion is plainly visible in his drama *Louder than Bombs* (*Głośniej od bomb*, 2001) and his bitter comedy *The Perfect Afternoon* (*Doskonałe popołudnie*, 2005), and he is gaining more and more support thanks to his vitality and common sense. Wojcieszek is opposed to the vision of Poland as a horrible place where everything is a failure. He asserts that, despite the general mess, overall degradation, disturbed outlook on life, political divisions, and economic fraud on an unheard-of scale, Poland is still a country that has been given a historic chance which should not be wasted. This is why his heroes suffer, hate and curse the place, but agree to stay there in the end. A new order is slowly emerging from the Polish dirt, boorishness and paranoia – a free, democratic, and better country. All you need to do is notice it.

Handsome, innocent gangsters

The Polish masses, meanwhile, have obviously been making completely different choices over the last two decades. Hungry for Hollywood-style entertainment, they were not

← *Louder than Bombs*, dir. Przemysław Wojcieszek

↓ *Killer*, dir. Juliusz Machulski

particularly interested in ambitious films by the masters (except Wajda's *Katyn* and Polański's *The Pianist*) or the difficult subject matter of films praised by the critics. Their first love in the early 1990s was the extremely young director Władysław Pasikowski, of whom Andrzej Wajda spoke jealously, saying that he knew things about the Polish audience that no-one else understood. Pasikowski was knowledgeable about one specific field of cinema: he made action films involving cops and robbers, lots of blood, corpses and shoot-outs. He made references to Tarantino but, unlike the illustrious American, was not at all interested in playing postmodernist games of form, and instead sought close contact with true-to-life reality that was as masculine, brutal and depraved as possible. The hero of Pasikowski's first big hit, the thriller *Pigs* (*Psy*, 1992), is a former secret serviceman fighting against his militia colleagues who have not passed the post-communist integrity tests. Pasikowski crossed Polish cinema's existing divide between noble members of the opposition and vicious law-enforcers. Casting the amazingly popular and charismatic star Bogusław Linda as a good secret serviceman, he wreaked havoc on the imaginations of the audience by making them identify with him being right. The martyrological ethos was thus demolished, and he introduced a new one that contradicted all traditions and ideological disputes.

The success of Pasikowski, who followed up *Pigs'* popularity by making a sequel, *Pigs 2: The Last Blood*, inspired other Polish filmmakers to develop and follow his lead. First of all, an array of variously talented directors started making gangster movie parodies. Among the most popular were Juliusz Machulski's *quid pro quo* pastiches *Killer* (*Kiler*, 1997) and *2 Killers* (*Kilerów 2-óch*, 1999), in which a decent Warsaw taxi driver is mistaken for a dangerous mafia boss. Another example is Olaf Lubaszenko's comedy *Boys Don't Cry* (*Chłopaki nie płaczą*, 2000), in which lovable criminals mostly fight over a stolen briefcase full of money. And when local inspiration was drying up, there was still fun to be had making local imitations of foreign hits like *Léon* (Maciej Ślesicki's *Sara*, 1997) or *Pulp Fiction* (Jarosław Żamojda's *Fast Lane* [*Młode wilki*, 1995]).

BIG-BUDGET COSTUME DRAMAS

Once the craze for action thrillers about the charms of mafia life (which the reviewers called "bandit movies") had passed, super-productions started to become incredibly popular. Three of these – Jerzy Hoffman's *With Fire and Sword* (*Ogniem i mieczem*), Andrzej Wajda's *Pan Tadeusz* and Jerzy Kawalerowicz's *Quo Vadis* – even managed to do better than James Cameron's Oscar-winning *Titanic*, which was watched by 3.5 million Poles. Twice as many people went to see Hoffman's costume drama (7.1 million), 6.1 million saw *Pan Tadeusz*, and 4.2 million watched Kawalerowicz's historical epic.

All these films were adaptations of well-known historical novels that had been eagerly read by successive generations of Poles. Made in order to "strengthen our hearts", their intention was to reinforce our sense of national pride. *With Fire and Sword* (1999) was

the last screen adaptation from Henryk Sienkiewicz's *Trilogy*, which also includes *The Deluge* (*Potop*, 1974) and *Colonel Wołodyjowski* (*Pan Wołodyjowski*, 1969). It was a reminder of the 17th century glory days when Polish troops crushed the Cossack uprising in Ukraine. However, fearing he would come across as anti-Ukrainian, the director changed the ending, and generally toned down several opinions that would have been controversial from a contemporary point of view, so that the film emphasises the heroism and courage of both sides.

Andrzej Wajda succeeded by making the actors in *Pan Tadeusz* (1999) speak the original text of the 19th century epic poem written in thirteen-syllable verse. The result was superb, but unfortunately rendered the delicacy of the concept untranslatable into foreign languages. Polishness was identified with an idyllic, mythical country where villains confessed their guilt as everyone else sat around the table at a wedding, forgiving one another for their sins, unlike the degraded Poland around them. It confronted the impoverished lives of ageing emigrants, recalling the idyllic days of their Parisian exile. Wajda's film hit a patriotic note and refreshed people's memories of an idealised past, yet on the other hand, it encouraged reflection on the changes wrought by history, the origins of certain attitudes, and the traditions Poles should identify themselves with nowadays.

Despite being a huge box-office success, only Jerzy Kawalerowicz's *Quo Vadis* (2001) failed to live up to the audience's expectations. Potentially, the film could have been a lot better. Unfortunately, this Polish adaptation of Henryk Sienkiewicz's most famous novel was simply not in the same league as its numerous Hollywood versions. Kawalerowicz intended his vision, depicting the martyrdom of the first Christians, to evoke the revival of faith through symbolic comparisons with the 20th century. Regrettably, instead of on-screen insights, there are decadent banquets, the naked breasts of Nero's concubines, and a model of Rome burning. It is hard to say what was most to blame: Kawalerowicz's poor form (he died shortly after the premiere, aged 85), the pretentious acting, or just the insufficient scale of the production, which reduced the whole novel to mere theatrical bombast.

Love and Dance,
dir. Bruce Parramore

For a long time afterwards, mass audiences were still partial to "school reading-list cinema" (as the fashion for these super-productions was sarcastically termed). Adaptations of 20th century classics (Stefan Żeromski's *The Spring to Come* [*Przedwiośnie*] directed by Filip Bajon) and older works (Józef Kraszewski's *An Ancient Tale* [*Stara baśń*] by Jerzy Hoffman and Aleksander Fredro's *The Revenge* [*Zemsta*] by Andrzej Wajda) were also popular.

OF LOVE, SEX AND SUCHLIKE

The heyday of entertainment cinema during the last twenty years also saw the birth of a new genre: Warsaw-style romantic comedies, which were just as well-liked by audiences. Middle-class melodramas made an unexpected comeback in Great Britain, particularly thanks to the comedy *Four Weddings and a Funeral* and Helen Fielding's bestseller *Bridget Jones's Diary*. As a result, this trend was willingly adopted, based on prose by Katarzyna Grochola and other syrupy Polish romance specialists. Several dozen such attempts have appeared in just the last few years, and their titles say it all: *Never Ever!* (*Nigdy w życiu!*, 2004), *Just Love Me* (*Tylko mnie kochaj*, 2006), *Don't Lie, Darling* (*Nie kłam, kochanie*, 2008), *Love and Dance* (*Kochaj i tańcz*, 2008) or *Why Not?!* (*Dlaczego nie!*, 2007). They always follow the same pattern. The husbands of beautiful fashion designers or women's magazine editors cheat on them in huge luxuriantly-decorated villas, so they have to find themselves a better man, and are helped to do so by their adolescent daughters or female friends. For this reason they go to the seaside and learn to dance or cook, and then along comes the perfect man, but unfortunately he is with another woman, who actually turns out to be his sister or a friend, so the way is wide open for a happy end.

Incidentally, it should be mentioned that this kind of film also served to teach the trade to a new marketing system which has become the mainstay of the revived Polish film business. In short, it relies on the effects of media synergy. A bestseller by a popular writer is adapted into a serial that must involve trendy, popular actors and compulsory large doses of product placement in order to reduce production costs significantly. Before its television premiere, a film version is released, which has previously been widely advertised in connection with the serial. Because the producer and distributor, and the owner of a multiplex network, television station and a popular women's magazine (whose readers are potential viewers of the adapted book) generally tend to be one and the same media group, the costs of releasing the film into cinemas are thus reduced even further. The advertising in itself is powerful anyway. It is difficult to judge whether this method is specific to Poland, or whether it is commonly applied everywhere else in Europe in order to make money quickly. Nevertheless, the mechanism works so efficiently that there is no end in sight for the production of romantic comedies.

Two amateurs have become kings of the Polish romantic comedy: Tomasz Konecki (a trained physicist who has adapted extremely well to the role of director) and ex-film critic Andrzej Saramonowicz (who retrained as a playwright and scriptwriter). Two of their comedies have made it into the all-time hall of fame. *Testosterone* (*Testosteron*, 2007) with 1.4 million viewers, and *Ladies* (*Lejdis*, 2008) with 2.5 million viewers, are both unconventional, "hit farces" about failures in love. The first is about men's erotic complexes, while the second deals with women's. Both of them describe sexual phobias and awkward morality issues in the style of Woody Allen, which sets them apart from their provincial competition who still mindlessly copy the western model. In *Testosterone*, Konecki and Saramonowicz expose the infantilism of male dreams of untamed sexual potency. They shatter the myth of harmony between the heart and the mind, and ridicule the enduring stereotypes concerning married life. They even equate contemporary Polish infidelity with the curious rituals of various species of animals, ranging from chimpanzees and gorillas to dragonflies, dolphins and bison. Our rules of love would seem to be like those of wild animals, just as determined, selfish, and designed purely for passing on genetic material. But still, they joke, that should not be the case, since we consider ourselves to be refined, spiritual beings, and by how much we differ from them thanks to our passionate foreplay.

One unquestionable advantage of Saramonowicz and Konecki's comedy was the way they set abstract contemplations about sex drive being superior to social standards into the context of a classic Polish archetype – a wedding reception. Seven men of varying ages, sitting at a table laden with food, bemoan the complex art of attracting fiancées, lovers and wives, which only leads to mass adultery (research says that 70 per cent of married women do not remain faithful to their partners anyway). One of them fails to get married after discovering that his true love's heart belongs to another as he stands before the altar. Seeking solace, he hears confessions from his equally painfully-experienced friends. Not an original idea, but still brilliant, because even if the film lacks any obvious references to Jerzy Andrzejewski's *Pulp* (*Miazga*) or Stanisław Wyspiański's *The Wedding* (*Wesele*), educated cinemagoers will catch the right associations anyway in some of the situations.

In *Ladies*, issues about the consequences of male-female struggles also come across in an interesting way, this time from the perspective of self-sufficient, spiritually-liberated and sex-starved thirty-something women. However, this did not save Konecki and Saramonowicz from the wrath of some aggressively-minded feminists, who accused them of laughing at their movement. "The 'ladies' of the title", complained one of them, "have no professional aspirations. Their liberation boils down to them swearing like troopers, drinking, smoking like chimneys, and having sex reasonably freely." It is worth reiterating that no other Polish filmmakers had ever attempted to analyse men's fears of the incomprehensible, demonic nature of femininity so candidly, so the commercial success of both films was assured in advance.

WE LOVE THE POPE

During the period we are discussing here, films with a religious theme were especially successful. Appetites had already been whetted by Jerzy Kawalerowicz's aforementioned super-production *Quo Vadis*. In the past, dramas like Jerzy Łukaszewicz's *Faustyna* about the blessed mystic Helena Kowalska, or Teresa Kotlarczyk's *The Primate* (*Prymas. Trzy lata z tysiąca*, 2000) about primate Stefan Wyszyński's arrest and imprisonment in a Stalinist jail, had brought in sizeable revenues. However, the trend for religious cinema only took off seriously following the death of Pope John Paul II. Three Pope-related films were produced very rapidly by western television channels as co-productions with Poland: Giacomo Battiato's *Karol: A Man Who Became Pope* (2005) and *Karol: The Pope, The Man* (2006), both starring Piotr Adamczyk in the title role, and *Pope John Paul II* (2005) by John Kent Harrison, starring Jon Voight. All three were shown in Polish cinemas and achieved remarkable success, with each film being watched by over 1.5 million people. Similarly, Rafał Wieczyński's *Popiełuszko: Freedom is Within Us* (*Popiełuszko. Wolność jest w nas*, 2009), a biopic about the murdered priest Jerzy Popiełuszko, was mostly made using state funds.

Supported by lavish media campaigns, the artistic quality of these films generally left a lot to be desired. Simplified and tailored to suit the average consumer, they were more social than artistic achievements. Their weakest points were definitely their discrete, politically correct treatment and avoidance of the most awkward theological, ethical and political issues. However, it must be remarked that Poles watched them with great emotion.

If one adds to this list the most outstanding auteur works and successes of individualists (such as Jan Jakub Kolski, Lech Majewski, Dorota Kędzierzawska, Andrzej Barański, Kazimierz Kutz, Wojciech Marczewski and Grzegorz Królikiewicz), or the remarkably talented wave of new filmmakers (including Borys Lankosz, Xawery Żuławski, Magdalena Piekorz, Michał Rosa and Greg Zgliński), as well as promising work by representatives of the younger generation (e.g. Anna Kazejak, Jan Komasa or Filip Marczewski), then the future of Polish cinema is assured.

Translated by Mark Bence

STRATEGIES OF POLISH COMMERCIAL CINEMA AFTER 1989

MAŁGORZATA SADOWSKA

A real revolution came to Polish cinema in 1989. The centralised film industry based on state financing and censorship ceased to exist. For many years there was no effective national institution supporting the development of Polish cinema. In the new market economy appeared the first private producers whose limited resources required support from the state, television stations (which slowly began financing filmmaking, the first public television station TVP and later Canal+), and sponsors. Insufficient funding made producers reluctant to accept ambitious, experimental projects by auteurs as there was little promise of return on the initial investment. The situation of directors also changed radically. Thus far they had enjoyed a special status – their political and social mission was well defined and they were on good terms with their audience who easily made sense of the Aesopian language developed over the years of struggle with the state. With the fall of communism this ideological, or even spiritual relationship between the artists and the audience was disrupted. The former were released from their obligations towards their country and suddenly felt lost. The latter, tired with politics, no longer needed moral authorities and their guidance, needing only to be entertained. A whole new generation of adults did not remember the Solidarity movement and were not at all interested in settling historical accounts. Cinemas and the newly established rental video phenomenon were flooded with hitherto unavailable Hollywood productions. Marek Haltof in his book *Polish National Cinema* (Berghahn Books, 2002) estimates that in 1991, "60 per cent of the Polish repertoire consisted of American films (as much as 73 per cent in 1992). They were heavily promoted and well distributed. The average number of prints used for the release of an American film ranged from twenty to fifty. Only five to fifteen copies of films from Poland and other parts of Europe were distributed on release." In this climate of financial collapse, distrust toward local artists, and a necessity to compete with American productions, there emerged a new generation of filmmakers who accepted the necessity to cater for the needs of a mass audience. Jacek Skalski, Władysław Pasikowski, Maciej Dutkiewicz, Jarosław Żamojda, Maciej Ślesicki and Łukasz Zadrzyński were the first to embrace previously derided genres like action movies and implemented tried and tested Hollywood formulae for the local market. This was this group of directors who after the change shaped Polish cinema.

Pigs gorge themselves

Jarosław Żamojda, the director of one of the most commercially successful films of the 1990s, *Fast Lane* (*Młode wilki*, 1995), said in an interview given to the monthly *Cinema* magazine, "Speaking of the Americanisation of cinema, we should not underestimate the fact that our everyday life has become Americanised too. [...] We put on clothes from other countries and wear them as our own, the same applies to the reception of art." ("I don't make it easy", *Cinema* 01/2001). Many of his colleagues would agree with this opinion, as they also turned to American formulae to please fans of *The Terminator, Die Hard, Speed* and Spielberg movies. For financial reasons Polish filmmakers were unable to provide similarly spectacular entertainment, but they heavily replicated the narrative patterns of Hollywood productions and indeed, "wore them as their own". A young audience and the new generation of filmmakers were brought together not only because of their passion for Hollywood but their belief that entertainment is the way for cinema to go. They united against authorities and high culture, sometimes also against school. These old institutions and values seemed inadequate in new times. New cinema strengthened the contempt the young audience expressed for "old farts" (we see the recurring theme of conflict between the old and the young in many films, including *The Bash* [*Balanga*] by Łukasz Wylężałek, *Fast Lane* [*Młode wilki*] by Jarosław Żamojda, and *Bitter-Sweet* [*Słodko-gorzki*] by Władysław Pasikowski). A famous sentiment of Andrzej Wajda's from an interview was often quoted, "Pasikowski as such is not purely my interest. I am more interested in his audience. He knows something about this audience that I do not know, something I may not even want to know" (*Kino*, 04/1993). Pasikowski himself did not make a secret of what he knew about the typical viewer of his films. "For me history is 1956 and for him it is 1981. He can choose from twenty channels of satellite TV where the longest take lasts six seconds [...] His world is not divided between the west and the wast but between the good and the bad. He has a passport at hand and is wise enough to learn English, but most importantly he is longing for basic values: love, peace, honesty, family, justice", he said in an interview for *Film* (04/1994).

To this viewer, familiar with pop culture and fascinated by it, Pasikowski and his colleagues offered a cinema which was more or less a successful copy of American action movies, full of references to Hollywood blockbusters. Polish "American" films created Hollywood-type heroes, but they were set in a familiar Polish reality – like the greatest blockbuster of the 1990s, even today boasting the status of a "cult" movie, *Pigs* (*Psy*, 1992) by Władysław Pasikowski. Interestingly, Pasikowski always invented foreign sounding names for his protagonists: Alex, Andre, Kroll, Berger, Mayer, Keller. The names alone were references to the "better" film world.

Controversially, the main hero of *Pigs* is a former officer of the Security Service of the People's Republic of Poland. Franz Maurer, charismatically portrayed by Bogusław Linda is a well known "loser" from American films who finds himself in the specific situation of a Poland in transformation. This was another meaningful decision by Pasikowski, since thus far Linda had been an actor-symbol associated with the "cinema of moral anxiety", previously cast by Kieślowski and Holland and whose many films were withdrawn from distribution at the request of the censorship office.

Franz starts working for the police and soon has to face a dangerous gang set up with the help of some of his unemployed colleagues from the secret service. A bloody battle ensues. Brutal (and well-executed for the screen) skirmishes with ex-friends are not the only difficult experiences shaping the identity of our hero. Maurer is betrayed by the country he was serving over the years, by his best friend and, of course, by his woman. The film world created by Pasikowski is dark and gloomy, immersed in chaos, lawlessness and deprived of hope. The only guidance for the hero is his own moral code and his set of principles. The director was often accused of using too much violence and coarse language, but also of nihilism and blasphemy. In one of the scenes he is said to have profaned the Solidarity protest song *Ballad on Janek Wiśniewski* (*Ballada o Janku Wiśniewskim*) devoted to a worker killed by the militia during the 1970 demonstrations in the northern Baltic coastal cities. Quite tellingly the same song was sung by Krystyna Janda in *Man of Iron* (*Człowiek z żelaza*, 1981) directed by Andrzej Wajda. Here the ballad was sung by drunk secret service officers who carry one of their colleagues on unhinged doors after a drinking session. "I was mocking those, who from December 1970 until now cannot get over this suffering and use it as a banner, even when half of them did not even know at the time where Gdańsk was", Pasikowski explains.

Wajda later admitted that he was so disturbed by the scene that he wanted to leave the cinema. However young audiences reacted enthusiastically to the screenings. It might have been that what they found particularly attractive was the assault on the older generation of their parents who cherished the myth of Solidarity.

With this type of film, critics coined the phrase "bandit cinema" and underlined that they glorified violence and made heroes of people closely related to the underworld, who often exceed the limits, who are guided by their own ambivalent moral codes and who are fascinated with violence and do not hesitate to use it. The image of a cynical thug clung to Linda for years. In the following films he portrayed similar heroes, in *Demons of War* (*Demony wojny według Goi*, 1998), *Operation Samoom* (*Operacja Samum*, 1999), and *Reich* (2001) by Władysław Pasikowski; *Private Town* (*Miasto prywatne*, 1995) by Jacek Skalski; *Sara* (1997) by Maciej Ślesicki; and in the co-production *Sekal Has to Die* (*Zabić Sekala*, 1998) by Vladimir Michalek.

Linda is the undisputed idol and icon of Polish cinema of the 1990s. Of this there are no doubts among critics and the audience. This exceptionally gifted actor was able to endow his somewhat conventional heroes with an unusual charisma. The nonchalance with which he imbued his lines (dozens of which became popular catch-phrases), the cynical smile, the subtle distance to the Hollywood heroes he himself was modelled on, all this effectively enticed the audience, both women and men. His heroes were bitter, experienced, and betrayed, hiding their sensitivity behind cynicism. These features

make an archetypical thug, but the directors put him in a Polish setting and ascribed his disillusionment to the political transformation. The actor himself declared, "People are fed up with martyrology, combatants and venality. They are mad about the situation the country is in. My character in *Pigs* is built from this anger and hatred toward the new reality". Doubtless, these emotions were shared by many Poles.

With time, film critics noticed that Linda, after Zbyszek Cybulski and Daniel Olbrychski, was the next embodiment of the Polish romantic hero who himself is an expression of the Polish fate. Interestingly, there was no-one to succeed Linda in this respect. It can be that the myth of a romantic hero in Polish cinema has lost its *raison d'être* forever, or at least for the time being.

HONESTY IS FOR SUCKERS

The unbelievable box-office success of *Pigs* (over 300,000 viewers) and prior to that of *Kroll* (where within the conventions of an action movie the director portrayed brutal relations in the army) resulted in a grand following of this formula. Pasikowski made a less accomplished sequel *Pigs 2: The Last Blood* (*Psy 2: Ostatnia krew*, 1994) which ranked still higher at the box office (684,000 viewers). In times when it was considered almost inappropriate to watch Polish films, this was an achievement.

Directors who came after Pasikowski also found inspiration in the clichés of action movies. The audiences were attracted by a combination of fast-paced action, violence, and a love story. The aesthetics of MTV and advertising were making their way into cinema: fast editing and scenes consisting of clusters of eye-catching takes.

The screens became populated by gangsters, Mafia soldiers, smugglers, corrupt politicians and businessmen with a connection to the underground: there were thugs and their trophy women ("bandit cinema" is typically misogynist, and this makes its male heroes even more stereotypically male).

In *Private Town* (1994) by Jacek Skalski, two backyard friends form a group that has now grown into a gang, fiercely fighting with one another to win control over the town and a woman. In *Night Graffiti* (*Nocne graffiti*, 1996) by Maciej Dutkiewicz the ex-captain of an élite commando unit declares war against drug dealers, and Łukasz Zadrzyński

Pigs,
dir. Władysław Pasikowski

in *Billboard* (1998) sends the protagonist, an advertising hot shot, into the dark world of the criminal underground and its attendant perversity, which is the reverse of the idealised and luxurious world known from adverts. The protagonist of *Amok* (1998) enters the world of temptation related to stock exchange activities.

As well as the leading stars created by action films and thrillers (Bogusław Linda, Marek Kondrat and Cezary Pazura) the directors cast other stars too. The leading roles in *Night Graffiti* (1996) by Maciej Dutkiewicz were played by the, at the time, extremely popular singers, Kasia Kowalska and Robert Janowski, who was well known from the greatly successful musical *Metro*. In *Billboard* (1998) by Łukasz Zadrzyński two music idols of the young generation were featured, Paweł Kukiz and Justyna Steczkowska. Producers and directors started to perceive music as a magnet for attracting audiences. Well-known artists wrote songs for films and soundtracks; those hits were later released commercially. Rock group Various Manx appeared on the soundtrack to the cult classic *Fast Lane* (1995) by Jarosław Żamojda, the soundtrack to *Billboard* contained songs by The Ramones, Paweł Kukiz and Nick Cave. On the *Night Graffiti* soundtrack there were songs by Kasia Kowalska and again Various Manx. Casting the music world's top stars and utilising music in film for the sake of promotion is now a standard marketing practice, but in the 1990s it was a novelty.

In "bandit cinema" there was a sub-genre focusing on teenagers. Some of the films claimed to be speaking on behalf of the generation, like the brutal *The Bash* (1993) by Łukasz Wylężałek, where the new Polish reality was shown as the setting of a brutal battle (literally) between the frustrated older generation and the young, deprived of guidance. Wylężałek squarely lays full responsibility upon the adults for the evil and violence in this brutal and nihilistic film. In *Bitter-Sweet* (1996) Pasikowski adopted the same convention and portrayed the environment of alienated teenagers – proving he can approach the subject matter gently. The greatest teenage blockbuster remained *Fast Lane* (1995) by Jarosław Żamojda and its sequel *Fast Lane ½* (*Młode wilki ½*, 1997). The director claimed he was pressured by the young who flooded him with hundreds of letters. "You've got to live fast and hard while you're young", "we study life", "there was no yesterday, there will be no tomorrow, there is only today" – are some of the lines from the film that many people accepted as their personal motto (from among 550,000 of those who watched the original and 600,000 viewers of the sequel). Both parts, inconsistent in terms of the script and the directing, portray the life of a group of high-school students who join

Night Graffiti, dir. Maciej Dutkiewicz

a gang of smugglers. This youth-action movie combined with a love story provided the young audience with a life lesson; the adults were bad, but taking shortcuts in life was no better. It created a new idol – Jarosław Jakimowicz, who in the 1990s was the number one heart-throb of Polish cinema. This charisma-deficient blonde actor who made his *début* in the film became an idol, not only thanks to his good looks. The hero he was playing was cynical but also sensitive, he was a party-goer displaying a weakness for fast cars and even faster money, but deep inside he was appreciative of real friendship. Żamojda managed to combine contrasting extremes: a contempt for dirty money with a fascination for the lifestyle, of which weekends at expensive hotels, rides in luxurious cars, lavish parties, and posh clothes were the inseparable elements. He suggested that it is worth being honest, but more frankly, that honesty is for suckers.

Emotions and money

A separate issue for the cinema of this period and this genre in particular was money. Not only because Polish cinema suddenly enjoyed an influx of dollars, which indicated that Polish cinema was a part of a better reality with a stable currency, but also signalled that Polish cinema was "American", to the same extent that McDonald's and Coca-Cola became "Polish". This dissonance in relation to money in films (negative) and in reality (positive) was an interesting phenomenon.

A new generation of filmmakers clamorously declared that cinema was subject to the rules of the market – which at the time was perceived as arrogant and cynical. It brought new ways of debating cinema. "We finally have in Poland the rules common to most countries in the world. Money has become the most important measurable value", Żamojda said in one interview (*Cinema*, 01/2001). "I want this work to bring me joy and money, and stir the emotions of the viewers", was the definition of a director's role by Maciej Dutkiewicz (*Machina*, 03/1997). "If there are producers who give me money because they think they will make a profit, and top stars want to act in my films, and if I myself am still having fun with this, then I don't see the point in discussing other stuff", was the way Maciej Ślesicki cut short any further enquiries concerning his films (*Cinema*, 05/1997).

All this talk about the profitability of filmmaking was meant to signal the great return of Poland to the family of civilised countries. However, money was also the anti-hero of cinema in the 1990s. In the films of this period wealth was suspicious and rich people were nothing but common criminals, with the exception being that they wore good suits. Greed was the source of conflict, drama and misfortune, first in *Pigs*, and then in *Private Town*, *Billboard*, *Fast Lane* and *Amok*. In the latter, the symbol that embodies evil is the stock exchange. Placing the devil right here, Natalia Koryncka adds a diabolical slant to the newborn capitalism of Poland. The trick Łukasz Zadrzyński makes use of in *Billboard* is similar – here advertising is like the icing-sugar on an evil reality. Again, lucrative ventures (that of an advertising agency) and striving to make it a means to an end, leads people astray and even pushes them into degeneracy. Money means depravity, money means crime, money means boorishness – such were the ways of perceiving wealth by Poles who had lost out economically during the transformation, who had not made it in the new system, and whose attitudes were so well exploited by the money-oriented directors of commercial productions. Or maybe not? It might have been, that even though cynical, the directors properly construed the world view of the audience.

From today's perspective we can clearly see that this cinema, even if detached from reality and limited by convention (it is worth remembering though, that Polish "bandit" films were more of a mix of various conventions), still reflected the emotions of Poles at the time. It produced a pessimistic and gloomy picture which in itself was a declaration of a mistrust in reality. Its protagonists lived in chaos and they felt betrayed. Similar were the emotions of many Poles after 1989 when it appeared that, contrary to expectations, the world did not rapidly change, unlike the values, authorities, customs and ideas. Many felt disillusioned with politics and the so called "thick stroke" – a decision by Tadeusz Mazowiecki's government to hold former activists of the communist regime unaccountable for any damage done to the country. The Polish films of that time reflected this void in political life, and the "grey sphere" in which many found themselves suspended, between the old and the new. *Pigs* in particular seems surprisingly astute today and stands as a fine description of the transformation period when political decisions affecting the present reality were made. Its infamous director, Władysław Pasikowski, appeared to be not only a good craftsman in following American film formulae but also an acute observer of and commentator on Polish politics.

Fast Lane,
dir. Jarosław Żamojda

The birth of commercial cinema at the beginning of the 1990s ushered in a new language, new topics and a new style of debate on films and changed the way films were perceived. They were no longer mere works of art, they were also commodities tailored to the expectations of an audience, attractively designed, well marketed and sold in large quantities. Yet another thing happened at this time. The alliance of filmmakers and critics so significant during the time of the Polish People's Republic came to an end. This was specifically the case for those directors who chose to produce commercial films. Their films met with harsh and vicious criticism and the directors' subsequent commentaries show how heated this conflict was. In interviews, time and time again, the question was repeatedly asked as to why young directors were not willing to speak "their own" language, produce "real" and "truly important" films. "I don't perceive my profession as a vocation. I am not here to present the entire nation with some mission, to transmit something important, some universal truth …", said Ślesicki (*Cinema*, 05/1997). "My mission is to tell interesting stories in an attractive fashion, that's all", added Pasikowski (*Kino*, 02/2001). "As long as the money came from the state, money you didn't have to account for, you could despise commerce. Today it is all about the audience. If you don't want to account for what you have done, then it's easiest to say "I make artistic films", which in the Polish reality means you are doing it for no one", was how Żamojda explained his professional choices (*Kino*, 01/1998). "Kurt Vonnegut said somewhere that the only sensible work of an artist is to bring people pleasure and make their life more bearable. I totally agree with this, although I don't see myself as an artist", opined Maciej Dutkiewicz (*Film*, 05/1999).

Indeed, directors denounced their role as "artists" and consistently stressed the fact they were only craftsmen. Zadrzyński, Ziemiński and Żamojda were working both in the filmmaking industry and in advertising. It was a completely new phenomenon considering that the prestige and strength of Polish cinema was wrought by such names as Wajda, Zanussi, Kieślowski and Holland. The rejection of the professional ethos which made cinema a bearer of important messages from ultimately committed artists, was probably due to pragmatic reasons and partially due to a fascination with the possibilities of the market economy. No matter how aware the rebellious directors, they definitely brought a substantial change to the ways of communicating with the audience. They rejected the predominant discourse shaped by the intelligentsia and invented a new language of communication with the audience. It was both the coarse language and the predictable narrative that the audience felt comfortable with. The idea was to speak in the simplest and most understandable way so that it could be accepted by the biggest possible young audience which even today constitutes the majority of movie-goers. Social dialogue was abandoned in favour of a partnership relation, flattering to the young, but based on a marketing decision. "*Night Graffiti* is addressed to a viewer who goes to the cinema. And we know who goes to the cinema from market research", Maciej Dutkiewicz openly admitted (*Express Wieczorny*, 03/02/1997).

Today, popular cinema has become a part of the day-to-day cultural landscape, as in everywhere else in the world. Critics are no longer so emotional discussing it and being a director of romantic comedies or action films is no longer a betrayal of the profession and the Polish tradition of filmmaking. The gap between critics and directors and their mass audience is of course still there.

FILM ENTERTAINMENT

"It is 1997. Times are bad, so films should let people take a break from reality. When we become a society where no problems exist, it will be the time for more serious productions," prophesied Jarosław Żamojda (*Kino*, 06/1997). Time has proven that he was wrong. The audience now expects even more productions that allow them to take a break from reality, and movies that are even more frivolous.

Action cinema had consumed all of its potential by the end of the 1990s. The change of atmosphere, stabilisation in politics and the economy, the increased affluence of society – all these factors influenced the needs of the audience. The new, gloomier action films were no longer attractive and the directors themselves felt that the formula of this cinema had become stale. The last production of Władysław Pasikowski (in the gangster genre), *Reich* (2001), was unintentionally seen as a parody of previous films and the stardom of

Bogusław Linda began to wane. His thug was no longer convincing. He was pompous, hurt and in as much pain as ever, but this time he was also funny, if not pathetic. Linda himself got tired of the image of the thug and distanced himself from this character. His image started to change with Maciej Ślesicki's *Sara* (1997) which was a freestyle mix of clichés, narrative patterns and threads inspired by popular productions such as *The Godfather, The Bodyguard* or *Léon*, bearing a marked resemblance to the films of the new icon of cinema, Quentin Tarantino. The film was a light comedy, and Linda, who was a bodyguard dating the teenage daughter of his boss (this by the way was a scandal which provided much-needed publicity), had an opportunity to play around with his image.

Sara heralded changes in filmmaking. The mass audience was already familiar with the new reality and accepted even the negative changes brought about by the transformation. It no longer demonised the world around it and no longer perceived it as evil. Lighter shades were expected from cinema as well. This was well understood by Maciej Ślesicki, who said in an interview, "I am really not into the problems of our businessmen, former secret service agents, the poor and workers who get up early to work, because I, Maciej Ślesicki, wouldn't like to watch anything based on that in a movie" (*Cinema*, 05/1997).

The end of the action film trend in Polish cinema came on the heels of a new phenomenon in world (or strictly speaking American) cinema. After Tarantino, directors could no longer take stories about gangs and the sad fates of gangsters seriously. To follow the new flavour – and to make money – Polish filmmakers started to reach for new and already exploited formulae in American cinema. The success of *Sara* was proof that playing with genres was the right thing to do, and its director argued that "people will still watch our films if we stop preaching and treating them like dummies" (*Machina*, 04/1997).

A revelation of this new strategy was the cult film, *Killer* (*Kiler*, 1997), by Juliusz Machulski, dealing a death-blow to "bandit" cinema by ridiculing its formula. Winking at the audience had become a recipe for gaining mass approval. Machulski was probably the right director to begin this trend, as in the 1980s he produced cult comedies with political undercurrents: *Sexmission* (*Seksmisja*) and *King Size* (*Kingsajz*). The title itself suggested the director was mocking real killers. The hero, taxi driver Jurek Kiler, is mistaken for a serial killer. The film is a parade of grotesque characters: clumsy policemen, brain-dead mafiosi and their bimbo wives. Cezary Pazura was cast as Kiler and he immediately became a new idol that suited those new times. Revealing his talent for comedy, Pazura skilfully parodied idols of the past and appeared to be the perfect embodiment of the average Pole. Not a hero but a coward, not a gangster but a taxi driver, not a womaniser but a man no-one would notice on a street. Though embroiled in a criminal affair, he had nothing to do with the thugs from American films. He was a homeboy – and that brought him stardom. The new idol was flexible, cunning, and lacking principles. This, and not weaponry, allowed him to save his bacon.

The new directors of comedies were not only quoting, borrowing and playing with clichés, but also convincing audiences that reality is not quite as dangerous as they might expect after watching the news. They gave them confidence that no matter what the difficulty, one could save one's skin and even gain from it.

Similar to this was the lesson of *Fluke* (*Fuks*, 1999) by Maciej Dutkiewicz. This gangster movie/romantic comedy was advertised as "Good fun with no limits" and the producers made sure that the soundtrack was hip enough for its young audience. It included songs of De Mono, Golden Life, Muniek Staszczyk and Kora Jackowska. The film's success was also due to the great acting team of Agnieszka Krukówna and Maciej Stuhr, who played their roles with grace and fluency. Stuhr was immediately cast by Olaf Lubaszenko, who himself tried to follow the success of Machulski and Dutkiewicz. He produced comedies which were very popular among a younger audience and much disparaged by critics, such as *Boys Don't Cry* (*Chłopaki nie płaczą*, 2000), *Coyote's Morning* (*Poranek kojota*, 2001), *E=mc2* (2002), and his *début Cheat* (*Sztos*, 1997) which was a nostalgic journey back to the times of the Polish People's Republic, and evocative of this era's underworld. Coarse humour, dialogues based solely on wisecracking banter, trivial narrative, clichés and stereotypes delighted the audience with little or no effort towards artistic production – these were the ways to pander to low tastes.

It had to be funny no matter what, and this constraint made the films look like parodies of skits. Gangster stories were mocking previous films by Pasikowski and Żamojda. They neutralised all real-life conflicts and put the audience at ease with the underworld. Lubaszenko's gangsters were likeable and harmless, and even if daft, they always managed to outwit students, artists and other "mugs" who considered themselves to be smart. The young audiences were pleased with the director who finally approved their fascination with easy money and the life of the *nouveau riche* that they aspired to.

Boys Don't Cry,
dir. Olaf Lubaszenko
↗

Teaching the elite a lesson

Making references to what seemed so homely ensured financial success, and from now on the familiar character of the "homie" constantly returned to the screen. It began with the already mentioned *Cheat* by Lubaszenko – an enjoyable portrait of thieves and gamblers, and found its climax in *The Career of Nikos Dyzma* (*Kariera Nikosia Dyzmy*, 2002) by Jacek Bromski – a story with Cezary Pazura as the main protagonist, a boor and a gravedigger who accidentally finds himself frequenting political circles and forges an astonishing political career. The actor's image clung to this type of hero for years to come. All his protagonists are nobodies, who, thanks to their cunning and cynical calculating, as opposed to knowledge or talent, manage to succeed in life. These creations were much applauded by the audience. They shared the belief that an average man can be powerful and they shared a dislike and distrust of the élite – a combination of the two was a guarantee of financial success.

Bromski drew inspiration from the renowned TV series by Jan Rybkowski and Marek Nowicki titled *The Career of Nicodemus Dyzma* (*Kariera Nikodema Dyzmy*, 1980) based upon the famous book of the same title by Tadeusz Dołęga-Mostowicz. It was a scathing satire of short-sighted political élites who could revere a fool as if he were a genius

and allow him to take control of the country. This message was meaningful, both in the original book published before World War II and in the TV series, but Bromski moved it to contemporary times and rendered it much simplified. *The Career of Nikos Dyzma* provides a populist commentary (as happens in politics, everyone is a corrupt stooge) that is poorly produced and caricatured, which makes a rather unsophisticated cabaret of it. Instead of raising concerns about the nature of politics, Nikos Dyzma was presented as a friendly figure, who, being a representative of the people, managed to teach the élite a lesson. In Polish mass cinema, directors all too often allied with the audience behind the back of the intelligentsia, and as in this case, even against it.

In mass cinema, homeliness and Polishness, two sources of our identity, are opposed to what is foreign, alien, new and unknown. Bromski achieved commercial success with the conflict between "us" and "them". The success came with *In Heaven as it is on Earth* (*U Pana Boga za piecem*, 1998), a nostalgic and light-hearted comedy, and was repeated twice more when the two other parts of the trilogy were produced, *God's Little Garden*

The Career of Nikos Dyzma, dir. Jacek Bromski
↑

(*U Pana Boga w ogródku*, 2007) and *God's Little Village* (*U Pana Boga za miedzą*, 2009). All three stories are set in a secluded provincial town run by the mayor, chief police officer, and the priest. The structure of the story is always the same. Every part begins with the arrival of an "intruder" who disturbs the peaceful life of the locals. The locals, despite their flaws, are portrayed as warm and good-hearted. The message is clear, and clearly conservative: evil always comes from the outside, and it comes with new ideas and with change. The best course to take is to avoid contact and wait for the strangers to be expelled, and if necessary to protect the status quo guaranteed by the Church and the Catholic faith. "Let there be war in the world, as long as the Polish village stays calm", wrote the poet Stanisław Wyspiański in his famous drama written at the turn of the 20th century (and later filmed by Andrzej Wajda). If, however, Wyspiański was waxing ironic, it is not the case with Bromski. The audience happily accepted the idyllic and idealistic image of the Polish countryside, which is of course a microcosm of Poland. The film critic Tadeusz Lubelski said, "The authors are not disrespectful of the plagues infesting people at the end of the century: their feeling of insecurity, their fears concerning organised crime and unemployment, their insecurity resulting from the erosion of beliefs formerly found in the Ten Commandments and the degeneration of democracy. In *Heaven as it is on Earth* we see all these plagues, but as in any typical fairy-tale, they are finally overcome and tamed by good men" (*Kino*, 12/1998).

Bromski fully recognised the demands of the audience who, after years of devouring western productions, finally felt the urge to return home, back to Polish tradition and landscape. This need was also answered by Wojciech Adamczyk who directed another successful homespun film, *Howling Wolf Ranch* (*Ranczo Wilkowyje*, 2007). Again, we are served a comedy depicting the idyllic Polish countryside, resistant to novelty and treasuring the most important values: family and faith.

The fairy-tales provided an antidote to Polish complexes: it is true that we are not wealthy or well educated, maybe it is true that we fall behind the rest of Europe – but our homeland is hospitable, warm, and familial. It is a space that provides shelter.

OBLIGATORY READINGS

Comedies depicting the Polish countryside were by no means original inventions of contemporary filmmakers. In fact, they echo the very successful, endlessly repeated

TV trilogy by Sylwester Chęciński: *Our Folks* (*Sami swoi*, 1967), *Take it Easy* (*Nie ma mocnych*, 1974), and *Big Deal* (*Kochaj albo rzuć*, 1977). The trilogy concerns two feuding peasant families who, after being removed from the eastern territories, settle down in the so-called "Regained Territories" incorporated into Poland after the Second World War, in return for the territories annexed by the Soviet Union. Chęciński's comedies were amusing for subsequent generations of viewers and no doubt inspired Bromski and Adamczyk to create their own contemporary versions.

As I have mentioned, financial gain and box office records were not important criteria in the Polish People's Republic: however even this era had its blockbusters with an audience of a couple million. Among them were not only the comedies of Chęciński, but also film adaptations of great works in Polish literature, namely the trilogy (is it just a coincidence that trilogies always ensure success?) by Nobel prize winner Henryk Sienkiewicz. In 1969 Jerzy Hoffman directed *Colonel Wołodyjowski* (*Pan Wołodyjowski*) and in 1974 *The Deluge* (*Potop*). The last part of the trilogy was left unfinished until 1999 when producers considered that it was the right time to bank on the huge popularity of the previous films. Once again Jerzy Hoffman approached the task and the producers did not skimp on the budget. *With Fire and Sword* (*Ogniem i mieczem*, 1999) gained the status of a blockbuster. The film started a new trend in Polish commercial cinema. From now on, the directors eagerly approached works of literature, which, by the way, and not at all accidentally, were obligatory texts in schools. Screenings for classes ensured a high box office turnout and, ultimately, financial success. Andrzej Wajda tried to flirt with the young, mass audience in 1996 when he made *Miss Nobody* (*Panna Nikt*). It was a flop. The book by Tomek Tryzna that the film was based on was a bestseller, however the adaptation was received coldly and critics exposed its shortcomings. Following the fiasco, Wajda decided to leave the young audience to directors of commercial cinema. He felt much more comfortable with adaptations of obligatory texts and decided to adapt one of the most important works of Polish romanticism, the epic poem by Adam Mickiewicz, *Pan Tadeusz*. This time Wajda had a success on his hands. Produced in 1999, *Pan Tadeusz* together with *With Fire and Sword* brought an audience of over 13 million people to theatres. Thanks to Wajda and Hoffman "Polish cinema shared an unprecedented 60 per cent of the local market", writes Marek Haltof in his book *Polish National Cinema* (p. 259). Interestingly, if we look at the charts, Wajda is the undisputed king of the box office after 1989. In the top ten films we find three of his: *Pan Tadeusz*, *The Revenge* (*Zemsta*), and the Oscar nominated *Katyn* (2007). Drawing inspiration from the national literary canon was certainly a good way of enticing an audience to cinemas. The only question is whether box office success translates into a deeper and more real relationship with the audience. There is an opinion that the adaptations allowed some directors, especially those who could not find themselves in the new reality, to reach into the pockets of the audience, while at the same time avoiding contact with their hearts. Adaptations should be seen more as a refuge for those directors who were confused as to what to produce in the reality of cinema "after Pasikowski".

Hot on the heels of Wajda and Hoffman came other directors willing to choose this well-travelled path: Filip Bajon directed *The Spring to Come* (*Przedwiośnie*, 2001) based on a novel by Stefan Żeromski, Gavin Hood (the same who was later awarded an Oscar for *Tsotsi!*) filmed his adaptation of Henryk Sienkiewicz's *In Desert and Wilderness* (*W pustyni i w puszczy*, 2001) (there already existed a film based on the novel, an ever-popular version from 1973), and Marek Brodzki attempted a screen adaptation of the contemporary classic fantasy book by Andrzej Sapkowski, *The Hexer* (*Wiedźmin*, 2001). Jerzy Hofman directed *An Ancient Tale* (*Stara baśń*, 2003) by Józef Ignacy Kraszewski, and Andrzej Wajda shot *The Revenge* (*Zemsta*, 2002) by Aleksander Fredro (one of the main parts in the film was played by Roman Polański). All the above titles were major productions because, unlike before, producers managed to get support from other institutions. During this period banks were very generous and other sponsors were also willing to fall in with these prestigious and safe, as it seemed, investments. Such backers included cosmetics companies, airlines and insurers. This golden period in filmmaking ended with the production of *Quo Vadis* in 2001, the most expensive film ever made in Poland. Its budget amounted to 68 m zloty (although there is no precise figure), which is about $18 m (while the average budget of a film in Poland is around $800,000). The adaptation of this novel by Henryk Sienkiewicz was a dream come true for the director of *Mother Joan of the Angels* (*Matka Joanna od Aniołów*, 1960), Jerzy Kawalerowicz, and it was this director who at the age of 79 made an attempt to take control of this gigantic production. The film was a box-office success mainly because schools made extensive use of it. Artistically speaking, it was yet another failure in Polish cinema. More importantly, however, the financial troubles with the production made investors from outside of the normal funding system extremely cautious and reserved, and thus this golden era of financing came to an end.

What made the Polish audience flock to home-grown blockbusters? It was definitely nostalgia for the legendary productions of the Polish People's Republic, and in part also due to the fact that the films were adaptations of the national literary back-catalogue. Apart from that, according to Marek Haltof, "The commercial success of film adaptations in Poland is almost guaranteed. Regardless of their artistic merit, these films will serve many generations of Poles as handy, albeit sometimes naïve, illustrations of the national literature and the national past" (*Polish National Cinema*, p. 260).

Unquestionably, even if well-known literary names appeared in the credits, new adaptations did not contribute to any social discourse. Their directors did not argue with the authors and did not make their works relevant to the present day. As some critics claim, the success of such blockbusters is a result of a longing for the lost grandiosity of a mythical golden era when heroes were real, as opposed to nowadays when they are non existent, both in reality and in the cinema. These "romantic-nostalgic" films, according to Haltof, were intended to reassure the audience rather than challenge them by asking questions and raising doubts.

A spin-off of this trend in popular cinema was biographies of "the greatest" – naïve, simplified, glorifying, but most importantly profitable to producers and popular among the audience. There were films on the life of Chopin – *Chopin: Desire for Love* (*Chopin: Pragnienie miłości*, 2002), on Jerzy Popiełuszko, a Catholic priest associated with the Solidarity opposition and murdered by the secret services in 1984 – *Popiełuszko: Freedom is Within Us* (*Popiełuszko: Wolność jest w nas*, 2009), on the legendary general of the Home Army Emil Fieldorf – *General Nil* (*Generał Nil*, 2009), and finally a few popular yet lacking in artistic merit co-productions on John Paul II, to name but two: *Karol: A Man Who Became Pope* (*Karol – człowiek, który został papieżem*, 2004) and *Karol: The Pope, The Man* (*Karol – papież, który pozostał człowiekiem*, 2005). With the increasing growth of patriotism among the young and a growing interest in the past and its heroes, we can expect more productions on national history directed at a mass audience.

Just love me

If in the case of blockbusters it is difficult to verify the real reason for their box-office success (knowing for example that many schools organised obligatory trips to cinemas, not to mention army units and workers who received tickets from the workers' social fund), however in the case of romantic comedies we can have no such doubts. Here we have to presume the audience go to cinemas voluntarily. No matter the many shortcomings of romantic comedy films, these productions are among the most successful. As film critic Grażyna Stachówna ironically writes, the artistic refinement of Polish romantic comedies proves that their producers are deeply convinced that "their audience – mostly women – will be satisfied with anything, that they have little or no familiarity with well-made foreign comedies, that they are so frustrated with their lives that anything will do to comfort them and to let them escape from reality into a safe and kitschy dream world" ("The dreams of beauty and love of life", *Kino*, 2008). So how bad are these films? They are so bad that some creators are ashamed to sign their scripts with their real names, as is the case of Ryszard Zatorski in *Why not?!* (*Dlaczego nie!*, 2007).

Sure there are agile creators of the genre, like the duo Tomasz Konecki and Andrzej Saramonowicz, who use typical narrative structures of well-known romantic comedies, but direct their urban love-story films toward a more refined audience who easily recognises the references and direct quotations, who values witty dialogue and good acting, who understands such concepts as "feminism" and who does not leave the cinema when confronted by an on-screen lesbian. In the comedies *Testosterone* (*Testosteron*, 2007), *Ladies* (*Lejdis*, 2008), *The Perfect Guy for My Girlfriend* (*Idealny facet dla mojej dziewczyny*, 2009), Konecki and Saramonowicz willingly play with the extremes and achieve comic effect by juxtaposing feminists and Catholics, the woman's world and the man's world. Even if more modern and more "liberal" in substance and more professionally made, these comedies still refer to the same world of values as their inferior counterparts, the world of values where ultimately it is love that matters and where its purest expression is found within the family.

The first directors of this long-neglected genre ("After 1945, melodramas were banned for being a bourgeois genre, and comedies were intended to lash society with satire", says Stachówna) were Krzysztof Lang with his *Paper Marriage* (*Papierowe małżeństwo*, 1991) and Piotr Wereśniak with *In Love* (*Zakochani*, 2000). The real surge begun a couple of years later and is still ongoing today. This includes melodramas like Waldemar Krzystek's *Little Moscow* (*Mała Moskwa*, 2008), a winner in the 2008 Polish Feature Films Festival in Gdynia, or *Solitude @Net* (*Samotność w sieci*, 2007) by Witold Adamek (based on a bestselling romance by Janusz L. Wiśniewski).

How can one explain the popularity of these films knowing they lack artistic merit? One thing is that the producers have properly sensed the audience's urge to escape from other issues. A case in point was the success of titles by Katarzyna Grochola, the author of novels depicting the lives of mature women, who, after divorce, get their second chance in life and find new love. On the other hand, it might have been due to the growing popularity of soap operas; *L for Love* (*M jak Miłość*) created by Ilona Łepkowska, the "queen of Polish soap opera", attained its peak popularity in 2005 with over 12 m viewers. No wonder then, that producers preferred to exploit successful television formulae and employ experienced television directors. Both Ilona Łepkowska and Katarzyna Grochola joined these new productions as scriptwriters and producers. *Never Ever!* (*Nigdy w życiu!*, 2004) by Ryszard Zatorski, *I'll Show You!* (*Ja wam pokażę!*, 2006) by Denis Delić, *Just Love Me* (*Tylko mnie kochaj*, 2006) and *Why Not?!* (*Dlaczego nie!*, 2007) by Zatorski, *One More Time* (*Jeszcze raz*, 2007) by Mariusz Malec, *Expecting Love* (*Mała wielka miłość*, 2008) by Łukasz Karwowski, *Midnight Talks* (*Rozmowy nocą*, 2008) by Maciej Żak, *Don't Lie, Darling* (*Nie kłam, kochanie*, 2008) by Piotr Wereśniak, *Love and Dance* (*Kochaj i tańcz*, 2008) by Bruce Parramore – the list of productions gets longer by the year. The TV audience can see on the big screen what they already know and like – "simple and predictable narratives, uncomplicated heroes, melodramatic solutions, stereotypes, no authenticity and aesthetic kitsch", enumerates Stachówna.

↑
General Nil,
dir. Ryszard Bugajski

→
Little Moscow,
dir. Waldemar Krzystek

The transfer from television to cinema does not only concern the ideas, narrative, conservative message and film style employed in the original soap operas. There is also the transfer of soap opera actors, an interesting phenomenon taking into account that in America, film actors, and soap opera and sitcom actors are two separate entities: the cases of transfers are rare and always well discussed, as occured with George Clooney or Jennifer Aniston. In Poland, a soap opera actor's popularity opens the door to cinema, because a well-known face is a guarantee of box office success. Besides, the producers of romantic comedies pay attention to the way they can imperceptibly transfer viewers from the world of soap opera to the world of film, which of course resembles that of a soap opera. Moreover, cinema has become a part of a promotional strategy of media concerns such as TVN, which advertise *their* actors, programmes and vision of the world in films. The finest example of such a practice is *Love and Dance*, a poorly made and extremely popular film promoting TVN programmes *You Can Dance* and *Dancing with the Stars* (*Taniec z Gwiazdami*).

The success of Polish romantic comedies is not only the result of flattering the tastes of soap opera viewers, but can also be ascribed to the marketing practice of selling to the audience particular aspirations in a fashion similar to that of popular magazines. The readers of those magazines cannot afford the advertised clothes and cosmetics, but the magazine itself is a substitute for an imagined luxury and prosperity. The same applies to the films which often depict urban life. It is described as if the cities were filled solely with office buildings made of glass, apartment buildings and stylish blocks of flats, and as if these were inhabited by their equally stylish and wealthy residents – the heroes of our dreams. More than love, romantic comedies promote a lifestyle associated with specific products and brands. One may sometimes get the impression that the scripts were hastily written to accompany the product placement, which is present in these films on an unprecedented scale (it first appeared in Polish cinema in the mid-1990s, initially clumsily in the films of Władysław Pasikowski). Stachówna claims there were ten companies advertised in *Never Ever!* and in *I'll Show You* there were twelve. True love needs packaging – filmmakers create the illusion that you can start from the packaging and when the initial requirements of a certain lifestyle are met, the feeling will arise automatically to fill the void. Love is transformed into a commodity and films metamorphose into advertisements of the consumerist lifestyle. Producers make money,

TV stations promote themselves at the lowest possible cost, and a cheerful audience gets its portion of beautiful illusions. It would be a lie to suggest that in the past Polish viewers never allowed themselves to be deceived. But they definitely have never allowed themselves to be deceived so easily.

A list of films made after 1989 with the biggest audience figures (source: PISF, January 2010):

With Fire and Sword (*Ogniem i mieczem*, 1999) directed by Jerzy Hoffman, audience: 7,151,354
Pan Tadeusz (*Pan Tadeusz*, 1999), directed by Andrzej Wajda, audience: 6,168,344
Quo vadis (2001), directed by Jerzy Kawalerowicz, audience: 4,300,351
Katyn (2007), directed by Andrzej Wajda, audience: 2,763,592
Ladies (*Lejdis*, 2008), directed by Tomasz Konecki, Andrzej Saramonowicz, audience: 2,530,066
In Desert and Wilderness (*W pustyni i w puszczy*, 2001) directed by Gavin Hood, audience: 2,227,228
Killer (*Kiler*, 1997), directed by Juliusz Machulski, audience: 2,200,943
The Revenge (*Zemsta*, 2002) directed by Andrzej Wajda, audience: 1,976,984
The Spring to Come (*Przedwiośnie*, 2001) directed by Filip Bajon, audience: 1,743,933
Just Love Me (*Tylko mnie kochaj*, 2006) directed by Ryszard Zatorski, audience: 1,669,259

Translated by Bartłomiej Reszuta

TRADITION AND DIVERSITY: AN OUTLINE OF POLISH FILM EDUCATION

KRZYSZTOF ŚWIREK

Before 1989 there were only two professional ways into the film industry in Poland: one was the National Higher School of Film, Television and Theatre in Łódź, and the second was the Faculty of Radio and Television at the University of Silesia. Both of these were state schools and both were afforded university status. Twenty years after the political transformation, there has emerged a strongly-developed private sector and the educational opportunities are now more varied. The schools boasting long traditions in the education of filmmakers are still of a great importance; however, film education is no longer limited to these institutions alone.

Who is the camera?

The National Higher School of Film, Television and Theatre in Łódź has a history that can be both inspiring and intimidating to students. It was one of the first of its kind in the world; among its graduates were Andrzej Wajda and Roman Polański, and a long-standing professor was Wojciech Jerzy Has – a representative of auteur cinema and director of *The Saragossa Manuscript* (*Rękopis znaleziony w Saragossie*, 1964) and *The Hour-Glass Sanatorium* (*Sanatorium pod klepsydrą*, 1973). Among the graduates of its Cinematography Faculty were several directors of photography who later achieved international acclaim: Andrzej Bartkowiak, Jerzy Zieliński, Sławomir Idziak, Piotr Sobociński and Andrzej Jaroszewicz. A student entering the school grounds is aware of the continuity of the tradition of film art – just as it was understood in the great times of auteur cinema. This awareness incites great ambitions and is a great challenge: a challenge to find one's own place in this great history and to equal those who follow the same path.

The school was established in 1948 in order to provide staff for Poland's film industry, which was set up after the war. At that time, Poland was behind the iron curtain and the film industry was nationalised. The sole film producer was the state and cinema was implemented as a propaganda tool. Its creation was assigned to a group of activists from the "Start" organization of film buffs, which was active before the war and associated with the communist left. Already before the war this group was engaged in the promotion of the idea of establishing a "socially useful" and artistic film industry and was involved in the popularisation of western and Soviet avant-garde cinema, which was nearly unheard of in Poland. The state authorities were convinced that the choice of a politically-engaged management for the school was an ideal solution.

However, the effects of their work fell short of expectations. The school trained the representatives of the later avant-garde of Polish artistic cinema, but not propagandists: Andrzej Wajda, director of *Ashes and Diamonds* (*Popiół i diament*, 1958) and *Man of Iron* (*Człowiek z żelaza*, 1981); Kazimierz Kutz, director of *Nobody's Calling* (*Nikt nie woła,*

1960), a film telling the story of Polish resistance soldiers; and Andrzej Munk, who in his comedy *Bad Luck* (*Zezowate szczęście,* 1960) discussed the problem of political opportunism. The first generation of graduates was able to undertake work at exactly the right time, namely when Stalin died and when political terror and censorship started to loosen their grip. New films had political underpinnings but reflected the political "thaw" in spirit.

From the beginning the school's idea of teaching was to merge humanities with practice and workshop skills. Students attended courses in film history, art and philosophy. Equally important as the basics of lighting the scenes in a film, or operating a camera, was developing one's taste in film. Of course instead of making films and working in the film industry, most camera operators and directors find their place in television or advertising. Is it likely then, that this refined taste is more of a handicap rather than an advantage in such a business? Absolutely not, suggests one of the graduates of the directing department – the skills acquired in a full immersion programme may be well applied to less demanding work. It is enough to mention classes teaching students how to express ideas in short films. Even first-year students produce short *études*, which are often shot in one well-planned take and feature an interesting story. These lessons on precision and accuracy provided by the representatives of auteur cinema can be well used in advertising. "The school's aim is to provide students with workshop skills that can be later used in many fields", claims another student – in television, advertising, and in the case of directors, also in theatre.

Practical assignments are essential for training and, though costly, work on film stock is seen as necessary for a high standard of education. This is not an option in private schools. We might think that in the age of the digital camera, the experience itself is not that much of a necessity. However, students emphasise its importance. Shooting with film stock is a different kind of production, accompanied by a different approach by the crew, and – most importantly – a unique "feeling". "This is magic", says Bolek Kielak, a student in the cinematography department, "you can shoot film like Woody Allen or Antonioni. If you have a good idea, you can make it work at a very low cost, but on the other hand, it is an exceptional feeling when it is screened in a cinema and you watch your film, recorded on film stock and projected from a real film copy." As we might have expected from a student of cinematography, the speaker underlined that "what you do and how you do it are equally important".

To provide the unique experience of work with film stock, the school maintains a highly professional infrastructure: analogue and digital cameras, editing rooms, sound stages – all this to get students used to the equipment and professional work, and to let them learn through their own mistakes. Jakub Piątek, a student in the directing department (who produced a 15-minute film at the end of his 3rd year, the so-called "minor diploma") stressed that it is easier to forgive mistakes made with a school crew, which is prepared for the uncertainty of students taking their first steps on the film set. "It shouldn't get professional too quickly", he adds. The school is often described as a "blasting ground", a place where various solutions are tested with a certain margin for error. At the school, the number of professional filmmakers present during shooting is intentionally limited. A film by a student in the directing department will therefore be shot by a beginner camera operator and edited by a full-time student in the editing department. These *études*, even if produced with limited budgets, can still be professional.

The idea behind education at the NHSFTT (PWSFTViT) is to create space between the rules of craftsmanship taught by professors and the individuality of students. Out of one hundred and fifty applicants who wish to undertake studies at the directing department, only six or seven are admitted (a similar ratio can be found in the department of cinematography). As a result, those who passed their finals feel highly distinguished but immediately clash with lecturers who teach them to be critical and to respect basic tenets. "Films obey certain rules, they are usually 90 minutes long, they have three acts, the beginning, the middle and the end", says Marcin Malatyński. Studying is based on a "master and his/her follower" relationship – during the five years of education, each student makes three films, documentaries and feature films, each under the supervision of a different tutor.

As students recall, the first two years of studies call for 12-hour working days. This period of time is necessary to pass on basic workshop skills to the students and to begin shaping their creative sensitivity. Even a single consultation can be of great importance, as can work on a single project or grappling with a single problem. Jakub Piątek recalls the inaugural question asked by Jolanta Dylewska, director of documentary films and director of photography on *Tulpan* (2008) by Siergiej Dworcewoj, "Who is the camera in this take?". Similar is the role of tutors who often criticise the "minor diploma" and graduation works of their students. Just as certain questions and advice increase sensitivity and develop the imagination, the advantage of these unusual dialogues is a critical consideration of one's own work, which is very useful when it comes to control of the subject matter in film narrative, because without answers to even simple questions the film will not be successful. Possibly the first person to have had that influence on students of the directing department is Grzegorz Królikiewicz, who is well known for his artistic refinement, which allowed him to undertake quasi-philosophical reflections of the existential problems of his protagonists in *Through and Through* (*Na wylot*, 1972) and *The Case of Pekosinski* (*Przypadek Pekosińskiego*, 1993), but also for the discipline

characterising his analyses of the masterpieces of cinematography, later published in a series of books often comprising detailed reconstructions of the key sequences of a film. The potential influence of Królikiewicz is realised through his ability to develop artistic ambitions and to teach humility toward classic works.

Just as important is the role of younger tutors who supervise work for "minor diplomas". Among these are Mariusz Grzegorzek and Łukasz Barczyk, who represent the middle and young generations of Polish filmmakers. Both are known as uncompromising and consistently struggling to work solely on their own terms, often facing the difficulties of the contemporary film industry. They teach their students honesty towards one's own vision, and towards the final effect of the students' work, which also has to be honestly evaluated. In those first years, students have the possibility to appreciate one advantage of their education, which is also true of other schools: they learn that school requires a formal regime, forcing students to translate their ideas into real works. The pressure of deadlines and the critical attention of others are among the mobilising factors.

Escape from Liberty Cinema, dir. Wojciech Marczewski
↑

Pornography, dir. Jan Jakub Kolski
↓

The final years in the directing and cinematography departments are when workshop skills are supplemented with meetings with the most experienced filmmakers. Students of the directing department enter master classes held by Robert Gliński, Wojciech Marczewski and Jan Jakub Kolski. Each of the directors presents a different strategy for the auteur's presence in film. Gliński represents film tracing social transformations; his films are "popular" in form, but they take on difficult issues, such as poverty in *Hi, Tereska* (*Cześć Tereska,* 2001), or more recently, child prostitution in *Piggies* (*Świnki,* 2009). In Wojciech Marczewski's work, political and personal threads are intertwined; the analysis of life under an oppressive political regime is at one level a bitter counterpoint to the maturing process (in *Shivers* [*Dreszcze,* 1981]), while on another level it is an excuse to present ironic reflections on the mechanisms which enslave the mind (in *Escape from the Liberty Cinema* [*Ucieczka z kina Wolność,* 1990]). Jan Jakub Kolski in turn represents a variant of magic realism, set in the reality of the Polish countryside. In his films he aspires to universalism and his stories make use of narrative threads which unfold from one film to another. Thus, tutors help students find their own voice, and only secondarily do they provide help with diploma works. In the cinematography department, courses in recent years have been led by Jerzy Wójcik (who collaborated with some of the great names of the Polish School: Andrzej Wajda, Kazimierz Kutz and Andrzej Munk), Witold Sobociński (the director of photography of *Frantic* by Polański and *The Hour-Glass Sanatorium* [*Sanatorium pod klepsydrą*] by Wojciech Jerzy Has) and, since 2009, Jerzy Zieliński (among other things the director of photography of *Washington Square* by Agnieszka Holland). These courses have more to do with the philosophy of motion pictures than an initiation into the secrets of the workshop. The five-year-long studies correspond with the stages of the maturing process and provide time to not only learn the basic rules but also to learn for what they are going to be used.

The annual output of the school is fifteen to twenty full feature films, which makes it the largest producer of film in Poland. "Those films", as Marcin Malatyński reminds us, "are among the competitors in the student film category at many major film festivals: in Cannes, Venice, Berlin, Brest and Oberhausen". The school organises film screenings and the Festival of Theatre and Film Schools. It is worth remembering that the school releases only 10–20 per cent of the films made. The festivals and screenings of *études* are necessary ways of promoting graduates who otherwise would find it difficult to enter the market. Challenged by the effort to produce so many films, the school relies almost exclusively on state grants, 90 per cent of which come from the Ministry of Culture.

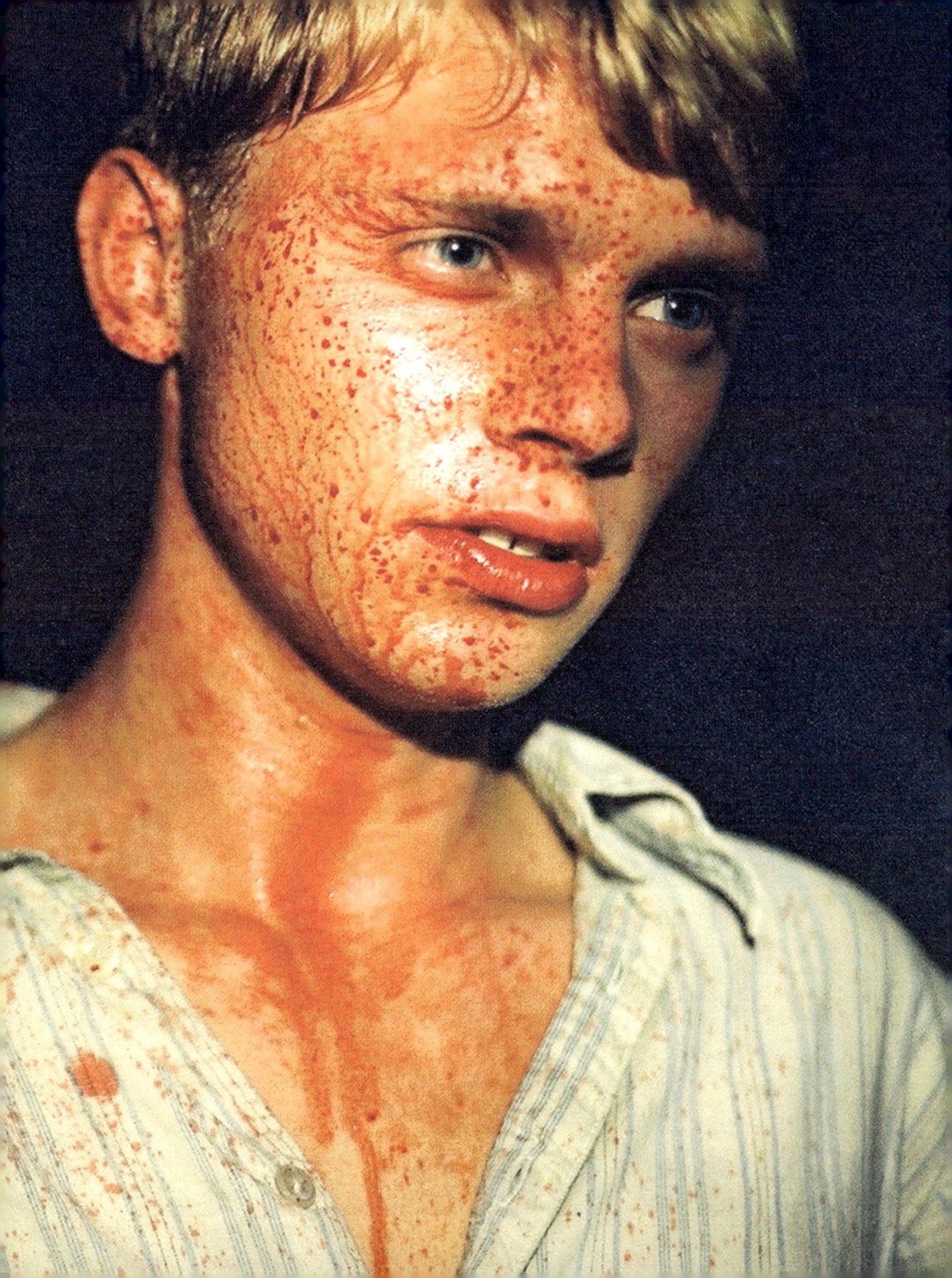

Malatyński claims that the money received from public sources is still insufficient but acquiring support from private investors is even more difficult. Still, the school is developing – new buildings are erected and equipment is replaced.

Highly important are contacts throughout the world. The school is already international in character – in terms of students' admittance – and now is the time for international co-production and cooperation with other institutions. "One weakness of Polish cinema is its seclusion", states Malatyński. One attempt to address such needs is a workshop known as "Passion to market", which is organised in cooperation with schools from London and Paris. It is targeted at teams consisting of three members (director, screenwriter and producer) selected from the submitted applications. The programme creates new possibilities for the students and forces them to deal with problems they will inevitably face – difficulties in entering the market, lack of team spirit, and challenging work conditions on first projects. Without the adequate preparation of specific projects and creating opportunities for their development, there is little use for even the best education system for young filmmakers.

The tradition of teaching at the school is seen less as an advantage than a problem requiring new solutions. "The tastes of the audience change as do the students themselves", remarks Malatyński. Moreover, those enrolling in the school are getting younger year by year. Several years ago the average age of an applicant was about twenty-four. Principally, studies in the Directing Department were a second faculty to most applicants, and it was required that they already had some experience to draw upon in writing scripts and producing their first films. Today, when graduates find it more difficult to take up studies at a second faculty (as students generally enter the labour market just after finishing their first faculty) there are "more younger people admitted who have too little life experience", grieves Malatyński. All this makes the old model of education derelict. Young students want to play moviemaker rather than treating it as a vocation. There are, of course, certain limits to compromise, but as Malatyński notes, "we need to find a golden mean – while still thinking of film as art we need to look for the possibility to get in touch with a mass audience". Though exemplary, the model of education at the school is now the object of severe criticism for this very reason. In his expertise in film education, Wojciech Marczewski, a film director and experienced pedagogue, mentions for example the prolonged five-year period of education which he believes is unnecessary but enforced by Bologna accords.[1] He would prefer to see a three-year education in film open to graduates of different faculties.

---

[1] W. Marczewski, Expertise on Education for Film Related Professions, a conference paper, Congress of Polish Culture (Kraków 2009) http://www.kongreskultury.pl/library/File/RaportSzkolnictwo/Marczewski_ekspertyza.pdf, p. 2.

ONE FORMULA

The Faculty of Radio and Television at the University of Silesia, the other public film school in Poland, differs from the Łódź school mainly in the scale of its production. Though the faculty has a small infrastructure, it is not at a disadvantage since students receive money for their films and rent equipment from professionals. The faculty was established in 1978 with the goal of training professional television footage producers. The greatest influence on the faculty was Krzysztof Kieślowski – a graduate of the Łódź school. The director, who later gave us *The Decalogue*, produced several films for TV in the 1970s, including some highly valued documentaries. He portrayed the life of "simple men" and, as a result, he was seen as a "politically engaged" director. It might have afforded him good standing with the authorities, but had little to do with Kieślowski himself – who was distanced from politics.

> I was interested in reality and in showing its truth. If someone called this "engagement" that was his business. I was and I am still an observer. My place is on the sidelines.[2]

He had a specific understanding of his profession, and this can be traced back to his student days when, while at the Łódź school, he met Kazimierz Karabasz, the Polish documentary film director. It was in his films (for example in *The Musicians* [*Muzykanci*, 1960]) that Kieślowski observed Karabasz's style of accompanying people with the camera, telling a story in a warm and empathic, yet formally disciplined and masterful way. Recalling the film courses led by Kieślowski at the University of Silesia and in West Berlin in the 1980s, his former students mention one distinctive trait: the author of *Camera Buff* (*Amator*, 1979) and *Blind Chance* (*Przypadek*, 1981) believed that filmmaking is a moral act. Some students also recall his constantly recurring questions: *Why are you making this film, what is interesting to you in this story?* Kieślowski did not consider his filmmaking a means to achieving professional perfection. It was a test in undertaking the most important and most difficult subjects. He influenced his students not because he was a professional; more important was the consistency in the general attitude visible in his work and in life. "We had our eyes fixed upon him, he was our absolute idol",[3] recalls Piotr Łazarkiewicz (Łazarkiewicz graduated from the Katowice school and later directed films about youth rebellion, *The Wave* [*Fala*, 1986], or the problem of social aggression against HIV carriers, *A Time for Witches* [*Pora na czarownice*, 1993]).

---

2 Krzysztof Kieślowski, One on One, a conversation led by Stanisław Zawiśliński, in: *Kieślowski. Without End* (*Kieślowski. Bez końca*), Skorpion, Warsaw 1994; p. 19.

---

3 A. Gwóźdź (ed.), *In Krzysztof Kieślowski's Circle* (*W kręgu Krzysztofa Kieślowskiego*), Silesia-Film, Katowice 2006, p. 99.

The Dean of the Faculty of Radio and Television, professor Krystyna Doktorowicz, admits that the formula of education in Katowice is similar to that of the school in Łódź. In both schools the emphasis is on auteur cinema and in both there are courses on feature films and documentaries. The most important part of the education is personal contact with experienced filmmakers. They shape students' perspectives on filmmaking and influence their choices. This similarity is also the source of a fundamental difference: the emphasis on auteur cinema translates into specific visions of the cinema among individual lecturers at both schools. In the Directing Department the tutors supervising work on feature films are Krzysztof Zanussi, Jerzy Stuhr and Filip Bajon, and work on documentaries is overseen by Andrzej Fidyk, who has for a long time been associated with Polish Television.

For Zanussi, cinema is a medium designed for pondering moral choices; his protagonists (e.g. in *Camouflage* [*Barwy ochronne,* 1976]) are representatives of the intelligentsia who choose between conformity on the one hand, and moral principles and the mission of their social group on the other. Jerzy Stuhr became famous first as an actor and later started directing films influenced by Kieślowski's vision of empathic cinema. Filip Bajon intensely outlines historical contexts, and in form his films are close to traditional film epics. Starting from these simplified characteristics we may attempt to define the differences in the vision of cinema that the two schools represent. In the Łódź school we may observe the influence of people like Grzegorzek and Królikiewicz, known for their stylistic refinement and devotion to the auteur vision of film, while in comparison, the vision of the Katowice school is closer to "base level" as it intensely accentuates psychological realism and dialogues as ways to convey its meaning. The Łódź school is thus closer to film, meaning that its foundation is the relating of stories through pictures, while the Katowice school leans towards emphasising the story-telling mechanics of literature. Of course the two models are not mutually exclusive nor do they determine the students' achievements. However, the works of students surely bear their school's trademark.

There are not many students each year – eight of them in the Directing Department and a similar number in each of Television, Film and Cinematographic Production. Participation in festivals is also very important. The curricula at the Katowice school are designed to teach students not only the language of film but also to be familiar with television formats and advertising. Through international contacts, the emphasis is on cooperation with audiovisual schools rather than just film schools.

Students of the faculty are steered towards learning practical skills common to both directors and cinematographers. Katarzyna Kural, a student of cinematography, was a participant in one of these projects: directors and cinematographers were paired and each was involved in making one part of an *étude*. This workshop included work on the screenplay, production and post-production, giving students a great opportunity to learn how to work on a film set. Future directors and cinematographers learn teamwork and the skills necessary for better communication.

The faculty maintains close cooperation with the Fine Art Academy in Katowice – starting in 2010 there will be integrated workshops for students of the Department of Directing, along with students of the Department of Scenography and the Department of Cinematography, with students of the Department of Fine Arts.

Just as in the case of the Łódź school, acquiring workshop skills is not an aim unto itself but is subjected to the particularly defined ethos of the artist. In their book *Cinema – The Eye (Kino – oko)*, Bogdan Dziworski and Jerzy Łukaszewicz – cinematographers and lecturers at the Katowice school – claim that the primary aim of artistic activity is a *subordination of the world*. As experienced educators, the authors of the book face a fundamental question – is it not the case, that by teaching workshop skills they enslave the individuality of their students?[4] Is it not the case that by passing to students the very strict rules of the art they curb the imagination of young cinematographers? To answer these questions they present the example of *a craftsman*, who, thanks to an adept command of his/her skills, can put the world in order by the very act of creativity. This short description alone is enough to imagine what their total programme of education consists of: it starts from craftsmanship and ends with metaphysics.

It happens that studying at a smaller school with limited resources can be a mobilising factor – in recent years, at least a few of the graduates of the Katowice school have made an impact on Polish film.

MASTER SCHOOL

The Andrzej Wajda Master School of Film Directing was established in 2001, and since its beginning it has offered a documentary course and a course on feature films designed for people who already have a university degree or artistic achievements. The one-page-long application form requires the specification of a film project a student is willing to work on.

---

[4] B. Dziworski, J. Łukaszewicz, *Cinema – The Eye. Workshop of a Cinematographer* (*Kino-Oko. Warsztat operatora filmowego*), WAiF, Warsaw 2006, p. 83.

Andrzej Wajda has long criticised the Łódź school where he was himself a student. He claimed the studies were prolonged and the school itself was isolated from the outside world. He also claimed that it suffered from overgrown administration. "Nobody takes care of the students. All the doors in front of them are locked. The school is completely dependent on its administration ... . Its recent graduates from the Directing Department have the mentality of civil servants."[5] According to the director of *Ashes and Diamonds* (*Popiół i diament*), the best solution would be to open multiple educational programmes and new schools, including private ones. His Master School was thus established to implement new ideas; what matters there is the artistic effect, and the school is closer to the filmmaking industry, offering help in finding film producers or even producing films on its own.

The main pedagogical body consists of four lecturers: Andrzej Wajda, Wojciech Marczewski, Jacek Bławut and Marcel Łoziński. As we can observe, what comes with these names is a functional division of competences. Wajda and Marczewski are authorities in feature films and the other two lecturers are influential directors of documentaries, who in their own distinctive ways explore the limits of documentary form. Marcel Łoziński has worked out a formula of film experimentation; he employed a psychodrama to depict the mechanisms of collective oppression (in *Happy End and How To Live* [*Jak żyć*]), and investigated the media and political manipulation (in *Workshop Practice* [*Ćwiczenia warsztatowe*] and *How It's Done* [*Jak to się robi*]). Jacek Bławut is well known for building lasting and profound relationships with his protagonists, sometimes refusing to maintain distance and becoming involved in the story (e.g. in *Rat in the Crown* [*Szczur w koronie*], a story of the self-destruction of an alcoholic), and sometimes even more intensely delves into the environment of his protagonists. He is focussed on the private stories of people representing the margins of society. The educational programmes of both directors are diametrically opposed and this is also the case with the directors of feature films who lecture there. It is clear that the Master School of Film Directing is founded on the individualities of its directors.

The school's curriculum takes into account what are likely to be the most difficult moments in the careers of future filmmakers, before and after finishing their studies. First, there is a course titled "Film Preschool" directed at students and high school pupils interested in film but unfamiliar with its production. Originally there were two courses, one on documentary films and the other on feature films, both designed to help with specific projects and directed at students who already have some achievements in filmmaking, such as young filmmakers, scriptwriters and writers.

5
Krzysztof Krubski *et al.*, *Film School: The Story of the Łódź Film School* (*Filmówka – powieść o łódzkiej szkole filmowej*), Prószyński i S-ka, Warsaw 1998, p. 233.

The Master School is designed as a place to consult on these projects and to work in teams on specific materials, but it avoids teaching workshop skills. In "Film Preschool", students learn the general idea behind what it means to be a filmmaker. The documentary course and the course in feature film, like the school's "EKRAN" (SCREEN) project, which is directed at professionals, are intended to teach film structure and to help find the best formula for a given story. These courses provide more advanced knowledge on designing film stories.

Magdalena Kowalczyk, the daughter of documentary film director and film editor Katarzyna Maciejko-Kowalczyk, completed both "Film Preschool" and the documentary course. Her *étude By the River* (*Przy rzece*) won the award in the student competition at the festival in Wiesbaden. Apart from making her own films, she works as a cinematographer in other student projects. From "preschool" she remembers the basic principles of directing, which are understood not as a road to achieve a goal, but as a professional and creative attitude. "Andrzej Wajda used to repeat that we have to put in much effort to show respect to people with whom we work", she recalls. Equally as important as practical advice was the way lecturers prepared for the classes. "One of the 'preschoolers' was doing a project on a young Polish writer. After just one week Andrzej Wajda knew all of the writer's books. And so did other lecturers." The necessity of collecting materials for the project, to build relations of trust among the team and, in the case of documentary films, with protagonists, were the essentials she learned at "preschool". At first the classes were led by the aforementioned lecturers. Today what the school offers is limited in this respect. The first limitation is that most courses are on documentary films only, and the second, that the classes are held by graduates of the school who have experience in filmmaking.

The documentary course offers assistance *from idea to production*. It no longer provides basic workshop help, e.g. with choosing the time for shooting scenes, the ways of building relationships with protagonists, or making documentation. "In preschool you are led by the hand, whereas in the documentary course you work on the message, the structure of your film, and you assess whether the protagonist is right for the story", compares Kowalczyk. The feature film course focuses on single takes, rehearsals with the actors, improving the script. The school helps find producers and recently declared it will produce the most interesting projects. During work on a project the tutors suggest solutions and the effects of work are discussed in groups. The school provides a friendly environment and ensures the students feel safe. It is supposed to lessen the stress of individual work, to allow for confrontation with the opinions of others while protecting the autonomy of the creator. All this is difficult in a situation where directors work with producers.

Among the lecturers, Wojciech Marczewski has the richest experience in teaching. He lectured in Great Britain and Denmark and held intensive courses for film students in many western European countries. In Poland he was a tutor of the last-year students at the directing departments in Katowice and Łódź. Adam Guziński, a graduate of the Łódź school recalls that consultations with Marczewski were an invigorating part of the film education. "He provided a space in which students could show their sensitivity. He was interested in what we had to say." His formula for education at the school was based upon the idea of intensive courses and the use of materials provided by students. It was a liberal education where the tutor and the young filmmaker developed partnership relationships. When asked about the source of these ideas, he said it goes back to the 1980s.

In those days, because of political reasons, many filmmakers left Poland to work abroad, some of them in film education. Because of competition they needed to offer something

The Boy on the Galloping Horse, dir. Adam Guziński

special. Workshops combining theory and practice were a novelty. Marczewski soon started working together with other filmmakers from Poland. The courses were getting popular and the news about new formulae was spreading quickly. Above all, they had little in common with typical courses at universities. Students worked on specific materials (e.g. literature) and during coursework they learned much from the lecturers' own experience, especially about work on film sets. What was particularly surprising was the openness with which Polish filmmakers revealed their "professional secrets"; they shared their craftsmanship which was usually acquired through professional work. "In the west this was not so obvious", Marczewski reminds us. Filmmakers there believed this knowledge was their greatest asset and their key to professional success, so they kept it secret. It was considered foolish to give it away for free, especially to future competitors. Why then did Polish filmmakers adopt a different approach? It seems that for them filmmaking was not a zero-sum game, where the success of one artist means failure for the others. "We were a close-knit group", recalls Marczewski, "partly for political reasons". In the authoritarian regime behind the "iron curtain", the successes of filmmakers' were arguments in ongoing negotiations with the state where freedom and independence were at stake. The success of a single filmmaker was seen as a victory for all and, as an incentive to increase output, never the subject of jealousy. Moreover, filmmakers were organised in institutions called Film Groups. They were not an equivalent to today's production studios but rather associations of filmmakers under the supervision of an experienced director. They were working in cooperation with writers, who were literary directors, and together they formed an environment for filmmakers to produce their films. Films were thus works of individual authors, but they were also the works of Film Groups, which had some institutional form. Artists formed groups, and their members knew each other and cooperated. To be admitted to a group required not clout but, as Marczewski says, "a little talent and a little decency. The Film Group 'Tor' was a real film school to me."

According to Marczewski, the western system of producing films was too hastily introduced after the transformation and since its inception it proved inadequate in local conditions. The Groups were dissolved, followed by the appearance of the unknown institution of the film producer, whose influence was equal to today's creative producers. The only problem was that in Poland there were no creative producers and the only producer in the socialist system was the state. Work on the film set was managed by a director of production who was more like the manager of a company and nothing like a "creative supervisor" who cares not only about the costs but also about the whole project.

Deprived of a friendly environment, the filmmakers were to negotiate the terms and conditions of their work individually, knowing that when production begins they are on their own. Master courses at the Wajda School fill this gap. There is a creative environment in which films can be elaborated on while still in development; unconventional solutions can be tested in comfortable conditions before the actual work on the film set begins. Wojciech Marczewski stresses that the similarity in the school's structure to that of the former Film Groups is not a manifestation of a belief in the superiority of the old system of production. It is more about gap-filling in the existing model of production. That is also the reason why there should be courses in production directed at professionals to accompany courses in directing. The idea is to enrich producers' competences and match them to the vast scope of their powers, which include making decisions in artistic matters. A telling example, Marczewski says, is the changing of scripts by producers who have their own idea of the film but neither the professional knowledge nor the ability to analyse text.

The Master School of Film Directing is not yet another school where workshop skills are taught, or a school endorsed by big names, promising to help establish connections in the film industry. Teaching programmes were designed to address specific problems and they are based on analysis of the situation in the Polish film industry with due respect to effective solutions from the past. They may contribute to films being thought of as works of art made with the help of many people and resulting from numerous discussions.

NEW SOLUTIONS

To shoot his film on genuine film stock, Artur Wyrzykowski launched a website where he spoke about his plans to make a movie and asked visitors for support. Instead of conforming to the possibilities he has been offered, he was looking for money outside school – and raised it. He wants to make films independently, but, as he remarks, fully professionally, with a good crew, professional equipment and as large scale productions.

Everything, dir. Artur Wyrzykowski
→

Before he made his first film he finished "preschool" at the Andrzej Wajda School, knowing that he wants to be a filmmaker but not at the expense of four years' studies at a state university. He was advised to enter the Warsaw Film School – a private school of art set up by two renowned representatives of Polish commercial cinema – actor and film director Bogusław Linda and film director Maciej Ślesicki. "This school was recommended to me because of the new quality it brings in", he recalls. The novelty was the school's focus on teaching practical skills and a reduction of theoretical subjects to a minimum, together with the assumption that after only two years of intensive studies students will be sufficiently prepared to start work in the film industry. This seemed perfect to those who were not so much interested in receiving a university diploma but instead wanted to develop filmmaking skills and to start working in the business.

Wyrzykowski recalls that the first year of studies was laborious. Courses were held every day, often also at weekends, and the emphasis was put on regular film assignments completed individually by students on digital equipment provided by the school. In the directing course, the curriculum covered a vast scope of subjects – the founders of the school assumed that a director must be knowledgeable on every part of the filmmaking process. There were courses preparing students for working with actors, courses on sound design, preparing storyboards, as well as acting assignments and workshops with experienced artists. It was underlined that, contrary to public schools, criticised for their strict theoretical approach, people lecturing at the Warsaw Film School were making their own films.

According to Wyrzykowski, this approach results in a good command of filmmaking skills. Assignments are thoroughly analysed and mistakes pointed out. Students are offered

solutions to make it more professional and improve the way the story is told. "Every decision must agree with what is being told is what the school preaches. This is something you have to begin with", Wyrzykowski says today; a film is not a collection of well-made scenes. On a higher level of thinking about the story, the craft must be of secondary importance, while more general aims related to the construction of the story must come to the fore. Looking back at his time at the Warsaw Film School he recommends the school and knows that it was an important part of his artistic development. However, he remarks, "We were not taught the magic, no secrets were revealed". This shortcoming is quite telling in itself, although in his case it may be the result of the path he has chosen or his personal ambitions. It raises the question as to whether it is possible to learn the "magic" of filmmaking in only two years. Still, there are people who can benefit from this formula, those who feel they do not need a long education in which to mature, but need to get acquainted with the film set and test their imagination.

Krystyna Ślązak found her way into filmmaking through the Kraków Screenplay School, where she attended a one-year course to develop a submitted project. It was a weekend course combining workshops devoted to students' projects with film studies, analyses of films and guest master lectures given by well-known directors and scriptwriters. The lecturers were names we know from the Łódź school: even professor Grzegorz Królikiewicz, who analysed *Citizen Kane*. Simultaneously students were working on scripts. They started with a three-sentence description of the future film and ended with a script ready for a complete feature film.

The idea was to follow the American model of a three-act structure for a film, or the model of classical drama. To accompany the workshops where students develop their projects, the school organises film language courses and courses on film history which provide future scriptwriters with the basics to work in the film industry. The idea underpinning the school's curriculum is to set state-of-the-art standards and ultimately create a core group of future professionals.

Krystyna Ślązak, today an alumnus of the school, thinks the idea is ambitious, if not overambitious. To finish a good script in just one year is a daring enterprise. Still, the very idea of a screenplay school seems to reflect the actual problems afflicting Polish cinema. It has long been observed that there is a lack of professional scriptwriters and good scripts.[6] Producers tend to be idle, and wait for directors to come up with a script. Only every now and then are we rightfully reminded of the fact that there should be professional scriptwriters and that a director is not necessarily a specialist in this field. Following

---

6
See: R. Kurkiewicz, Do Scriptwriters Exist at All? *Kino* 09/2009.

this line of reasoning, the Łódź school set up its own screenwriting department and the Warsaw Film School introduced a course in scriptwriting.

The Kraków Screenplay School was the first and so far the only school specialising solely in this field. Beginning in 2009 it has been a part of the Film and Audio-Visual Communication School in Kraków, which introduced two new departments – production and directing. Both are designed in a fashion similar to that of the Screenplay School, with a focus on workshops. Even if there are differences there is also one similarity, which is filling in the space left by public schools. In this space we find the aforementioned Warsaw Film School and the Film and Theatre Academy in Warsaw.

The latter, no matter the department (directing, cinematography, screenwriting, editing or production), offers joint courses and lectures to first-year students, and this way provides basic knowledge to all students. The specialisation begins after the first year. The graduates I spoke to mentioned the emphasis on photography and availability of digital equipment. The schools mentioned here offer more or less extensive courses providing students with basic workshop skills and exposing them to the most important tools.

Future cinema

The questions concerning film schools now and in the future are in fact questions about the shape of future cinema. On the one hand, film education must correspond to reality and keep up with advances in the field, but on the other, education itself is the agent of change because the curricula of film schools will influence future filmmaking and the future choices of festival organisers.

There are two main approaches to the issue of continuity versus change in film studies. The first approach is to seek a balance between adaptation and tradition – this is the approach of traditional public schools. The second approach is to find a niche in the market and respond to current needs – this is the approach of private schools which have appeared in Polish education in the last several years. Their offer significantly differs from that of public schools. There are courses providing basic skills for working on a film set, and there are master classes open to graduates and professionals.

Today's students at the various film schools take their first steps toward the filmmaking industry while still in a high school. The people I spoke to – both students and graduates – rarely had the experience of studying at one school only. They usually started with film "Preschool" or post-secondary courses and spend one or two years here and there. Their education is spread over time as they try different possibilities or simply take a year or two to prepare for the exams of the faculty they dream about. New private schools offer a shortened route to the film industry to those who already have some artistic achievements (e.g. they have worked in theatre or published a book), but it is often a stopover before traditional public school or a part of yet another path where there are no effective shortcuts. When one looks at this path, one question arises: what exactly do film schools offer to someone who wants to make films? To put it more bluntly, what do we need film schools for in the age of digital technology, which makes filmmaking an egalitarian mode of expressing oneself?

The most interesting answer to this question reverses its logic: film schools are necessary because filmmaking is egalitarian thanks to the availability of digital cameras. Why? To tell the professionals apart from the crowds of amateurs. In brief, entry into the film industry is a means to an end. For only in a professional film is there the "magic" referred to by one of the students of cinematography at the Łódź school. The subsequent stages of complexity in film production are to many a rite of passage: amateur means are finally abandoned, the crew gets bigger, the tension and the motivation are on the increase, and there is a different quality of work on the film set.

Another answer I received seems more modest: attending school is a mobilising factor thanks to contact with people who are interested in film. This contact does not necessarily have to be with the professionals. Equally important is contact with other enthusiasts, which can sometimes result in interesting cooperation and which would not be possible without school.

What then, is the vision of future cinema? The ethos of auteur films promoted in public schools will probably continue. This model will likely result in an artistic cinema bent towards social issues. This cinema will comply with the motto of one of the most famous graduates of the Łódź Film School and currently the patron of the Katowice school, Krzysztof Kieślowski, who claimed that the job of a filmmaker is to *depict reality*.

The second model will probably fall in line with the remarks of Marcin Malatyński, who said that cinema today must work out a *golden mean* formula to combine artistry with popular entertainment. This is also the direction Artur Wyrzykowski wants to follow. "The films I intend to make will attempt to reach a mass audience and to be a memorable experience."

The two models seem to be natural responses to the question about the future of filmmaking. Both use understandable codes. In the case of the first one the code is set in the tradition of Polish auteur cinema. In the case of the second it results from attempts to meet the requirements of the market, where ambitions relate both to the size of the audience and the quality of the experience provided by cinema.

Bibliography

Dziworski B., Łukaszewicz J., *Cinema - The Eye. Workshop of a Cinematographer* (*Kino-Oko. Warsztat operatora filmowego*), WAiF, Warsaw 2006.
Gwóźdź, A. (ed.), *In Krzysztof Kieślowski's Circle* (*W kręgu Krzysztofa Kieślowskiego*), Silesia-Film, Katowice 2006.
Janicka, B. (ed.), *Filmmakers: Polish Cinema According to its Creators* (*Filmowcy. Polskie kino według jego twórców*), Association of Polish Filmmakers, Warsaw 2006.
Klejsa, K., Nurczyńska-Fidelska, E.(eds.), *Polish cinema: Reinterpretations. History- Ideology- Politics* (*Kino polskie: reinterpretacje. Historia, ideologia, polityka*), RABID, Kraków 2008.
Krubski, K., et al., *Film School: The Story of the Łódź Film School* (*Filmówka – powieść o łódzkiej szkole filmowej*), Prószyński i S-ka, Warsaw 1998.
Kurkiewicz R., Do Scriptwriters Exist at All? *Kino* 09/2009.
Marczewski, W., Expertise on Education for Film Related Professions, a conference paper, Congress of Polish Culture (Kraków 2009) http://www.kongreskultury.pl/library/File/Raport Szkolnictwo/Marczewski_ekspertyza.pdf, p. 2.
Krzysztof Kieślowski, One on One. A conversation led by Stanisław Zawiśliński, in: *Kieślowski. Without End* (*Kieślowski. Bez końca*), Skorpion, Warsaw 1994.

Translated by Bartłomiej Reszuta

CONTRIBUTORS

Michael Brooke

is the Screenonline curator at the BFI National Archive. He has written extensively about central European cinema for *Sight & Sound* and *Vertigo* magazines, including interviews with Jerzy Skolimowski, Jan Svankmajer and Andrzej Wajda, and sits on the advisory board of the journal *Studies in Eastern European Cinema*. He is also the producer of the BFI's DVD compilations Quay Brothers: *The Short Films 1979-2003* and Jan Svankmajer: *The Complete Short Films*. He is currently contributing to BFI Publishing's forthcoming book on the post-war British documentary movement.

Mariusz Frukacz,

born in 1976, is a film theorist and critic, and a promoter of animated film. Since 2000 he has been a programme director of the National Festival of Author Animated Films OFAFA in Kraków. Since November 2008 he has been a member of the management board of the International Animated Film Association (ASIFA). In addition, he was the editor of the dictionary entry for 'Animation' in the *Tekstylia Bis Dictionary of Polish Youth Culture* (Kraków, 2006) and co-author of the book *Polish Animated Film* (Warsaw, 2008). More recently, he authored the book *24 Frames Per Second: Discourses on Animation* (Kraków, 2009).

Andrzej Kołodyński,

a film critic holding PhD in film theory and art. He is editor-in-chief of *Kino* monthly and the author of numerous publications on film, including *Searching For the Truth: Theory of Documentary Films (Tropami filmowej prawdy: teoria dokumentu,* 1981), *The Heritage of Imagination. History of SF Films (Dziedzictwo wyobraźni. Historia filmu SF,* 1989), *Dictionary of Film Adaptations* (*Słownik adaptacji filmowych,* co-author, 2005), *The History of Polish Cinema* (*Historia kina polskiego,* editor and co-author, 2007). He is also a translator of books on film as well as novels, an editor of collective works, and the author of several dictionary entries (e.g. *Speelfilm Encyclopadie,* 1988, *Encyclopaedia of Religious Films* [*Encyklopedia filmów religijnych,* 2007] and *Bond. Lexicon* [*Bond. Leksykon,* 2009]). He currently lectures at Warsaw University and Cardinal Stefan Wyszyński University in Warsaw (teaching film history and film criticism).

Anita Piotrowska,

a film critic for the *Tygodnik Powszechny* and a columnist for the psychology monthly *Charaktery*. She also contributes to *Film* and *Kino* monthly magazines. She is a lifetime member of the Kraków Film Foundation Programme Council and Revision Commission and a member of FIPRESCI. She has sat on the juries of many film festivals including those in Karlovy Vary, Moscow, Istanbul, Oberhausen, Viareggio and Ankara. She is also the Polish Film Institute's expert on feature and documentary films and the author of numerous publications on film.

Jerzy Płażewski,

born in 1924, a film historian and film critic. Since 1968, he has been the editor of the international section of *Kino* monthly. He is the author of 22 books on film and film history, including *The Language of Film* (*Język filmu*), *A History of Film 1895-2005* (*Historia filmu 1895-2005*), *History of French Film* (*Historia filmu francuskiego*), and *Andrzej Munk*. He is an initiator of the Independent Critics Awards and the Festival of Film Festivals, as well as the former president of the Polish Federation of Film Discussion Clubs and the president of the Academic Council of the National Film Library. In addition, he is the founder and manager of Good Films Cinema in Warsaw, the vice-president of the Polish section of FIPRESCI, and a jurist or president of the jury at many festivals, including Cannes, the Berlinale, Venice, Karlovy Vary, San Sebastian and Mar del Plata.

Joanna Rożen-Wojciechowska
is a film theorist and editor, and since 2008, the programme director at Telewizja Kino Polska. For years she has actively promoted independent cinema in Poland. From 2003 to 2008 she was the Editorial Director of Telewizja Kino Polska's Young Cinema, where she created and produced author programmes devoted to young independent cinema ("fringe" cinema) – KinOFFteka and Young Staff (Młode kadry) directed at young professionals in the field. She has also been a creator and coordinator of the "Young Staff – Debuts" ("Młode kadry – Debiutanci") Screenplay Competition. Until 2003 she was the organiser of the KRAKFFA Kraków Independent Film Festival. She has sat on the juries of many independent film festivals and is the author of commentaries on Polish cinema, interviews and TV series.

Małgorzata Sadowska
is culture section editor-in-chief of the weekly publication *Przekrój* as well as one of its film reviewers. Previously associated with *Film* monthly, she has also been published in *Kino* monthly and in the *Gazeta Wyborcza* daily. She is the co-author of a book on Polish documentary films, *Chełmska 21* (the address of the Documentary Film Studio), which received an honourable mention at the competition for young film critics under the patronage of Krzysztof Mętrak. Together with Jacek Rakowiecki she hosts a radio programme on film airing on Chilli Zet radio.

Krzysztof Świrek
is a film critic, assistant at the Institute of Journalism at Warsaw University, and a student of the Institute of Sociology at Warsaw University. Since 2007 he has been a columnist for *Kino* monthly. A laureate of the Krzysztof Mętrak competition (2009), he was also a member of the film critics jury at the 9th Era New Horizons International Film Festival in Wrocław.

Andrzej Werner,
born in 1940, is a film and literature critic and historian. A professor of the Literature Research Institute at the Polish Science Academy, he is also head of the 20th and 21st Century Literature Department as well as a lecturer at the Theatre Academy. He is the author of such titles as *The Usual Apocalypse: Tadeusz Borowski and His Vision of Camp Life* (*Zwyczajna apokalipsa. Tadeusz Borowski i jego wizja świata obozów*, 1971, 1981); *Polskie, arcypolskie...* (1987); *Passion and Boredom* (*Pasja i nuda*, 1992); *Blood and Ink* (*Krew i atrament*, 1996); *A Film Decade. The Crisis of Culture in the Cinema of the 1960s* (*Dekada filmu. Problem kryzysu kultury w kinie lat sześćdziesiątych*,1997); and *On the Writing of Jan Józef Szczepański* (2004).

Mateusz Werner,
Ph.D., born 1970, is a film critic and writer. He lectures at Cardinal Stefan Wyszynski University in Warsaw. Editor of the philosophical quarterly *Kronos*. Author of a book *Facing up to Nihilism. Gombrowicz, Witkacy* (*Wobec nihilizmu. Gombrowicz, Witkacy*), on the phenomenon of nihilism in literature (Sic! Publishing House, Warsaw 2009); editor of *What Kieślowski Tells Us Today?*

(Warsaw 2008, in Hebrew) and a series *Young Polish Cinema* (Warsaw 2004-2008, in French, German, English, Russian). He edited DVD compilations *Polish Shorts 2008*, *Polish Shorts 2009*. He was a member of editorial board of *Film* weekly and *Film Around the World* (*Film na Świecie*) magazine. Co-created and compered a popular television programme *The Picture Show* about the cinema for Polish public television (TVP Channel 2). Contributed to international film magazines e.g. *Cahiers du cinéma*, *Close Up* (Italy). Member of The International Federation of Film Critics FIPRESCI and Polish Filmmakers Association.

Janusz Wróblewski
born in 1963, is a film journalist with a degree from the Faculty of Polish Philology at Warsaw University. During the late 1990s he directed the TV programme Pegaz and is currently a member of the editorial board of Polityka weekly. His writing has appeared in *Życie Warszawy*, *Kino*, *Playboy*, *Film*, *Film na świecie*, *Dialog*, *Zwierciadło* and *Machina*. He is a member of the jury at the FIPRESCI festivals in Cannes and Venice and is the author of *The Magic of Cinema* (*Magia kina*).

DVD

This publication features 2 DVDs containing 21 short films, which, I believe, represent the best achievements in Polish cinema over the last 20 years. In these short pieces we can see reflected a great variety of subjects, intellectual ambitions and the continuing search for new formal means characteristic of Polish cinema from 1989 until today.

Mateusz Werner

1989 RACE, 6'
WYŚCIG

A grotesque vision of competition between the representatives of various social groups and professions. A brutal and ruthless struggle for an illusory victory.

Direction, script, animation, production design: Marek Serafiński
Director of photography: Jan Maciej Ptasiński
Music: Janusz Grzywacz
Production: Studio Miniatur Filmowych (Warsaw)

1990 – Leipzig (IFF) – Golden Dove
1990 – Huesca (International Short Film Festival), Award of the Aragonian Federation Film Society

1990 THE ABNORMAL, 78'
NIENORMALNI

A dramatized documentary created at a centre for mentally handicapped children in Kozice Dolne. The filmmaker invited handicapped children to play themselves. The storyline is simple – a new music teacher arrives and intends to teach the students the fundamentals of rhythm and how to play musical instruments in one month. At first, the teacher's work has no effect, but later he begins to understand his unconventional charges and to accept them. The children also change, first withdrawn and wary, they completely open up to him and each other.

Direction and script: Jacek Bławut
Director of photography: Jerzy Rudziński
Production: Jacek Bławut Film Production, Educational Film Studio (Łódź), STO Films, Shop-Tronik

1990 – Gdynia (Polish Feature Film Festival) – Special Award for the Biggest Art Event of the Festival
1991 – San Sebastian (International Film Festival) – Special Jury Prize
1991 – Mannheim-Heidelberg (International Film Festival) – FIPRESCI Award
1991 – European Film Award (nominee)

1991 FRANZ KAFKA, 16'

A fantasy biography of Franz Kafka, bringing to life the writer's diaries and photographs. The film's technique requires each phase of movement to be engraved on plasterboard painted black and then captured by the camera.

Direction, script, animation, production design: Piotr Dumała
Director of photography: Jan Maciej Ptasiński, Adam Dąbrowski, Barbara Stankiewicz, Adam Mickiewicz
Music: Janusz Hajdun
Production: Studio Miniatur Filmowych

1992 – Kraków Film Festival – Bronze Dragon
1992 – Kraków Film Festival (International Shorts) – Don Quixote Award, International Federation
    of Film Societies (IFFS) Award

1992 DIM., 10'

The lives of two lonely puppets are slowly coming to an end. They brighten up only when they can feed a bird which comes to the window of their apartment. However, one day the bird doesn't show up.

Direction: Marek Skrobecki
Script: Maciej Bełdycki, Marek Skrobecki
Director of photography: Zbigniew Kotecki
Production design: Marek Skrobecki, Krystyna Rostworowska
Animation: Adam Wyrwas
Music: Wolfgang Amadeus Mozart, Michał Lorenc
Production: Studio Małych Form Filmowych Se-Ma-For

1994 – Brussels (International Film Festival of Fantasy, Thriller & Science Fiction) – Honourable Mention
1994 – Kraków Film Festival (International Shorts) – Honourable Mention of the Jury
1994 – Zagreb (World Festival of Animated Films) – Honourable Mention
1994 – Espinho (International Animated Film Festival) – Honourable Mention

1993 89 MM FROM EUROPE, 12'
89 MM OD EUROPY

Brest – a checkpoint between Poland and the former Soviet Union. The standard-width European train tracks end, and from here on in the gauge is wider. In Europe the gauge is 1435 mm and in the former Soviet Union it is 1524 mm. The difference is the eponymous 89 mm. Every day, Belarusian workers change thousands of wheels under the wagons of international trains as French, German, and Dutch passengers watch from inside their compartments. Is this the border between two worlds?

Direction and script: Marcel Łoziński
Director of photography: Jacek Petrycki, Artur Reinhart
Production: Kalejdoskop Film Studio, Polish Television

1993 – Oberhausen (International Short Film Festival) – Grand Prix
1993 – European Film Award – Best Documentary Film (nominee)
1994 – Leipzig (International Film Festival) – Golden Dove
1994 – Clermont-Ferrand (International Short Film Festival) – Special Jury Prize
1994 – Oscar (Academy of Motion Picture Arts and Sciences) – Best Documentary, Short Subjects (nominee)
1994 – Montreal (International Film Festival) – Grand Prix
1994 – San Francisco (International Film Festival) – Special Mention
1995 – Sydney (Flickerfest International Short Film Festival) – Best Documentary Film

1994 STENCH, 16'
SMRÓD

A wino bumps into a 25-year-old man waiting at the train station. This accidental encounter turns into an escalating conflict and eventually the young man runs and hides in the public toilet. What imbues the situation with meaning is the fact that none of the people watching the scene finds the courage to intervene.

Direction, script, production design: Artur Urbański
Director of photography: Mariusz Prokop
Cast: Igor Bartosik, Stanisław Sobola, Daniel Olbrychski, Grażyna Torbicka.
Production: The National Polish Film, Television and Theatre School in Łódź

1995 – New York (International Student Film Festival) – First Prize
1996 – Brno Film Festival – Special Mention

1995 MISSY, 14'
PANCIA

Sylwia is 13. One day, her dog accidentally wanders into a neighbouring flat, where Sylwia encounters a priest anointing the sick. She falls in love with the priest and soon decides to meet him again to confess her feeling to him.

Direction: Iwona Siekierzyńska
Script: Iwona Siekierzyńska
Director of photography: Marek Wieser
Music: Grzegorz Zgliński
Cast: Sylwia Karczmarczyk, Piotr Dumała
Production: The National Polish Film, Television and Theatre School in Łódź, Canal+ Polska, Yleisradio Oy The Finnish Broadcasting Company

1996 – Oscar (Academy of Motion Picture Arts and Sciences) – Student Film Competition, (nominee)
1996 – Munich (The Munich International Festival of Film Schools) – Special Prize of the Jury President
1997 – Bornholm ("Balticum" Film Festival) – Student Film Award
1997 – Montecatini Terme (Film Festival) – Jury Award
1997 – Ludwigsburg (IFF) – Jury Award
1997 – Ebeltoft (CILECTu Mini Festival) – Kodak Award

1996 HAIRDRESSER , 5'
FRYZJER

Animation. A lonely hairdresser in a forsaken salon escapes into a world of imagination so he can once again feel the emotions he used to feel at work. This is the graduation *étude* of a student of the Faculty of Graphic Arts at the Jan Matejko Academy of Fine Art in Kraków.

Direction and script: Robert Sowa
Director of photography: Piotr Rusnarczyk
Production: Academy of Fine Art in Kraków

1997 – Kraków (Polish Animated Film Festival) – Grand Prix

1997 SILENCE, 12'
CISZA

A portrait of a family living in a village in Masuria. A short impression of everyday family joys and sorrows. The true dimension of a life immersed in nature and silence; a slow pace, filled with monotony and lethargy. A story without words.

Direction: Małgorzata Szumowska
Script: Małgorzata Szumowska
Director of photography: Michał Englert
Production: The National Polish Film, Television and Theatre School in Łódź

1998 - Tel-Aviv (International Student Film Festival) - Best Documentary
1998 - Neubrandenburg (Dokument-Art Festival) - Grand Prix
1998 - Łódź ("MediaSchool" International Film and TV Schools Festival) - Grand Prix
1998 - Bologna (European Festival of Film Schools) - Special Jury Prize
1998 - Angers (IFF) - Special Jury Award for Student Film
1999 - Tampere (IFF) - Best Documentary
1999 - Mexico (IFF) - Grand Prix
1999 - Mexico (IFF) - Best Cinematography

1998 JACOB, 16'
JAKUB

This is the story of a 13-year-old boy neglected by his father. The boy is aware of his parents' marital crisis and adds to the family conflict. As a result, a teacher is called upon for help. After speaking to the pedagogue, the father begins to pay more attention to his son. He buys him an accordion and from now on they can play together.

Direction and script: Adam Guziński
Director of photography: Wojciech Staroń
Music: Zbigniew Ignaczewski
Cast: Jakub Rogala, Małgorzata Hajewska, Mariusz Jakus, Aleksander Bednarz, Marek Sławiński, pupils of Primary School No. 150 in Łódź

1998 - Cannes (IFF) - First Prize Cinéfondation in Student Film category

1999 SUCH A BEAUTIFUL BOY I GAVE BIRTH TO, 25'
TAKIEGO PIĘKNEGO SYNA URODZIŁAM

He was a cute baby. He had these funny bowlegs, but eventually they straightened out. And now? He is a moron, a slacker, a half-wit, an idiot, a scoundrel, a bloody scumbag, a loser, a womaniser, a mediocrity, an eternal student, and God forgive him - a cinematographer. The above is what a somewhat domineering mother makes of her son's life. The son is Marcin Koszałka, and he gives us "a portrait of a family from the inside" in the middle-class family home he shares with his parents.

Direction, script, photography: Marcin Koszałka
Production: Telewizyjna Agencja Produkcji Teatralnej i Filmowej, Polish Television - Channel 1

2000 - Berlinale (Prix Europa) - Special - TV Non-Fiction
2000 - Kraków Film Festival - Honourable Mention
2000 - Kraków Film Festival (International Shorts) - Honourable Mention of the Jury
2003 - Nyon ("Visions du Reel" International Documentary Film Festival) - Prix Etat de Vaude

2000 TUNING THE INSTRUMENTS, 15'
STROJENIE INSTRUMENTÓW

The film shows that events and facts are relevant, while situations and feelings are nothing but temporary. The role of coincidence is exposed for comedic effect and to show how dramatically coincidental human life can be. The events take the form of an "audio-visual symphony".

Direction and script: Jerzy Kucia
Director of photography: Janusz Wierciak
Animation: Jerzy Kucia
Music: Wadim Chrapaczow
Production: Polish Television – Film Agency (for Channel 2), Film Production Agency, Jerzy Kucia Film Production

2000 – Ottawa (International Animation Festival) – Craft Prize (Best Use of Music/Sound)
2000 – Leipzig (International Festival for Documentary and Animated Film) – Prize of Sparkasse Leipzig for an Animated Film
2000 – Kraków (Polish Festival of Auteurs in Animation) – Golden Line
2001 – Kraków Film Festival (national short film competition) – Silver Hobby-Horse
2004 – Kraków (Polish Festival of Auteurs in Animation) – Platinum Line for best film in the 10-year history of the festival

2001 A MAN THING, 25'
MĘSKA SPRAWA

Bartek is thirteen and lives with his poverty-stricken family in Łódź. His father, once an amateur footballer, is now unemployed, frustrated and abusive. Bartek constantly earns reprimands for his misbehaviour in class and disobedience during recess, or for his disgraceful ignorance of the volume formula for a regular tetrahedron – serious enough to justify parental wrath. The boy plays in the school football team which is run by a coercive and overambitious coach pushing the team to its fourth subsequent victory. This brings about more intimidation and humiliation.

Direction and script: Sławomir Fabicki
Director of photography: Bogumił Godfrejów
Cast: Bartosz Idczak, Mariusz Jakus, Marek Bielecki, Katarzyna Bargiełowska.
Production: The National Polish Film, Television and Theatre School in Łódź

2001 – Oscar nominee for Live Action Short Film (Annual Student Academy Awards)
2001 – Stuttgart/Ludwigsburg (International Film Festival) - Best European Short Feature
2001 – Edinburgh (International Film Festival) – Best European Short Feature
2001 – European Film Award (nominee)
2001 – Łódź ("MediaSchool" International Film and TV Schools Festival) – Grand Prix
2001 – Kiev ("Molodist" International Film Festival) – Grand Prix and Audience Award
2001 – Teheran (International Short Film Festival) – Best Feature Film
2001 – Mexico (IFF) – Best Feature Film
2001 – New York (International Short Film Festival) – Best Feature Film
2001 – New York (International Student Festival) – First Prize
2001 – Moscow (VGiK Student Festival) – Best Foreign Film
2002 – Clermont-Ferrand (International Short Film Festival) – Critics Award and Young Jury Prize
2002 – Taipei (International Student Film Festival) – Golden Lion First Prize

2002 THE CATHEDRAL, 7' KATEDRA

On a distant planet, a lone wanderer approaches the doors of a mysterious building which resembles a medieval cathedral. Lighting his way with a scant torch flame, he enters and walks along gigantic columns which seem alive. Upon reaching the nave, he stops above a precipice, and just then the sun rises, its light changing the pilgrim into another living column that this amazing temple is constructed of. The script is based on a story by Jacek Dukaj.

Direction and animation: Tomasz Bagiński
Script: Tomasz Bagiński, Jacek Dukaj
Music: Adam Rosiak
Production: Platige Image

2002 – Oscar (Academy of Motion Picyure Arts and Sciences) – Short Animated Film Category (nominee)
2002 – San Antonio (Siggraph Computer Animation Festival) – Best Animated Short
2002 – Animago Main Award
2002 – Bradford (Film Festival) – Best Digital Short
2002 – Barcelona (ArtFutura Festival) – Best of the Show
2003 – Kraków Film Festival (national short film competition) – Silver Hobby-Horse

2003 A BAR AT VICTORIA STATION, 55' BAR NA VIKTORII

The film tells the story of two young men from Kluczbork, a small town near Opole, who are looking for work in London. Their foreign adventure begins at Victoria Coach Station, the main destination of buses from Poland. Piotr and Marek come here in hope of earning a better living. Their home Kluczbork, struggling with unemployment and poverty, does not offer much, so they decide that leaving for London is the only solution. They believe they can make it and their dreams are not unreasonable, "money, a decent flat, a good car, and their own business of some kind".

Director and screenplay: Leszek Dawid
Music: Bartek Straburzyński
Production: The National Polish Film, Television and Theatre School in Łódź

2004 – Neubrandenburg (Dokument-Art Festival) - Main Award
2004 – Wiesbaden (Festival of Central and Eastern European Film) – Honourable Mention of the Jury
2004 – Kraków Film Festival (international competition) - Silver Dragon for "pulse and energy"
2004 – Łódź ("MediaSchool" International Film and TV Schools Festival) – Main Award
2004 – Ińsko Film Summer – Main Award

2004 TELEFONO, 2'

Patty Diphusa is an erotic film star created by Pedro Almodovar. One day she comes to Poland, because the script says so. She waits for the man of her dreams, but he doesn't arrive. So, she calls Almodovar...

Direction and script: Marcin Wrona
Director of photography: Paweł Fils
Cast: Ewa Kasprzyk, Marcin Kwaśny
Production: Andrzej Wajda Master School of Film Directing

The film was made for The European Film Academy and was shown during the Award Ceremony in Barcelona (December 2004).

2005 – Kraków (KRAKFFA) – Third Prize for a Student Film
2005 – Warsaw (OFFskar) – Third Prize in Best Student Film category

2005 MELODRAMA, 19' MELODRAMAT

14-year-old Tadek has no parents. He lives with his older sister in a shabby house in a bad neighbourhood. But for Tadek the sister is not so much a mother as an object of sexual desire. It is this secret passion which becomes the main focus of the story. But this is also a tale of Tadek's friendship with a young female neighbour and his uneasy contacts with the sister's boorish fiancé, of whom he is jealous. Everyone here longs for something, seeking love or acceptance. Everyone is struggling to be noticed by others. And the stakes are high – it is a game for love, as all melodramas are.

Direction and script: Filip Marczewski
Director of photography: Radosław Ładczuk
Music: Paktofonika
Cast: Alan Andersz, Agnieszka Krukówna, Paweł Królikowski, Sylwester Maciejewski
Production: National Polish Film, Television and Theatre School in Łódź, Quartet

2005 – Kiev ("Molodist" International Film Festival) – Best Student Film
2005 – Moscow (International Student Film Festival) - Honourable Mention
2005 – Warsaw ("Łodzią po Wiśle" Review) – Grand Prix
2005 – Kraków (Kraków Film Festival, national competition) – Best Short Feature Film
2006 – Oscar nominee – Best Student Film
2006 – Brussels (Festival du Court Metrage de Bruxelles) – Honourable Mention of the Jury
2006 – Huesca (International Short Film Festival) – Best Short Film
2006 – Barcelona (Short Film Festival) – Grand Prix
2006 – Kyoto (International Student Film Festival) – Second Prize
2006 – Munich (The Munich International Festival of Film Schools) – Best Cinematography Award
2007 – Berlin (BerlinerFilmFenster – grenzenlos) – Main Award

2006 TAKING CARE, 13'20"
POD OPIEKĄ

A portrait of a young doctor who cares for terminally ill children, patients of the Gajusz Foundation in Łódź.

Direction: Jan Wagner
Director of photography: Tomasz Nowak
Production: National Polish Film, Television and Theatre School in Łódź

2006 – Warsaw ("Łodzią po Wiśle" Review) – Grand Prix
2006 – Łódź ("Human in Danger" Media Festival) – Honour Diploma

2007 SEEDS, 27'09"
NASIONA

In a remote village cottage, surrounded by the Altai Mountains, somewhere on the border of Russia and Kazakhstan, lives a large family that is totally rejected by the village people. They live on the verge of poverty, barely making ends meet. Once, a great tragedy happened here and now everybody, both the parents and children, lives in its shadow. The main protagonist is the father, a former sailor, who himself says that he loses four hours a day on the preparation of meals for his children and his sick wife. He has something of an old saint in him, someone who is called a "jurodiwyj" in Russia.

The film was created as part of the "Russia – Poland. New Gaze" cycle organized by the Adam Mickiewicz Institute and Eureka Media.

Director and screenplay: Wojciech Kasperski
Cinematography: Szymon Lenkowski
Music: Philip Glass (Koyannisqoatsi)
Production: Eureka Media, Polish Television

2006 – Kraków Film Festival (national competition) - Golden Hobby-Horse
2006 – Perm ("Flahertiana" International Documentary Film Festival) – Big Silver Nanook – Award for Best Documentary
2006 – Illinois Big Muddy Film Festival – Award for Best Short Film
2006 – Washington (AFI/Discovery Channel "Silverdocs" Documentary Festival) – Main Award in the documentary category
2006 – Berlinale (Prix Europa) – Special Mention
2007 – Missoula, Montana (Big Sky Documentary Film Festival) – Special Award of the Jury
2007 – Pärnu International Documentary and Anthropology Film Festival – Grand Prix

2008 THE CALF, 4'
CIELAK

A small village, a sleepy winter landscape, a dairy farm. Suddenly one of the calves is taken away from its safe home and put in a tractor trailer. This short film is a mixture of genres: a comedy, social drama and even ... a thriller.

Direction: Marek Marlikowski
Photography: Rafał Zgud
Production: Andrzej Wajda Master School of Film Directing

2009 WHERE THE SUN DOESN'T RUSH, 18'
TAM GDZIE SŁOŃCE SIĘ NIE SPIESZY

Places like this are scarce. Time in this mountain village in Slovakia goes by with its own lazy rhythm. Its blissful tranquillity is occasionally interrupted by announcements of the Funeral Society on the local radio. Nearly every inhabitant of the village is elderly, and all the while, more and more space is taken up at the local cemetery. This modest film by Bobrik manages to merge documentary attentiveness with warm, and at times, sarcastic microscopic observation.

Direction and script: Matej Bobrik,
Director of photography: Artur Sienicki,
Music: Michał Marecki.

2009 – Warsaw ("Łodzią po Wiśle" Review) – Grand Prix
2009 – Kraków Film Festival – Maciej Szumowski Award
2009 – Minsk ("Kinogran" Minsk Open Student Film & Video Festival) – Best Documentary 2009 – St. Petersburg ("Beginning" Open Student Film Festival) – Grand Prix in the documentary category

Film descriptions have been elaborated with help of www.filmpolski.pl

INDEX OF NAMES

Adamczak, Jacek →84
Adamczyk, Piotr →192
Adamczyk, Wojciech →211–212
Adamek, Witold →108 →215
Andrzejewski, Jerzy →67 →191
Antkowiak, Dawid →137
Arnold, Agnieszka →48 →70
Ash, Timothy Garton →9
Baar, Kamila →138
Bagiński, Tomasz →91–92 →96 →252
Bajon, Filip →12 →73 →78 →154 →190 →213 →219 →230
Baka, Mirosław →137
Balabanov, Alexei →35
Barański, Andrzej →96 →114 →154 →157 →192
Barciś, Artur →137
Barczyk, Łukasz →120 →224
Bardem, Juan Antonio →10
Bareja, Stanisław →15 →148
Bartkowiak, Andrzej →221
Bartkowicz, Rafał →84
Bartosik, Izabela →96
Battiato, Giacomo →192
Bąkowski, Wojciech →96 →100
Becker, Wolfgang →28–29
Bendazzi, Giannalberto →81 →102
Białoszewski, Miron →114
Błaszczyk, Anna →96
Bławut, Jacek →54 →232 →247
Bodrov, Sergei →35
Borcuch, Jacek →17 →19 →144
Borowczyk, Walerian →23
Borowski, Paweł →91
Borzęcka, Ewa →52 →121
Bosacki, Piotr →101
Bosek, Małgorzata →100
Braun, Ewa →174
Bromski, Jacek →18 →209–212
Bruszewska, Balbina →95
Brzozowski, Andrzej →62
Bugajski, Ryszard →11 →12 →23 →61 →73 →218
Bujak, Jan →123
Bukojemski, Michał →47
Buñuel, Luis →10 →113
Burski, Juliusz →153
Buzek, Agata →114

Chęciński, Sylwester →15 →28 →212
Ciechanowicz-Sarata, Aleksandra →49
Cielecka, Magdalena →113
Cummings, Neil →123 →132
Cybulski, Zbigniew →105 →200
Cywińska Izabella →116 →124
Czeczot, Andrzej →89
Czekała, Ryszard →86 →87
Czyżewska, Elżbieta →105
Ćwiek, Maciej →84
Damięcki, Mateusz →138
Dammas, Jacob →48
Dancewicz, Renata →110
Darday, István →33
Dąbrowski, Waldemar →156
Dejczer, Maciej →28
Delić, Denis →215
Dizdar, Jasmin →36
Doktorowicz, Krystyna →230
Donnersmarck, Florian Henckel von →28
Dorociński, Marcin →137
Dragojević, Srđan →35
Drążewski, Marek A. →49
Drozdowicz, Tomasz →123
Drygas, Maciej J. →12 →49 →51 →75
Dudziewicz, Michał J. →49
Dumała, Piotr →87–89 →93 →247 →249
Duraković, Jasmin →36
Dutkiewicz, Maciej →195 →200 →201 →203 →205 →206 →208
Dworcewoj, Siergiej →223
Dwurnik, Edward →96
Dylewska, Jolanta →46 →47 →70 →223
Dymna, Anna →113
Dzida, Franciszek →131
Dziworski, Bogdan →231 →241
Edelman, Marek →46
Edelman, Paweł →174
Falk, Feliks →12 →31 →148 →182 →183
Feldman, Krystyna →114 →179
Ferens, Anna →73 →74
Fidyk, Andrzej →42 →51–54 →230
Figura, Katarzyna →108–110 →125
Fijołek, Radek →137
Ford, Aleksander →62
Forman, Miloš →10

Fredro, Aleksander →78 →190 →213
Frycz, Jan →124
Gajewski, Dariusz →17 →141 →144 →145
Gavras, Costa →154
Gebert, Konstanty →66
Gębski, Józef →45 →46 →71
Giersz, Witold →81 →84
Giżycki, Marcin →81 →83
Gliński, Robert →20 →71 →125 →179 →180 →225
Głodek, Tomasz →100
Gombrowicz, Witold →105 →182 →244
Gosieniecki, Andrzej →92
Gotkowski, Hubert →146–148
Gowin, Aleksandra →117
Gretkowska, Manuela →112
Grochola, Katarzyna →111 →190 →215
Gross, Jan Tomasz →70 →174
Grottger, Artur →105
Grudzień, Regina →138
Gruza, Jerzy →15
Grynberg, Henryk →48 →67 →69
Grzegorzek, Mariusz →117 →224 →230
Grzyb, Ireneusz →117
Guziński, Adam →234 →235 →250
Haltof, Marek →29 →195 →212-214
Haneke, Michael →36
Harrison, John Kent →192
Has, Jerzy Wojciech →10 →105 →221 →225
Hoffman, Jerzy →19 →23 →25 →76 →77 →160
    →188 →190 →212 →213 →219
Holland, Agnieszka →29-31 →34 →106 →112 →171
    → 173 →196 →206 →225
Idziak, Sławomir →221
Iwaszkiewicz, Jarosław →114 →124
Jabłoński, Dariusz →46 →47 →68 →69
Jackowska, Kora →208
Jacob, Irène →173
Jadowska, Anna →17 →117 →144 →145
Jakimowicz, Jarosław →203
Jakimowski, Andrzej →20 →31 →32 →36 →144 →183
Jancsó, Miklós →10 →33
Janda, Krystyna →106 →114 →197
Jankowski, Łukasz →89
Jankowski, Wojciech →49
Janowski, Robert →201
Jaroszewicz, Andrzej →221

Jaruzelski, Wojciech →28
Jasińska-Koronkiewicz, Joanna →92
Jędrusik, Kalina →105
Jonkajtys, Grzegorz →96
Kabaj, Marcin →148
Kamiński, Janusz →174
Kane, Sarah →179
Karabasz, Kazimierz →229
Karwas, Piotr →90
Karwowski, Łukasz →215
Kasprzyk, Ewa →113 →253
Kassovitz, Mathieu →137
Kawalerowicz, Jerzy →77 →114 →174 →188 →189
    →192 →213 →219
Kazejak, Anna →192
Kędzierzawska, Dorota →16 →114 →116 →192
Kielak, Bolek →222
Kieślowski, Krzysztof →15 →23 →24 →29 →30
    →34 →84 →120 →132 →154 →164 →171-174
    →196 →206 →229 →230 →240 →241 →244
Kijowicz, Mirosław →81 →87
Kijowski, Janusz →68
Kiwerski, Krzysztof →86 →100
Kofta, Krystyna →112
Kokoryn, Krzysztof →89
Kolski, Jan Jakub →15 →16 →68 →192 →224 →225
Kołakowski, Leszek →84
Komasa, Jan →192
Komorowska, Maja →113
Konchalovsky, Andrei →35
Kondratiuk, Andrzej →108
Konecki, Tomasz →24 →110 →111 →123 →191
    →214 →215 →219
Konieczny, Zygmunt →100
Konopka, Bartosz →55 →56
Konwicki, Tadeusz →10 →14
Korejwo, Aleksandra →84
Koryncka, Natalia →204
Koszałka, Marcin →52 →53 →121 →250
Kotecki, Zbigniew →84 →248
Koterski, Marek →24 →179 →182 →183
Kotlarczyk, Teresa →73 →192
Kowalczyk, Magdalena →233
Kowalewski, Zbigniew →45
Kowalska, Helena →192
Kowalska, Kasia →201

INDEX OF NAMES 258

Kox, Bodo →17 →137
Koza, Janek →89
Kozak, Tomasz →90
Kozyra, Katarzyna →127
Krafftówna, Barbara →105
Kraszewski, Józef Ignacy →77 →190 →213
Krauze, Krzysztof →20 →24 →34 →73 →114 →164 →178 →179 →183
Królikiewicz, Grzegorz →14 →75 →192 →223 →224 →230 →238
Krukówna, Agnieszka →208 →253
Krzystek, Waldemar →215 →218
Krzywiec, Piotr →134
Kucia, Jerzy →86–89 →93 →94 →251
Kukiz, Paweł →201
Kural, Katarzyna →230
Kusturica, Emir →25 →35
Kutz, Kazimierz →10 →12 →14 →23 →28 →73 →106 →110 →192 →221 →225
Kwiatkowska, Barbara →105
Kwieciński, Michał →24
Land, Julie →125
Lang, Krzysztof →215
Lankosz, Borys →114 →192
Lanzmann, Claude →63
Laudyn, Stefan →135
Lee, Bruce →134
Lehnert, Henryk →132
Lenica, Jan →87
Leto, Norman →96 →101
Lewandowska, Marysia →123 →132
Linda, Bogusław →34 →36 →107 →112 →142 →187 →196 →197 →200 →201 →207 →237
Lipiec, Grzegorz →134–136 →148
Loach, Ken →33
Lubaszenko, Olaf →18 →108 →109 →188 →208 →209
Lubelski, Tadeusz →73 →211
Łazarkiewicz, Piotr →68 →229
Łepkowska, Ilona →215
Łomnicki, Jan →15 →66 →67
Łoziński, Marcel →12 →45 →46 →48 →49 →54 →55 →69 →70 →72 →75 →120 →232 →248
Łoziński, Paweł →48
Łukaszewicz, Jerzy →192 →231 →241
Machulski, Jan →137

Machulski, Juliusz →15 →18 →23 →106 →108 →109 →111 →187 →188 →207 →208 →219
Maciejewski, Wojciech →49
Maciejko-Kowalczyk, Katarzyna →233
Majdrowicz, Piotr →123
Majewski, Lech →192
Majewski, Maciej →93 →96
Malatyński, Marcin →223 →225 →228 →240
Malec, Mariusz →215
Maleszka, Lesław →73
Manchevski, Milcho →24
Marczewski, Filip →253
Marczewski, Wojciech →74 →135 →147 →192 →224 →225 →228 →232 →234–236 →241
Marecki, Piotr →134 →139
Margolis, Hanna →96
Matwiejczyk, Dominik →134 →136–138
Matwiejczyk, Piotr →17 →125 →128 →134 →136 →137
Mendyk, Michał (Mendyk) →138
Menzel, Jiří →10 →24 →32
Michalek, Vladimir →197
Michałek, Bolesław →167
Mickiewicz, Adam →78 →105 →212
Mikhalkov, Nikita →24 →35
Miller, Marek →47
Miłosz, Czesław →10
Mitulescu, Cătălin →38
Morawska, Irena →121
Morawski, Jerzy →121
Możdżer, Leszek →94
Mucha, Stanisław →24
Mungiu, Cristian →25 →38
Munk, Andrzej →10 →11 →14 →152 →222 →225 →243
Muntean, Radu →38
Muratova, Kira →10
Muybridge, Eadweard →95
Najsztub, Piotr →135
Nałkowska, Zofia →67
Nekanda-Trepka, Michał →48
Nemescu, Cristian →38
Neumann, Hieronim →83 →84 →93–95
Niewolski, Konrad →144
Nowak-Tyszowiecki, Krzysztof →45 →71
Nyczka, Ryszard Maciej →127
Odorowicz, Agnieszka →156

Olbrychski, Daniel →200 →249
Osińska, Magdalena →95
Ostaszewska, Maja →113 →120
Pajek, Marta →93
Pankiewicz, Anna →93
Parramore, Bruce →189 →215
Pasikowski, Władysław →18 →34 →36 →107 →187 →188 →195-97 →200 →201 →204-206 →208 →213 →218
Paskaljević, Goran →36
Pazura, Cezary →137 →201 →207 →209
Petelska, Ewa →62
Petelski, Czesław →62
Piątek, Jakub →223
Piekorz, Magdalena →121 →125 →192
Piekutowski, Andrzej →41 →43
Piesiewicz, Krzysztof →172
Pięta, Ewa →120
Pintilie, Lucian →37
Piwowarski, Radosław →108 →112
Piwowski, Marek →12
Plucińska, Izabela →92 →93 →96
Polak, Joanna →95
Polak, Kamil →96
Polański, Roman →14 →25 →68 →164 →174 →175 →178 →187 →213 →221 →225
Polony, Anna →114
Polska, Agnieszka →101
Popescu-Gopo, Ion →37
Popiełuszko, Jerzy →73 →192 →214
Porumboiu, Corneliu →38
Prokofiev, Sergei →95
Puiu, Cristi →37
Pyjas, Stanisław →73
Quay, Brothers (Stephen and Timothy Quay) →101 →243
Raksa, Pola →105
Ravenhill, Mark →179
Rehme, Robert →10
Rogalski, Michał →121 →123
Rosa, Michał →28 →192
Rosłaniec, Katarzyna →149
Różewicz, Stanisław →10 →62
Rybczyński, Zbigniew →94
Saramonowicz, Andrzej →24 →110 →111 →191 →214 →215 →219

Sass, Barbara →106 →113
Schlöndorff, Völker →13
Segda, Dorota →137
Serafiński, Marek →82 →84 →87 →94 →96 →100 →101 →247
Shukshin, Vasili →10
Siekierzyńska Iwona →120 →249
Siwiński, Tomasz →93
Skalski, Jacek →18 →195 →197 →200
Skoczek, Zbigniew →51
Skolimowski, Jerzy →14 →28 →164 →178 →243
Skonieczny, Zygmunt →41
Skrobecki, Marek →84 →86 →93 →94 →248
Smarzowski, Wojciech →20 →21 →24 →28 →31 →32 →164
Smoczyńska, Agnieszka →125 →158
Sobociński, Piotr →221
Sobociński, Witold →71 →225
Socha, Michał →96
Sowa, Robert →94 →97 →249
Sowa, Wiola →94 →96 →97 →117
Spielberg, Steven →63 →154 →196
Stachówna, Grażyna →214 →215 →218
Stalińska, Dorota →106
Stankiewicz, Ewa →17 →73 →74 →144 →145
Stańczakowa, Jadwiga →114
Starski, Allan →174
Staszczyk, Muniek →208
Steczkowska, Justyna →201
Stokowski, Aleksander →49
Struzik, Justyna →125
Stuhr, Jerzy →148 →173 →174 →182 →230
Stuhr, Maciej →208
Svěrák, Jan →25 →31 →32
Svěrák, Zdenek →32
Szabó, István →24 →33
Szatlarska, Danuta →114
Szczechura, Daniel →81 →83 →93
Szpilman, Władysław →174
Szulkin, Piotr →108 →109 →112 →113
Szumowska, Małgorzata →21 →37 →116 →117 →120 →183 →250
Szymański, Zbigniew →100
Ślązak, Krystyna →238
Ślesicki, Maciej →18 →112 →147 →188 →195 →197 →203 →205 →207 →237

Tanović, Danis →25 →36 →173
Tarantino, Quentin →187 →207
Tarkovsky, Andrey →10
Tarło, Robert →95
Tarr, Béla →33 →34
Templeton, Suzy →95 →96
Treliński, Mariusz →124 →127
Tryzna, Tomek →212
Trzaskalski, Piotr →20 →179–181
Trzos, Tomasz (Trzos) →138
Turczanik, Edyta →94 →97
Turło, Robert →89 →90
Tykwer, Tom →172
Tyszkiewicz, Beata →105
Uklański, Piotr →110
Urbański, Artur →112 →113 →249
Urbański, Kazimierz →84 →93
Voight, Jon →192
Wajda, Andrzej →10–14 →19 →23 →25 →26
  →30–31 →34 →36 →37 →39 →46 →60–63
  →66 →67 →72 →76–78 →105 →106 →114
  →135 →147 →152 →156 →160 →164 →174
  →175 →187–190 →196 →197 →206 →211–213
  →219 →221 →225 →232 →233 →243
Wat, Aleksander →71
Watowa, Ola →71
Wawer, Zbigniew →45
Wawszczyk, Wojciech →91 →92 →96
Wereśniak, Piotr →215
Wieczyński, Rafał →73 →192
Wilczyński, Mariusz →89 →93 →97
Wilkoszewska, Natalia →95
Winterbottom, Michael →36
Wiśniewski, Janusz L. →215
Witkiewicz, Stanisław Ignacy (Witkacy) →124
Wojcieszek, Przemysław →17 →20 →120 →183
  →186 →187
Wojtyła, Karol (John Paul II) →10 →28 →192 →214
Wójcik, Jerzy →71 →225
Wójcik, Tomasz (Waciak) →138 →139
Wroniewicz, Olga →95
Wylężałek, Łukasz →107 →196 →201
Wyrwas, Adam →89 →248
Wyrzykowski, Artur →236–238 →240
Wyspiański, Stanisław →191 →211
Wyszyński, Stefan →73 →192

Zadrzyński, Łukasz →18 →195 →200 →201 →204
  →206
Zanussi, Krzysztof →15 →23 →30 →113 →123
  →132 →156 →164 →175 →206 →230
Zaorski, Janusz →106 →109
Zaręba, Andrzej →89
Zatorski, Ryszard →214 →215 →219
Zečević, Dejan →36
Zgliński, Greg →192 →249
Zieliński, Jerzy →221 →225
Ziębiński, Marcin →18
Ziółkowska, Iwona →135
Zmarz-Koczanowicz, Maria →70 →120 →121
Zmudziński, Bogusław →81
Zvyagintsev, Andrei →25
Zygadło, Tomasz →120
Žbanič, Jasmila →25 →36
Żak, Maciej →24 →215
Żakowski, Jacek →135
Żamojda, Jarosław →18 →188 →195 →196 →201
  →203–206 →208
Żeromski, Stefan →77 →78 →190 →213
Żuławski, Andrzej →23 →31 →112
Żuławski, Xawery →192

INDEX OF FILMS

12:08 East of Bucharest /A fost sau n-a fost? →38
14 Tales from Lailonia Kingdom →84
45–89 →49 →75
2 Killers /Kilerów 2-óch →109 →188
300 Miles to Heaven /300 mil do nieba →28
33 Scenes From Life /33 sceny z życia →21 →37
    →117 →118-119 →183
4 Months, 3 Weeks and 2 Days /4 luni, 3 săptămâni
    și 2 zile →25 →38
Across the Fields /Przez pole →87
After Apples /Po jabłkach →93
AlaRm →17 →142-143 →144
All That I Love /Wszystko co kocham →17 →18
All That Really Matters /Wszystko, co
    najważniejsze →70 →71
Amateur Photographer /Fotoamator →47 →68 →69
Amok →201 →204
Ancient Tale, An /Stara baśń →77 →190 →213
And the Body Lies Quietly in the Grave /I cicho ciało
    spocznie w grobie →49
Anger /Gniew →18
Angry Harvest /Bittere Ernte →171
Animation Films to Classical Music →84 →95
Aria Diva →125 →158 →159
Arizona →52 →121
Ark /Arka, The →96
Ashes and Diamonds /Popiół i diament →10 →11
    →61 →105 →221 →232
Autumn Almanac /Őszi almanach →33
Bad Luck /Zezowate szczęście →10 →222
Ballad of a Slightly Erotic Nature /Ballada o lekkim
    zabarwieniu erotycznym →121
Barber of Siberia, The /Sibirskiy tsiryulnik →35
Barefoot /Na boso →137
Bash, The /Balanga →196 →201
Beads of One Rosary, The /Paciorki jednego różańca
    →23
Beautiful →137
Beautiful People →36
Before the Rain /Pred dozhdot →24
Beijing: Gold of '83 /Pekin. Złota 83 →52
Bellissima →113
Beside the Railway Line /Przy torze kolejowym →62
Between Us /Pomiędzy nami →94
Beware of Fierce Dogs / Uwaga! Złe psy →93
Big Animal, The /Duże zwierze →174

Big Deal /Kochaj albo rzuć →212
Biggest Quarrel, The /O największej kłótni →84
Billboard →18 →201 →204
Birth /Narodziny →87
Birth Certificate /Świadectwo urodzenia →10 →62
Birthplace /Miejsce urodzenia →48 →69
Bitter-Sweet /Słodko-gorzki →196 →201
Black Burlesque /Czarna burleska →90
Blind Chance /Przypadek →173 →229
Blue Danube Waltz /Kék Duna keringő →33
Bolek and Lolek /Bennie and Lennie →87
Boogie →38
Border Street /Ulica graniczna →62
Born Dead →54 →54
Boys Don't Cry /Chłopaki nie płaczą →18 →108
    →188 →208 →209
Bread Rush, The /Gorączka chleba →45
Brother /Brat →35
Burial of the Potato, The /Pogrzeb kartofla →15
Burnt by the Sun /Utomlyonnye solntsem →24
Buy Now /Kup teraz →137
By the River /Przy rzece →233
Calendar, The /Kalendarz →101
California Dreamin' →38
Camera Buff /Amator →23 →132 →229
Camouflage /Barwy ochronne →23 →230
Canal /Kanał →10 →11
Capital, or How to Make Money in Poland /
    Kapitał, czyli jak zrobić pieniądze w Polsce →12
Career of Nikos Dyzma, The /Kariera Nikosia Dyzmy
    →18 →209-210
Carmen Torrero →84
Carousel, The /Karuzela →48
Case of Pekosinski, The /Przypadek Pekosińskiego
    →75 →223
Cat-Burglars, The /Pajęczarki →113
Cathedral /Katedra →91 →252
Cauliflower /Kalafiorr →17 →144
Chamanka /Szamanka →112
Changes /Przemiany →120
Cheat /Sztos →208–209
Cheerleader /Cheerleaderka →127
Chick, The /Laska →96
Chinacity →137
Chopin: Desire for Love /Chopin: Pragnienie miłości
    →214

263 INDEX OF FILMS

Chronicle of the Warsaw Ghetto Uprising According to Marek Edelman /Kronika powstania w getcie warszawskim według Marka Edelmana →46
Cinematograph /Kinematograf →96
City Sails On, The /Miasto płynie →95
Coal Miners '88 /Górnicy '88 →41
Code Unknown /Code inconnu →36
Collector, The /Komornik →182 →184
Colonel Kwiatkowski /Pułkownik Kwiatkowski →110
Colonel Wolodyjowski /Pan Wołodyjowski →189 →212
Coming Out Polish Style /Coming out po polsku →125
Condemnation of Franciszek Kłos, The /Wyrok na Franciszka Kłosa →61
Conductor, The /Dyrygent →23
Conductor Paradox /Paradoks o konduktorze →49
Constant Factor, The /Constans →23
Contract, The /Kontrakt →23
Controlled Conversations /Rozmowy kontrolowane →28
Convention: Behind the Scenes Or the Power of the Tape, The /Kulisy zjazdu czyli siał taśmy →141
Conversation with a Cupboard Man / Rozmowa z człowiekiem z szafy →117
Convert, The /Zawrócony →28 →73
Cornerhouse 360 degrees /Warzywniak 360° →96
Coyote's Morning /Poranek kojota →18 →208
Crime and Punishment /Zbrodnia i kara →88
Crimes in Kolyma /Zbrodnia w Kołymie →45
Criminal Section /Biuro kryminalne →138
Cross of Valor /Krzyż Walecznych →10
Crows, The /Wrony →16
Cupboard, A /Kredens →48
D.I.L. →144
Dad /Tato →112
Damnation /Kárhozat →33
Dark House, The /Dom zły →21 →28
Dark Side of Venus, The /Ciemna strona Wenus →112
Day I Die, The /Dzień, w którym umrę →135–136
Day of the Wacko /Dzień świra →179 →181 →183
Death as a Slice of Bread /Śmierć jak kromka chleba →10 →12 →13 →28 →73
Death of Mr Lazarescu, The /Moartea domnului Lăzărescu →37
Death with a Human Face /Śmierć z ludzką twarzą →53
Debt, The /Dług →20 →34 →178–179

Debutante /Debiutantka →106
Decalogue, The /Dekalog →23 →84 →171 →229
Deluge, The /Potop →23 →76 →189 →212
Demons of War /Demony wojny według Goi →36 →197
Depths /Toń →123
Devils, The Devils, The /Diabły, diabły →16
DIM. →84 →85 →248
Do Not Kill /Nie zabijaj →46
Dokumanimo →100
Dollybirds /Csinibaba →29
Don't Lie, Darling /Nie kłam, kochanie →190 →215
Double Life of Véronique, The /La double vie de Véronique/Podwójne życie Weroniki →23 →30 →164 →171 →173
Drowsiness /Senność →125
E=mc2 →18 →208
Edi →20 →180–181
Egoists, The /Egoiści →124
Elementary School, The /Obecná škola →32
Emilia →137
Envelope, The /Koperta →148
Eroica →10
Erotic Confessions /Erotyczne zwierzenia →89
Escape from the Liberty Cinema /Ucieczka z kina Wolność →74 →225
Esma's Secret /Grbavica →25 →36
Esterhazy →96
Europa Europa →30 →171 →172
Everything Flows /Wszystko płynie →94
Everything for the Eaglets /Wszystko dla Orląt →45
Exam /Egzamin →87
Excuse Me /Przepraszam →148
Existence /Istnienie →53
Expecting Love /Mała wielka miłość →215
Extras, The /Statyści →24
Fairy Tale Pictures /Märchenbilder →86
Fallen Art /Sztuka spadania →91
Fallow Land /Ugór →138
Family Life /Życie rodzinne →23
Far from the Window /Daleko od okna →68
Farewell to Autumn /Pożegnanie jesieni →124 →126
Farewells /Pożegnania →10
Fast Lane /Młode wilki →18 →34 →188 →195–196 →201 →204 →205
Fast Lane ½ /Młode wilki ½ →201

INDEX OF FILMS **264**

Faustyna →192
Female-Male Issues /Damsko-męskie sprawy →121
Femina →112–113
Few People, A Little Time , A/Parę osób, mały czas →114
Filaments /Druciki →117
Film About the Grim Reaper /Film o kostuchu →101
Film Found in Katyn, A /Film znaleziony w Katyniu →46
Film with no Sound, A /Film bez dźwięku →101
First Love /Pierwsza miłość →138
Flax /Len →92
Flight of the Bumble-Bee /Lot trzmiela →84
Fluke /Fuks →208
For My Mother and Me /Mojej Mamie i sobie →97
Forgotten Prisoners-of-War /Zapomniani jeńcy →45
Fourth Man, The /Četvrti čovjek →36
Frantic →225
Franz Kafka →88 →89 →247
From the Gulag Archipelago /Z Archipelagu Gułag →45
From the Gulag Archipelago to America / Z Archipelagu Gułag do Ameryki →45
Fur /Futro →123
Gates of Europe, The /Wrota Europy →71
Gdansk Station /Dworzec Gdański →70
Gdańsk Tapes, The /Gdańskie taśmy →49
General Nil /Generał Nil →61 →73 →214
Generation /Pokolenie →11
Gentleman's Romance /Romans dżentelmena →90
George the Hedgehog /Jeż Jerzy →101
Girls from Szymanów /Dziewczyny z Szymanowa →121
God Walks Backwards /Isten hátrafelé megy →33
God's Little Garden /U Pana Boga w ogródku →210–211
God's Little Village /U Pana Boga za miedzą →211
Gold Rush, The /Gorączka złota →45
Good Bye Lenin! →28
Hairdresser /Fryzjer →94 →249
Happiness →93
Happy End →232
Happy Man /Szczęśliwy człowiek →116
Happy New York /Szczęśliwego Nowego Jorku →109
Hate, The /La haine →137
Headless →92
Hear My Cry /Usłyszcie mój krzyk →12 →50 →51 →75

Hell /L'Enfer →173
Hen, The /Kura →87
Hexer, The /Wiedźmin →213
Hi, Tereska /Cześć Tereska → 20 →179 →181 →225
Hijacking of Agata /Uprowadzenie Agaty →12
History of Cinema in Popielawy /Historia kina w Popielawach →15–16
Hit the Bank /Vabank →15
Hobby →83
Holy Week /Wielki tydzień →67 →164 →175
Homo Father →127 →128 →137
Homo.pl →125
Hope /Nadzieja →24
Hour-Glass Sanatorium, The /Sanatorium pod klepsydrą →221 →225
House of Fools /Dom durakov →35
How It's Done /Jak to się robi →55 →232
How To Be Loved /Jak być kochaną →105
How To Live /Jak żyć →232
Howling Wolf Ranch /Ranczo Wilkowyje →211
Human and Bread /Człowiek i chleb →86 →87
Humps /Garby →84
I Am Yours /Jestem twój →117
I Served the King of England /Obsluhoval jsem anglického krále →32
I'll Show You! /Ja wam pokażę! →110 →215
I'm a Man /Jestem mężczyzną →120
I'm Looking at You, Mary /Patrzę na ciebie, Marysiu →120
Immoral Story, An /Historia niemoralna →106
I'm Still Waiting /Jeszcze czekam… →49
Ichthys →94
Identification Marks: None /Rysopis →178
Illumination /Iluminacja →23
Impressions →83
In Full Gallop /Cwał →30 →113 →175
In Heaven as it Is on Earth /U Pana Boga za piecem →210–211
In Love /Zakochani →215
In Memory of the Dead /Umarłym ku pamięci →49
In the Middle of Europe /W środku Europy →68
Interior Portrait /Portret we wnętrzu →94
Interrogation /Przesłuchanie →11 →23
Inventory of Traces /Inwentorium śladów →101
It's Me Now /Teraz ja →117
It's Me, the Thief /To ja złodziej →18

Jacek and Placek →87
Jam Session →92
Johnnie Aquarius /Jańcio Wodnik →14 →15
Joyets /Radostki →95
Just Beyond This Forest /Jeszcze tylko ten las →66 →67
Just Love Me /Tylko mnie kochaj →190 →215 →219
Jym & Jam /Reksio →87
Karol: A Man Who Became Pope /Karol - człowiek, który został papieżem →192 →214
Karol: The Pope, The Man /Karol - papież, który pozostał człowiekiem →192 →214
Katyn → 36 →39 →46 →72 →175 →187 →212 →219
Katyn File: Mass Murder as a Propaganda Tool, The /Katyń. Ludobójstwo i propaganda →46
Katyn Forest /Las katyński →12 →44 →46 →72
Kill Them All /Zabij ich wszystkich →17 →120
Killer /Kiler →18 →109 →188 →207 →219
2 Killers / Killerów 2-óch →109 →188
King Size /Kingsajz →207
King Ubu /Ubu król →109
Kizi Mizi →97
Kneeling-Moaning /Klęcząc jęcząc →137
Kolya /Kolja →25 →32
Korczak →23 →63 →64
Krasicki Reactivation /Krasicki Reaktywacja →96
Kroll →18 →107 →200
L for Love /M jak Miłość →215
Ladies /Lejdis →111 →123 →191 →215 →219
Landscape After Battle /Krajobraz po bitwie →23
Landscape of My Heart /Krajina mého srdce →32
Larks on a String /Skřivanci na niti →24 →32
Late Night Talks with Mother /Noční hovory s matkou →32
Level →100
Life and Extraordinary Adventures of Private Ivan Chonkin, The /Život a neobyčejná dobrodružství vojáka Ivana Čonkina →32
Life as a Fatal Sexually Transmitted Disease /Życie jako śmiertelna choroba przenoszona drogą płciową →30 →164 →178
Lining of God's Coat, The /Boża podszewka →116
Liquidation 08.1944 /Likwidacja 08.1944 →47
List of Adulteresses, The /Spis cudzołożnic →173
Little Moscow /Mała Moskwa →215 →219

Little Penguin Pik-Pok →84
Lives of Others, The /Das Leben der Anderen →28
Lonely Woman, A /Kobieta samotna →106
Lord's Lantern in Budapest, The /Nekem lámpást adott kezembe as Úr Pesten →33
Louder Than Bombs /Głośniej od bomb →17 →20 →120 →186
Love and Dance /Kochaj i tańcz →188 →190 →215 →218
Love Gamestation →91
Lovers of Marona, The /Kochankowie z Marony →124
Made in Hungária →29
Magritte →83
Maids of Wilko, The /Panny z Wilka →23 →114
Mall Girls /Galerianki →149
Man of Iron /Człowiek z żelaza →10 →11 →23 →106 →197 →221
Man of Marble /Człowiek z marmuru →10 →23 →106
Man on the Track /Człowiek na torze →11
Manhunter /Naganiacz →62
Manna →146 →147-148
Masks /Maski →89 →91
Mass /Masa →100
Maurycy and Hawranek →84
Medical Gymnastics /Ćwiczenia korekcyjne →101
Men's Bath-House /Łaźnia męska →127
Midnight Talks /Rozmowy nocą →24 →39 →215
Militiamen and Thieves /Milicjanci i złodzieje →101
Miracle at the Vistula River, A /Cud nad Wisłą →45
Miss Nobody /Panna Nikt →164 →212
Misunderstanding /Nieporozumienie →123
Moonlighting →28
Mordziaki →84
Mother Joan of the Angels /Matka Joanna od Aniołów →114 →213
Mother of Kings /Matka Królów →106
Mouse /Mysz →92
Musicians, The /Muzykanci →229
My Nikifor /Mój Nikifor →24 →114 →164 →179
My Roast Chickens /Moje pieczone kurczaki →120
Nafaka →36
Neighbours /Sąsiedzi →48, 70
New Bell, The /Nowy dzwon →87
Nervous Life /Nerwowe życie →88
Never Ever! /Nigdy w życiu! →110, 190, 215, 218

INDEX OF FILMS **266**

Next Door /Za ścianą →93
Night Graffiti /Nocne graffiti →34 →200-201 →202 →206
Nightmare of Last Winter /Koszmar minionej zimy →137
No End /Bez końca →23
No Man's Land /Ničija zemlja →25 →36
Nobody's Calling /Nikt nie woła →221
Nosebleed /Krew z nosa →137
Nothing /Nic →16 →116
Nothing But Fear /Tylko strach →113
Oasis /Oaza →96
Oil Gobblers, The /Ropáci →32
Old Lady Goes to See the Doctor, An /Przychodzi baba do doktora →88
Olivier, Olivier →30
On the Other Side of the Vistula /Z tamtej strony Wisły →52
One Day in People's Poland /Jeden dzień w PRL →49 →75
One More Time /Jeszcze raz →215
Operation Samoom /Operacja Samum →197
Our Folks /Sami swoi →212
Pan Tadeusz: The Last Foray in Lithuania →19 →25 →27 →31 →77 →78 →135 →160 →188-189 →212 →219
Paper Marriage /Papierowe małżeństwo →215
Paper Will Be Blue /Hîrtia va fi albastră →38
Parade, The /Defilada →42
Pearl in the Crown /Perła w koronie →73 →106
Peasant's Fate – a Film Triptych, The / Chłopski los – tryptyk filmowy →41
Penguin /Pingwin →92
Perfect Afternoon, The /Doskonałe popołudnie →186
Perfect Guy for My Girlfriend, The /Idealny facet dla mojej dziewczyny →111 →215
Peter and the Wolf →95 →97 →101
Pianist, The /Pianista →25 →68 →164 →174-175 →187
Piggies /Świnki →225
Pigs /Psy →18 →34 →107 →188 →196 →200 →204
Pigs 2: The Last Blood /Psy 2: Ostatnia krew →34 →35 →188 →200
Pit Bull /Pitbull →138
Players /Gracze →12
Pograbek →15
Poland as it Has Never Been Seen in the West /La Pologne comme jamais vue à l'Ouest →49 →75
Police, Adjective /Politist, adjectiv →38
Po-Lin. Slivers of Memory /Po-lin. Okruchy pamięci →46 →47 →70
Polish-Bolshevik War 1918-1921, The /Wojna polsko-bolszewicka 1918-1921 →45
Pope John Paul II →192
Popieluszko: Freedom is Within Us /Popiełuszko: Wolność jest w nas →214
Poster Girl /Dziewczyna z plakatu →120
Powder Keg /Bure baruta →36
Poznan '56 →12 →73
Pretty Village Pretty Flame /Lepa sela lepo gore →35-36
Primate, The /Prymas. Trzy lata z tysiąca →73 →192
Prisoner of the Mountains /Kavkazskiy plennik →35
Private Town /Miasto prywatne →18 →197 →200 →204
Professional /Zawodowiec →94
Queen of Angels, The /Królowa aniołów →117
Quo Vadis →77 →188-189 →192 →213 →219
R.O. Island /Wyspa R.O. →87
Rabbit à la Berlin /Królik po berlińsku →55 →57
Rabolatory Or a Tribute to Science /Rabolatorium czyli w hołdzie nauce →139 →141
Race, The /Wyścig →82 →87 →100 →247
Rat in the Crown /Szczur w koronie →232
Refrains /Refreny →94 →98 →117
Reich →197 →206
Remote Control →94
Return, The /Powrót →87
Return, The /Vozvrashcheniye →25
Revenge /Zemsta →78 →190 →212-213 →219
Reverse /Rewers →114 →115
Ring with a Crowned Eagle /Pierścionek z orłem w koronie →12 →60-61
Rondo Alla Turca →84
Rough Treatment /Bez znieczulenia →23
Salt of the Black Earth /Sól ziemi czarnej →73 →105
Salto →10
Salvation Opera /Opera ocalenia →90
Samson →62
Sara →18 →188 →197 →207
Saragossa Manuscript, The /Rękopis znaleziony w Saragossie →221

Sátántangó →33-34
Sauna →154
Saviour Square /Plac Zbawiciela →183
Schindler's List →63 →154 →155 →174
Scratch, The /Rysa →28
Scream, The /Krzyk →106
Sekal Has to Die /Zabić Sekala →197
Sequence /Sekwens →94
Seven Jews from my Class /Siedmiu Żydów z mojej klasy →48 →70
Seven Stations on the Way to Paradise / Siedem przystanków na drodze do raju →127
Sexmission /Seksmisja →15 →23 →106-107 →207
Shadowland /Kraina cieni →100
Shadows /Cienie →94
Shame /Wstyd →137
Sheriff Story /Sprawa szeryfa →52
Shivers /Dreszcze →225
Shoah →63
Short Film About Killing, A /Krótki film o zabijaniu →23
Short Film About Love, A /Krótki film o miłości →23
Short Hysteria of Time /Krótka histeria czasu →138
Siberians /Sybiracy →45
Silent Touch, The /Dotknięcie ręki →23 →30 →164
Silesian Business /Śląski interes →121 →122
Slaughterhouse One /Rzeźnia nr 1 →138
Small Apocalypse →154
Solitude @ Net /Samotność w sieci →215
Sour Soup /Żurek →109
Speed /Lotna →10
Spindle of Time, The /Wrzeciono czasu →108
Splinter /Drzazga →96
Spoken Movie /Film mówiony [Film mówiony 1, Film mówiony 2, Film mówiony 3, Film mówiony 4] →100
Spring to Come, The /Przedwiośnie →77-78 →190 →213 →219
Squint Your Eyes /Zmruż oczy →20 →144
Stiudent →148
Story of Sin, The /Dzieje grzechu →23
Stranger /Ono →117
Street Games /Gry uliczne →73
Strike /Strajk - Die Heldin von Danzig →13
String Movie /Film sznurkowy →101

Stupajkop →89
Such a Beautiful Son I Gave Birth To /Takiego pięknego syna urodziłam →53, 121
Summer Love →110
Sundial, The /Słoneczny zegar →109
Sunny Town /Słoneczne miasteczko →92
Sweet Emma, Dear Böbe /Édes Emma, draga Böbe →33
Sweet Rush /Tatarak →36 →114
Szczecin Album 17/12/70, The /Album szczeciński 17.XII.1970 →49
Szczepan and Irenka →89
Take it Easy /Nie ma mocnych →212
Tale of Great Shame, A /O wielkim wstydzie →84
Tales from the Golden Age /Amintiri din epoca de aur →38
Temptation /Pokuszenie →113
Testosterone /Testosteron →24 →39 →111 →191 →215
That Life Makes Sense /Że życie ma sens →135
Third Part of the Night, The /Trzecia część nocy →23
Thirteensome, The /Trzynastka →52 →121
Them /Oni →52
There Will Always Be Tomorrow /Zawsze będzie jutro →93
Things'll Work Out /Jakoś to będzie →53
Three Buddies /Trzech kumpli →73 →74
Three Colours: Blue /Trois couleurs: Bleu/Trzy kolory: Niebieski →23 →24 →164
Three Colours: Red /Trois couleurs: rouge/Trzy kolory: Czerwony →23
Three Colours: White /Trois couleurs: blanc/Trzy kolory: Biały →23 →30
Through and Through /Na wylot →223
Time for Witches, A /Pora na czarownice →230
Time to Die /Pora umierać →114 →116
Titanic World →96
Top Dog /Wodzirej →182
Touch Me /Dotknij mnie →17 →144 →145
Trans-Mission /Trans-misja →125
Tricks /Sztuczki →36 →183
Tulpan →223
Tuning the Instruments /Strojenie instrumentów →86 →87 →251
TV-Set /Telewizor →93
Ty tani K. Or Personal Selection /Ty tani K. czyli wybór własny →141

INDEX OF FILMS 268

Underground /Podzemlje →25 →35
Unfortunately /Niestety →97
Unmoved Mover /Nieruchomy poruszyciel →120
Uranium Rush, The /Gorączka uranu →45
Urga →24
Vibrating String /Drgająca struna →84
Walkover /Walkower →178
War /Voyna →35
Warm Heart, A /Serce na dłoni →123
Warning to the Living, A /Żywym ku przestrodze →49
Warsaw /Warszawa →17 →144
Warszawa. Année 5703 /Tragarz puchu →68
Washington Square →225
Wave, The /Fala →229
Way I Spent the End of the World, The /Cum mi-am petrecut sfârșitul lumii →38
Wedding, The /Wesele →21 →24 →164 →191
Welcome to Sarajevo →36
We're All Christs /Wszyscy jesteśmy Chrystusami →24
Where Is My Elder Son Cain? /Gdzie mój starszy syn Kain? →48
Why Not?! /Dlaczego nie! →110 →190 →214–215
Wistful /Smętna →137
With Fire and Sword /Ogniem i mieczem →19 →25 →76 →160 →188 →212 →219
Without Love /Bez miłości →106
Witness 1919 – 2004 /Świadek 1919 – 2004 →100
Witnesses, The /Świadkowie →69
Workshop Practice /Ćwiczenia warsztatowe →232
Year of the Quiet Sun /Rok spokojnego słońca →23
Zoopraxiscope →95

PHOTO CREDITS

Agencja Filmowa eRBe →35 →183 →202 →205 →209 | Agencja Media Plus →124 | Apple Film Production →113 | Andrzej Wajda Master School of Film Directing →159 | Bomedia →47 | Bow and Axe Entertainment →70 | Piotr Dumała →89 | Guy Ferrandis →176 | Film it/Fotos-Art. →21 | Filmoteka Narodowa →82 →85 | Filmotwórnia →142 | Jewish Museum of Frankfurt →69 | Fabryka Obrazu →27 →36 →77 →184 →188 →216 →226 | HBO Polska →122 | Piotr Jaxa →162 | Marcin Koszałka →53 | Jerzy Kucia →86 | Łyżka Czyli Chilli →139 | Muzeum Kinematografii w Łodzi →108 | Opus Film →180 →234 | Otter Films →57 | Paisa Films →146 | Platige Image →91 | Izabela Plucińska →92 | Prasa i film →18 | Remigiusz Przełożny →116 | Renata Rajchel →64 | Se-Ma-For →97 | Skopia Film →165 | Skorpion Art →219 | SF Kadr →66 →115 | SF Oko →156 | SF Perspektywa →60 →172 | SF Tor →13 → 224 | SF Zebra →20 →109 →173 →187 →198 | STI Studio Filmowe →118 | Studio Logos →50 | Paweł Śmietanka →30 | TVN →74 | TVP →14 →54 →145 →181 | Universal/Courtesy Everett Collection/East News →155 | Van Worden →110 | Video Studio A →98 | Adrianna Weryk →129 | WFDiF →43 →44 | Vision Film →210 | Przemysław Wojcieszek →186 | www.wszystko.net →237 | Wytwórnia Filmowa Czołówka →126 | Zodiak Jerzy Hoffman Film Production →19